STOP

Wasting Your Wealth in

MUTUAL FUNDS

Separately Managed Accounts—
The Smart Alternative

DON F. WILKINSON

Dearborn

Trade Publishing

A **Kaplan Professional** Company

D1446034

This publication is designed to provide accurate and authoritative information in regard to the subject matter covered. It is sold with the understanding that the publisher is not engaged in rendering legal, accounting, or other professional service. If legal advice or other expert assistance is required, the services of a competent professional should be sought.

President, Dearborn Publishing: Roy Lipner
Vice President and Publisher: Cynthia A. Zigmund
Senior Acquisitions Editor: Mary B. Good
Development Editor: Karen Murphy
Interior Design: Lucy Jenkins
Cover Design: Studio Montage
Typesetting: Ellen Gurak

Published by Dearborn Trade Publishing
A Kaplan Professional Company

Printed in the United States of America

06 07 08   10 9 8 7 6 5 4 3 2 1

Library of Congress Cataloging-in-Publication Data

Wilkinson, Don F.
  Stop wasting your wealth in mutual funds : separately managed accounts : the smart alternative / Don F. Wilkinson.
      p. cm.
  Includes bibliographical references and index.
  ISBN 1-4195-2018-0 (6×9 pbk.)
  1. Portfolio management. 2. Investment analysis. 3. Mutual funds. I. Title.
  HG4529.5W545   2005
  332.6—dc22

                                                                      2005015092

Praise for *Stop Wasting Your Wealth in Mutual Funds*

"Having been a comprehensive wealth advisor for more than 20 years, I am always looking for the best solutions for my high-net-worth clients. When I met Don Wilkinson several years ago, he convinced me that separate accounts were a superior solution for retirement planning. The media has told us that paying low fees, no commissions, and modest taxes, in addition to utilizing a good "stock picker," is critical to generating more return from our investments. Using separate accounts is the best approach available. Our clients are very happy with the benefits of separate accounts, as Don so convincingly explains in his new book. *Stop Wasting Your Wealth in Mutual Funds* gives the bottom-line answers as to why clients should be in separate accounts over mutual funds, and I agree."

Peter Tedstrom, CFP, owner, Brown and Tedstrom, Inc., one of the Robb Report's *Worth* magazine top 100 wealth advisors in the country

"A provocative guide for people who don't think they can pick mutual funds wisely or simply want more personal attention."

Russ Wiles, personal finance writer, *The Arizona Republic*

"Finally, there is a book that provides investors with a bridge to well-known, proven investment tools that have historically only been available to large institutional investors, and ultrawealthy individuals. Wilkinson is a nationally known expert in the area of separate accounts and shares his insights for the benefit of today's investor. His book gives investors factual, clear evidence of how owning individual stocks and bonds can be more tax-efficient, enhance overall performance, and reduce fees when compared to owning mutual funds. A must-read for anyone who has worked hard to build and accumulate wealth."

Keith Tigue, managing partner, Robinson, Tigue, Sponcil & Associates, Phoenix, Arizona

"Don is a leading expert in mutual funds and separate accounts. He has been exposing mutual fund problems long before they became a national concern. I would highly recommend that all individual investors and investment professionals read this book. Don takes the blinders off and gives us the straight truth!"

James P. Dew, ChFC, MBA, CFP, president, Dew Wealth Management

"Wilkinson's new book provides an extremely timely and comprehensive education on separately managed accounts and on managing one's wealth. Investors have been stung by the recent negative period in the market, combined with poor mutual fund performance. Now, with the revelations of overcharging, improper trading, and preferential treatment in the mutual fund industry, investors are searching for alternatives but feel trapped with the very people who 'did them wrong.' *Stop Wasting Your Wealth in Mutual Funds* provides a profitable alternative, supported by facts, history, and concrete advantages. As a bonus, you also receive a comprehensive overview of portfolio management and retirement planning in general."

Randolph Hinton, registered principal, United Planners Financial Services of America

"I am happy to report that Wilkinson's new book is a work of great value to the average investor. As a five-time published author, I can attest to his skill as a writer who makes his ideas clear, relevant, and of great value. As a major investor, I can state that Wilkinson has helped me personally in my investments and, at the core, has made me money. No other endorsement has more power than that statement in this field."

Morton L. Kurland, MD, board-certified psychiatrist and published author

Contents

Managing your assets can be incredibly frustrating. The language people use is needlessly confusing, the paperwork overwhelming. Deciding how to invest, where to invest, and who you can trust is no easy task. So what's a reasonable person to do? Ignoring the problem is no solution. After all, in this society, our financial well-being is in our own hands. If we want to own a home, have our children go to college, or retire comfortably, we all have to learn how to have our stock market assets managed correctly in a way that is acceptable to us.

Financial freedom can be yours, but it will require becoming educated, understanding how things work, and then making your money work for you the right way.

For many years mutual funds were the only investment solution for millions of investors; but the investment landscape has changed. Today, with the advent of technology, new investment alternatives are being offered to investors every day. Many of these can provide huge benefits to individuals striving to reach their financial goals. This valuable book provides insights into one of the most important investment developments in a generation—the separately managed account.

Don Wilkinson has worked with thousands of investors and investment professionals throughout his career, and his knowledge, experience, and humor shine through in this book. He provides a valuable service, sharing insights into how separate accounts work and how to determine whether investing this way is right for you. Most important, his down-to-earth, easy-to-understand style takes the confusion out of investing and shows in simple terms how separate accounts compare to mutual funds. He shares some of the truths about mutual funds that many in the investment world don't want you to know.

As you read this book, you will no doubt be surprised, educated, entertained, and, most important, enlightened. I have always loved Don's ability to take complex issues and simplify them; in this book he has provided another great resource for investors.

Most of us spend our lives working to make enough money to reach financial independence; making your money work as hard as you do is crucial to getting there sooner. Unfortunately, like dieting, there are no magic pills to investment success. However, if you take the time to learn, and have the discipline to apply what you have learned, you can have significant control over your financial freedom.

Joe John Duran, CFA,
author of *Start It, Sell It & Make a Mint* and
The First Time Investor's Workbook

I have always believed that the best way to simplify a complicated subject and make it instantly meaningful for the reader is through frequently asked questions (FAQs). By reading the answers to these questions, you can gain insight into the subject of separately managed accounts and quickly determine if you want to buy this book or not.

I hope you decide to read the rest of this book after you read the FAQs. It promises to establish a more secure financial future for you and your family through separately managed accounts so you can stop wasting your wealth in mutual funds.

What is separate account management? Separately managed accounts comprise individual securities owned directly by an investor(s) that are professionally managed to achieve higher performance with lower fees, increased tax efficiency, and heightened asset control. These and other features provide substantial advantages over mutual fund investing.

Who is investing in separate accounts? In decades past, separate accounts were the asset management strategy of choice for institutions and wealthy investors with $500,000 or more in investable assets. Today, it is a new ball game in which computers and other technological improvements allow investors with minimums of $100,000 access to separate accounts. This means over 37 million U.S. households now qualify to invest in separate accounts. Many high-net-worth clients are shifting from mutual funds to separate accounts. As a result, separate accounts grew by a whopping 29 percent during three quarters of 2000. In that same time period, mutual funds only grew 5.2 percent.

Why should I switch from mutual funds into separate accounts? Mutual funds have served their time well and will continue to do so for those individuals with modest funds to invest. But for affluent individuals whose mutual funds decreased in value and whose capital gains distribution increased in 2000, this is a wake-up call. The years 2000 and 2001 buried a lot of the gains achieved by mutual fund investors during the 1990s. Separate accounts, with the benefits of tax efficiency, asset control, customization, lower fees, and the services of professional money managers, offer knowledgeable investors all that mutual funds once promised but failed to deliver.

How much investment is necessary to establish a separate account? For the most part, a minimum of $100,000 of investable cash and/or securities is necessary to establish a separate account. However, there are available accounts per asset class with minimums in the $25,000 to $50,000 range. Low-end separate accounts (folios) are available through Internet financial companies offering lower minimums and lower fees. These usually do not include a high-end money manager.

How much will I pay to have a separate account? Unlike mutual funds with numerous fees and charges, you will pay one straight fee for the serving of your separate account. Expect to pay annually between 2 and 3 percent of total assets managed. The situation is fluid and the fee often is reduced through discounting and the size of the account. Discounts can be as much as 25 percent and even can be higher with more assets invested. What you receive for a straight down-the-line fee structure is trading, money management, custody, and consultation plus the benefits of the separate account infrastructure, such as tax efficiency, potential higher performance, customization, etc. If you chose not to employ an investment advisor you could bring your annual fee to approximately 1 percent of your separate account total assets annually.

Where do I find separate account management programs? As you might guess, the big stock brokerage houses—Salomon Smith Barney (29 percent), Merrill Lynch (22 percent), Morgan Stanley Dean Witter (10 percent), Paine Webber (9 percent), and Prudential (8 percent)—hold most of the separate account business. However, the regional brokerage houses—Raymond James, AG Edwards, Wheat First Union, etc.—are coming on strong and lock in 14 percent of the business. The remaining 8 percent is a mixture of financial service firms such as banks (Wells Fargo, Chase, etc.) and independent broker-dealers

(Linsco/Private Ledger, etc). These percentages will change as the big mutual fund houses—Fidelity, Oppenheimer, MFS, etc.—are scrambling to bring out their own managed account programs. According to the Financial Research Corp., the industry is expected to experience a 30 percent yearly growth reaching one trillion dollars in 2005.

What should I watch for in setting up my separate account? If you read the previous question, do your due diligence very carefully. With the abundance of vendors including broker-dealers who sell through independent investment advisors, banks, insurance companies, mutual fund companies, regional brokers, and the national wire houses such as Salomon Smith Barney, it will benefit you to research carefully before you take the plunge into separate accounts. There are more choices, levels of control, and prices for separate account management than ever before. Whether you are going it alone or utilizing a financial advisor, make your move wisely.

How do separate accounts work? Understanding the financial landscape of separate accounts means understanding who the players are. One of the major reasons for establishing a separate account is to obtain the services of a money manager who would not have been available to you through your previous investments. This money manager manages your portfolio on a daily basis to makes prudent investment decisions. The investor still retains control of his portfolio, even hiring a financial planner to function as a consultant to assist in creating a rational investment strategy. If you decide not to hire an investor advisor, then you will function as your own consultant. All in all, a separate account program includes the program sponsor (brokerage firm, etc.), money manager(s), and the financial advisor (if selected), all assisting the investor in enhancing his portfolio.

Who determines the asset allocation when setting up a separate account? First things first, you initially review your complete financial picture—goals, investable funds, performance requirements, time horizon, and tolerance for risk. This process is typically accomplished with a financial planner though you can choose to go it alone. The result of this process is the establishment of your investment policy statement that you then share with yourmoney manager. This statement determines your asset allocation between asset classes. Your investment policy statement is designed to keep you, your financial advisor, and your money manager(s) on the same track regarding your asset mix. Usually a separate account contains only about 50 stocks versus up to 150 in a mutual fund. Institutional money managers have as many as 15 advisors selecting stocks compared to one manager selecting the stocks in a mutual fund. Feel free to alter your plan as you go because you are in charge of your portfolio. However, your money manager and advisor will be there to provide the necessary advice to reduce the emotion and second-guessing involved in investment decisions.

How do I handle my taxes if I purchase a separate account?
Unlike mutual fund investors, separate account investors hold stocks in their own name. In mutual funds, investors are shareholders and have no control over the taxation of their funds. At the end of the year, new shareholders have to pay taxes on the same capital gains as investors who have been shareholders since January 1. Separate account managers perform "tax harvesting," offsetting gains with losses to deliver a higher after-tax return than mutual funds for their clients.

How do clients track their separate accounts?
What your money is doing is never more than a click away. The Internet makes it easy to check on your separate account regularly and make investment decisions as needed. Depending on the program, your investment advisor and money manager are usually a phone call away. You will receive full reports on investment activity usually quarterly.

How does the future look for separate accounts? It does not appear that the big leap from mutual funds to separate accounts through 2005 will falter. Cerulli Associates, the Boston firm specializing in researching the separate accounts industry, predicts separate accounts will average 30 percent growth per year with assets building to $2.6 trillion by 2010. Does this remarkable growth leave the mutual fund industry in the dust? No, because many mutual fund companies are establishing their own programs. The separate accounts process gives upscale, knowledgeable, take-charge investors access to the cream of the crop institutional money managers, a better way to manage taxes, and more control of their investments.

The idea for this book would have remained in my head were it not for the able assistance of many people. It was the support of these people that transformed this process from just thinking about writing a book about separate accounts to the actual book with words on paper.

In January 2002 while visiting my brother David who lives in Florida, I began to tell him in a quiet moment together about the many benefits separate accounts have over mutual funds. When the conversation was done, we decided we would write our first book. My brother, with many years of experience in journalism and marketing, agreed to assist me.

More than three years later, I can look back to the many people I owe credit. First, I am grateful to my brother for working long hours, meeting deadlines, and faithfully sending copies of drafts across the country from Florida to California.

During the time I presented the separate accounts proposal to publishers, it was Mary Good, acquisitions editor at Dearborn Trade Publishing, who recognized the need for the emerging affluent investor to be exposed to options more productive than mutual funds to build wealth. She and her staff, especially Karen Murphy, developmental editor, were most professional in helping me overcome the challenges offered by the unfamiliar territory of book writing.

During the actual writing of the book, I used many resources throughout the industry. I thank financial research organizations like Cerulli Associates, Morningstar, Strategic Research Corporation, DALBAR Research, Lipper, Inc., and Tiburon Strategic Advisors for presenting to me their best thinking on financial management.

To the people at Money Market Institute (MMI) and Investment Company Institute (ICI), I appreciate the support of your organizations and the valuable data from your respective vantage points representing the separately managed account industry and the mutual fund industry.

I especially wish to thank the independent financial advisors who utilize separate accounts for their clients. Whether they have taken on separate accounts as a new financial strategy or have been a bedrock utilizing separate accounts for years, they are the dedicated professionals who make tough choices to reduce investors' dependence on mutual funds and structure separate account programs for the sake of their clients who are better off for it. Throughout the pages in this book, you will meet some of these professional advisors who care about their clients and constantly look for ways to enhance their clients' wealth.

Finally, I wish to pay homage to the individual investors who are reading this book. By picking up this book, you must be seeking a better way to invest your wealth—to improve your performance returns by looking for the most appropriate asset management vehicle offering the lowest possible costs and the greatest tax efficiency.

I didn't begin my financial career urging millions of American investors to *stop wasting their wealth investing in mutual funds.*

In fact, a few short years ago, I would be applauding all those Americans who had their personal resources in mutual funds. For over 60 years this group has done just that, utilizing the mutual fund asset management strategy as they fueled their retirement, educated their kids, and purchased big-ticket items (cars, homes, etc.) so important for an affluent American lifestyle.

With the advent of 401(k)s and IRAs during the 1980s and 1990s, the assets plowed into mutual funds increased tenfold, exponentially creating an $8 trillion industry. Odds are you had or currently have a portion of your wealth in mutual funds. And why not? Funds have low minimums, give you a professional financial person to manage the account, and provide the option of redeeming your money if you need it in a few days. It was, for a time, the perfect wealth-building vehicle for millions of Americans anxious to get a piece of the action from the enigma of Wall Street.

STOP WASTING WEALTH IN MUTUAL FUNDS

During my 30 years in this business, my opinion of mutual funds has been highly positive and I have recommended that most of my clients invest in mutual funds. But during the 2002–2003 investment period, a combination of events occurred in the marketplace that made me reconsider the validity of recommending mutual funds for my clients. I became disillusioned with the mutual fund industry. My clients were complaining loudly about the poor performance of their funds and the huge capital gains taxes tacked on by the IRS. They were asking for more transparency in their funds so they could find out what specific stocks they were invested in. They felt they lost all control over the decision making regarding their funds.

Then, the mutual funds scandal broke in late 2003 and continues today, implicating some of the biggest, most respected mutual fund companies in the business. I decided during those months that my clients needed a better wealth-building philosophy if they were going to protect their assets and financial well-being.

SEPARATE ACCOUNTS: THE SMART ALTERNATIVE TO MUTUAL FUNDS

Separate account management, a managed money financial strategy in the marketplace for 30 years, was rising to new prominence and visibility among savvy clients who were disappointed with mutual funds and were looking for a better way to invest and protect their wealth.

This financial strategy of protecting and enhancing wealth is not new. It has been around almost as long as mutual funds, but it has remained obscure because until recently minimum requirements were in the millions of dollars, not a few thousand dollars like mutual funds. Separately managed accounts, or SAMs, once were reserved only for the ultrarich and large institutions.

I discovered that by opening a SAM, my clients could have access to the same top-grade money managers—some of the sharpest financial minds in the country—that the superrich and large corporations like the Ford Foundation have been enjoying for years. This type of asset management also allowed my clients to improve their tax efficiency and enjoy real-time reporting on their accounts—benefits to my clients that mutual funds could not offer.

After much due diligence researching the concept, I decided that separate account management was the wave of the future for knowledgeable medium-income to high-income individuals. At the same time, technology and computer software breakthroughs were happening, bringing separate account ownership down to a reasonable level for the new "emerging affluent."

THE NEW BEGINNING:
SEPARATE ACCOUNT MANAGEMENT

Due to past experience and in response to today's ever-changing financial climate, I am no longer a supporter of mutual funds. In this book, I will explain clearly the inequities of mutual funds such as escalating fees, crushing tax liabilities, and double-digit performance losses. The mutual fund companies' collective philosophy of doing business is "growth at all costs," an infectious greed that has been slowly poisoning this industry at the expense of the average mutual fund investor. To cap it off, in the last quarter of 2003, scandal rocked this once-pristine industry when some of the most respected names in the business—Bank of America, Janus Capital, Capital One, Strong Capital Management, Prudential Securities, Alliance Capital, and Putnam Investments to name just a few—were accused of deceiving the American investor.

USING THIS BOOK

I have divided this book into four parts. In Part One, I will explain the nature of the problems plaguing the mutual fund industry. In Part Two, I will introduce you to the SAM concept of investing and how it compares head-to-head with mutual fund investing. Thus, the purpose of this book is to document the problems of mutual funds and present a logical alternative: separate accounts. If I have presented a convincing argument, then continue on to Part Three for a how-to guide for setting up and maintaining a separate account. I have tried to present the SAM story in a friendly, informal style, jargon-free and with little academic excess. The final section, Part Four, will help you utilize the latest innovations and breakthroughs to keep you on top of your game and looking into the future.

Further, I included samples of useful tools at the back of this book that you will need when establishing a separate account, including a glossary of terms and resources for you to contact. I intended to give you a real-world feel in the book so you can easily determine if a separate account is for you. If a separate account is for you, then the book will show you how to set one up step-by-step.

Purpose of the Book

The reason for this book is simple: American investors are wasting their wealth in mutual funds. There is a logical asset management alternative for investors suffering from the instability and fluctuations of the market. It is called separate account management. It is the hottest concept in the financial industry today for investing your wealth. This book tells you why separate accounts have been increasing in assets, averaging 30 percent most years since 1999. More and more investors are discovering that there's a superior way of handling their wealth. I hope you do too. I want you to *stop wasting wealth in mutual funds.*

Part One

STOP WASTING YOUR WEALTH ON MUTUAL FUNDS

1

THE DOWNFALL OF MUTUAL FUNDS

He is now fast rising from affluence to poverty.

Mark Twain (Samuel Clemens)

George, 61, and Janice, 63, a few years older than the massive boomer generation coming up behind them, suddenly realized that they had never managed to put away the large investment egg they had always wanted. They had good intentions, but were not able to follow through. The kids, a mortgage, two cars, and all the necessities had siphoned off most of their extra money through the years.

Now they were in their 60s, retiring soon, and looking for a quick solution utilizing the $50,000 they had managed to save over the years in a bank account with low, single-digit interest.

George's brother, Edward, was an independent investment advisor who had been urging George for years to put his money in the stock market.

In November 1999, George made the call. On that call, Edward told George that his clients were getting double-digit returns with high-tech, dot-com mutual funds.

Edward told George that he had some strong high-tech mutual funds that were returning 12 percent to 14 percent per year, and increasing their value almost on a daily basis.

Figure 1.1 *George's Lament: High-Tech Mutual Funds Returns in 2001*

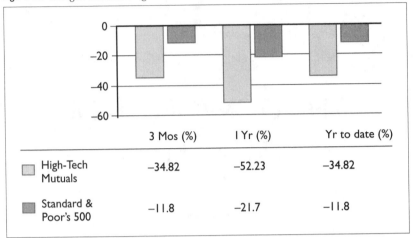

	3 Mos (%)	1 Yr (%)	Yr to date (%)
High-Tech Mutuals	−34.82	−52.23	−34.82
Standard & Poor's 500	−11.8	−21.7	−11.8

George wired his brother his entire $50,000 savings the next day, in spite of Janice's objections about risking all of their money in one sector of the market.

During the first months, the investments went well. Their value increased almost weekly. Edward had placed George's money into five mutual funds, $10,000 in each, to create diversification and to minimize risk. Of course, at that time, all funds heavily invested in technology were basically invested in the same companies. George didn't have any real diversification, a common situation with mutual funds in the same industry.

Early in 2001, things began to change. By November, George's initial investment of $50,000 had dwindled to $13,000. George placed a frantic call to his brother and was told it was a temporary market correction.

The market did not correct itself. From its March 2000 peak to the lowest point in October 2002, the Standard & Poor's (S&P) 500 had dropped approximately 47 percent, with dividends reinvested.

George and Janice ended up with five high-tech mutual funds that were worth about $2,600 each. (See Figure 1.1.) Another surprise came in January 2001. They learned that they owed $1,500 in capital gains taxes for the 2000 tax year, which essentially wiped out what was left of their life savings.

MILLENNIUM BACKLASH

Mutual funds have become the roadkill of the financial industry.

During 2000 and 2001, the financial damage became painfully apparent for 50 million American households. In the first years of the new millennium there were 6,000 equity funds, give or take. Of those thousands of funds, only about 20 percent performed well enough to earn back their fees and loads. Additionally, most investors had to contend with capital gains tax.

The U.S. stock market began the new century with three years of losses—a significant event that hasn't happened since the Great Depression. Mutual funds, a beloved investing institution for 63 years, lost money for most, if not all, of the 93 million shell-shocked Americans invested in them. In fact, February 2001 saw Standard & Poor's 500 Index drop 9.6 percent—the worst showing since 1998. The Nasdaq, comprised more heavily of tech stocks, posted a 22.39 percent loss.

A Wake-up Call

Investors have been dribbling away their wealth for many years in mutual funds, paying millions in excessive costs and taking untold risks in their pursuit to beat the market. During the go-go years of the 1990s when there were double-digit returns, hardly a murmur was heard about the inequities of mutual funds. But the first five years of the 21st century have caused the green light to flash red. Mutual funds, with their underperformance, hidden fees, higher income tax consequences, and lack of control, have caused wiser investors to realize that they're wasting their wealth in mutual funds.

IN THE BEGINNING: THE BRIGHT PROMISE OF MUTUAL FUNDS

Mutual funds didn't start out wasting the wealth of millions of investors. In fact, to give credit where it's due, mutual funds have oiled the fortunes of millions of Americans during their working life and retirement since 1940, when the Security and Exchange Commission (SEC) founded the Investment Company Act that created the concept of putting multiple stocks and/or bonds in separate funds. Mutual funds have been good for America for decades.

Mutual funds created an opportunity for average, middle-class Americans to invest like those with more substantial resources. Funds became the investors' best friend, offering professional management, wide choices, and, for a time, stress-free investing. It was truly a powerful force in the marketplace. These pools of equities offered investors diversification and more safety than most single securities, at a price that was affordable.

Mutual funds increased in popularity when the government offered retirement plans such as 401(k)s, SEPs, and IRAs. In fact, today, 38 percent of mutual fund assets come from 401(k)s. Minimums for IRAs were as low as $2,000, affordable for most middle-income Americans—a major reason vast sums of money were pumped into mutual funds.

At the same time, fund companies promoted mutual funds heavily. They promised excellent returns and safety for investor dollars, causing more Americans to wade in and believe the maximum return/minimum risk fantasy.

TODAY THE MASK IS OFF

Unfortunately, today mutual fund companies have changed. Although in earlier years they were all about making money for clients, now they're focused only on gathering as many assets as the law allows.

Face Facts

Year	Number of Funds	Value
1980	500	$100 Billion
1993	3,800	$1.6 Trillion
2001	8,200	$6.6 Trillion
2004	8,106	$7.0 Trillion
2005	8,300	$8.1 Trillion

Source: Investment Company Institute.

They're sidestepping the spirit of the 1940 mutual fund law. And as you'll see, they're also optimizing as much market share as they can—even if the law *doesn't* allow it.

Asset Gathering with a Wink

Before 2003, the worst thing about mutual funds is that *most* lost money. From 2003 on, you can say something even worse about mutual funds: A large number are losing money *fraudulently*.

Thanks go to the attorney general of New York State, Eliot Spitzer, whose crusading efforts in September 2003 put the brakes on the likes of major financial companies for improper trading of mutual fund shares. Blue chip companies—Bank of America, Bank One, Janus Capital Group, Strong Capital Management—were implicated along with small trader, hedge fund Canary Capital Partners in schemes to bilk investors of billions each year, according to Spitzer.

Spitzer exposed the more-than-60-year backside of an industry entrusted with nearly $7 trillion of the American public's money. Mutual funds used to be the investment vehicles investors relied on to finance the American dream—the home in the suburbs, the kids' education, and the comfortable retirement.

Today the nation's 93 million mutual fund investors are overwhelmed by competing claims of some 8,000 funds. Most of the time, these investors are clueless about how to enhance their wealth with mutual funds. The average stock fund lost 12 percent yearly during 2000, 2001, and 2002. And the last few years have not been much better, but investors are still in the game shelling out $14.7 billion of their wealth in 2004 to get into mutual funds—the best sales year for mutual funds since 2001.

Mediocrity Is Mutual Funds

Memories dim, and the thrill of the hunt is with all of us. The real fact is that investors pay out upwards of $72 billion in fund costs and fees. What do they get in return? They almost always receive mediocre performance, and when you factor in taxes, they actually suffer a financial loss. A stable bond fund, real estate, individual stocks, or even a

Treasury bill may perform as well as the average mutual fund with risky high-trading equities.

Read my lips: It's the expenses! Expenses are the real killer—those you see and those you don't. Average investors are so confused by these expenses that they have no idea what they are paying.

The sales commission for most actively managed funds is tacked on by the stockbrokers and is usually around 6 percent. The fund deducts at least 0.5 percent from your account for its service. Cash drag, which is a reserve set aside for "opportunity costs" or to pay off redemptions, adds another 0.6 percent.

The buying and selling of stocks that the fund manager performs all year long causes transaction costs. In fact, the average "turn" of a stock is 90 percent (or higher) yearly for nearly every stock in a mutual fund portfolio. By conservative estimates, this racks up an expense of 0.7 percent, not including capital gains taxes, which I will cover in Chapter 6.

Add another 1.5 percent for management fees and expenses including the dreaded 12b-1 marketing fee that those outside the industry criticize. Those inside the industry exploit it for all its worth.

Taxes, based on your tax bracket if you're a taxable investor, could be as high as 2.7 percent. Let's be conservative and say you will pay taxes on capital gains of 0.7 percent.

Here's the bottom line: Say your fund is generating a good return in today's market of 12 percent in total assets as a long-term investor. The commissions, costs, cash drag, and fees reduce this to 8.7 percent. In short, your fund manager has cost you 3.3 percent. Therefore, the fund is underperforming the market by 3.3 percent.

After taxes, which I estimated conservatively (0.7 percent), you will have no more than 8 percent of the original 12 percent. Only two-thirds of your fund's returns make it into your pocket, probably less.[1]

Funds cost too much. Simply put, mutual funds cost too much. The typical investor, which we will see in later chapters, is averaging 3.5 percent in costs. The reason that you're seeing conflicting fee charges for mutual funds is that there are multiple fee revenue streams and many fee charges are hidden. You will see that separate accounts—the investment alternative to mutual funds that were long thought to be a higher price investment strategy—have costs around 2.5 percent and all fees are out in the open.

Before I explain separate accounts in detail in Part Two, I want to spend a few more chapters detailing why investing in mutual funds is "wasting wealth."

2

THE HONEYMOON IS OVER, THE MARRIAGE ON THE ROCKS

Marriage is a mistake every man should make.

George Jessel

For over 60 years, American investors have had a love affair with mutual funds—until now. The honeymoon is over and the marriage is in serious difficulty. Since the millennium, the escalating fees, crushing tax liabilities, and double-digit losses I mentioned earlier have surfaced and slowly killed investors' affection for mutual funds. And in the final quarter of 2003, scandal rocked the once-pristine industry that will seriously test the future relationship American investors have with mutual funds.

IT'S FIVE O'CLOCK SOMEWHERE

No one can escape it. Turn on the radio and you'll hear what's going on in the stock market. Turn the dial, and you'll come across multiple syndicated investment programs pitching investment products and get-rich schemes. On TV, you can find three cable channels covering financial news exclusively. Slick literature, newsletters, magazine and journal articles, and puffed-up print advertisements constantly hammer home mutual fund investment opportunities. Financial Internet sites have become widespread, creating the largest e-business on the Web.

How'd You Hear About Us?

Ten years ago not one TV channel covered detailed market news. Today:

- Three major cable channels are devoted to financial news
- Hundreds of radio stations report financial news
- Most major and minor newspapers have business pages
- There are specialized financial newspapers and magazines
- Thousands of newsletters cover financial topics
- Hundreds of thousands of Web sites pertain to financial investments
- Advertisements, slick brochures, and mailing pieces abound with financial offers
- Financial salespeople do make calls

Source: Robert B. Jorgensen.

Literally hundreds of Web sites are positioned to reveal the latest hot investment opportunities. All of these triggering devices want you to believe they're the genie in the lamp—one rub will propel you to riches.

"Investors today are being fed lies and distortions, are being exploited and neglected," says Arthur Leavitt, former chairman of the SEC. "In the wake of the last decade's rush to invest by millions of households, and Wall Street's obsession with short-term performance, a culture of gamesmanship has grown among corporate management, financial analysts, brokers, and mutual fund managers, making it hard to tell financial fantasy from reality, salesmanship from honest advice."[1]

Getting Even, But for How Long?

Growing wiser and angrier after getting hit with double-digit losses and high taxes a few years back, disillusioned investors responded accordingly. They yanked record amounts of money out of equity funds. In July 2002 alone, they pulled out $52.6 billion, more than they withdrew during three of the worst months in recent stock market history—September 2001, August 1998, and October 1987—combined.

Face **F**acts

Mutual funds cost too much! With investment dollars pouring into the mutual fund industry—from $371 billion in 1984 to $8.1 trillion in 2005—you'd think the total cost of mutual fund investing would have gone down. The truth is that the average cost of mutual funds has never been higher. (See Figure 2.1.)

Figure 2.1 *Know the Truth about Mutual Funds or Suffer the Consequences*

The Tax Consequence: If fund managers sell stock at a profit, you take a capital gains hit even if your fund lost money that year.

The Quick Change Consequence: You invested in the fund to fulfill a certain investment strategy. Be careful; the manager can change the strategy.

The Power Vacuum Consequence: The fund manager makes all buy-and-sell decisions, not you.

The No Diversification Consequence: Unless you are diversified across fund sectors, you may wind up owning the same stocks in different funds.

The Name's the Game Consequence: A stock fund's name doesn't always reflect its investing intentions.

The Moving Manager Consequence: Managers come and go. If you lose your manager, your fund will probably suffer.

The Huge Fund Consequence: The more assets a fund takes in, the higher the chances of lower performance.

The Fee Consequence: You'll pay myriad fees and commissions.

The bottom line is that mutual fund companies fall short in regard to performance and returns with investors' stock funds, yet they're excellent at charging exorbitant fees and add-on charges. In short, mutual funds are a marketing success, not an investing success.

What does this mean to you as an investor in mutual funds? If you've entrusted any of your hard-earned wealth to mutual funds, you're being ripped off. This is surprising because we've always been told that the stock market is the single best place to build wealth for your families and your retirement.

This is true if you're getting the most bang for your buck by putting those dollars in the right investment vehicles. If you're not, your portfolio is on a treadmill going nowhere along with the assets of millions of other dejected mutual fund investors. The purpose of this book is to get you off the mutual fund treadmill. But first, a little history.

WHAT WENT WRONG WITH SOMETHING SO RIGHT?

In 2005 mutual funds had assets totaling over $8.1 trillion, up from $371 billion in 1984. This has caused fund companies' priorities to shift. It's evident that the mutual fund industry does not hold the individual investor in the highest regard. In fact, the industry treats the investor rather poorly.

Welcome to Business 101

John Bogle, outspoken critic of mutual funds and founder of Vanguard Financial, says his biggest complaint of the mutual fund industry is that it's now run like a business. Bogle traces the industry's demise to a 1956 federal court ruling allowing mutual fund firms to become public enterprises. This changed the playing field, according to Bogle. "That opened the door to look at this business as an entrepreneurial business in which the focus was on making money for the stockholders," he said. "Once you change the investment profession into a financial services business, you put management in the backseat and marketing in front."[2]

The Death of Mutual Funds?

These changes in priorities will hasten the downfall of mutual funds in much the same way that catastrophic changes in their environment wiped out the dinosaurs. This doesn't mean that mutual funds and the companies that promote and market them are going to become extinct.

In fact, the opposite is true. At the time of this writing, mutual fund companies are evolving. They're developing new alternatives and investment strategies in order to hold on to their client base and secure new clients. Eventually, though, mutual funds will take a backseat to new forms of investing for the emerging affluent investor. Mutual funds as we know them are going the way of the dinosaur.

Mutual funds are dying in their original state because of the unfairness of fees, unnecessary taxes, lack of investor control, and a host of other reasons. Investors have never grasped these points until now. Today, a lot of investors understand the drawbacks of mutual funds because the events of the last five years have brought the message home. They've discovered that they're paying out millions of dollars in excessive costs and running needless risks—all in the hope of outperforming the market.

Government Rises to the Occasion

As the government examines more critically the operating policies of mutual fund companies, things will change—in much the same way we transformed transportation from the horse and buggy to the automobile.

In 2003, the government (state government and the SEC) provided temporary fixes to mutual fund company abuses. Now, not only are government officials noting serious discretions throughout the industry and working to do something about them (with new regulations and stepped-up surveillance), but investors also are becoming outraged.

"I'm appalled," said one investor. "What a dupe. I've been thinking I was being afforded the same chances to win and lose." She was referring to the September 2003 scandal involving Canary Partners, a hedge fund, in which the attorney general of New York State accused Canary of trading after the market's 4 PM closing to make fast profits the next day on fast-breaking financial events. This is something strictly illegal under securities laws, and it is a trading scam that no small investors would be privy to.

Increased federal and state scrutiny will trigger more reforms that will probably get bogged down in Congress, like the Mutual Funds Integrity and Fee Transparency Act that the mutual fund industry successfully lobbied against.

In any event, the Canary that sang in 2003 will have mutual fund companies singing a different tune in the future.

Face **F**acts

A mutual fund portfolio that loses **25 percent** in a single year needs to return **33 percent** to get back to where it was at the beginning of the decline. The investor's solution: Save more (if you're building for retirement) or withdraw less (if you're already retired).

PAST PERFORMANCE IS NO GUARANTEE OF FUTURE RESULTS

In the meantime, underperformance is the norm. In recent years, mutual fund companies could perhaps be forgiven for the huge marketing expenses and the increasing salaries of their star managers if their product delivered as advertised. But this is no longer the case. With mutual funds, underperformance is the norm rather than the exception. It's a fact. In spite of a respectable past during the 1980s and 1990s, the average mutual fund today returns 2 percent less than the returns of the market each year.

> *In the mutual fund industry, we used to be in the business of long-term investing,*
> *and now we're in the business of short-term speculation.*
> **John C. Bogle, founder of Vanguard Financial**

Not only do fund managers tend to underperform the S&P 500 yearly, but the underperformance also is growing more pronounced over the years. The individual managers responsible for funds are marketed as "stars." But as John Bogle grumbles, "They're not stars but comets."[3]

Investors and potential investors are subjected to billions of dollars of advertising promoting the virtues of funds and mutual fund managers who are supposedly skilled in handling their money. As journalist Richard Karlgaard has written, the average mutual fund manager "hasn't beat a dart thrown by a drunk at a bus depot bar since 1994."[4] The chances of the fund manager beating the market are small—so small that the average mutual fund only outperforms the market two times out of every five, according to mutual fund researchers.

If you're still not convinced, consider the following:

F*ace* **F***acts*

Here's why you can't get ahead in today's markets with mutual funds:
Increased taxes (from frequent trading)
+ lower returns (from failing to buy and hold)
+ excessive fees and charges
= Unreasonably poor performance

- Through the end of 2001, there were 1,226 actively managed stock funds with a five-year record. Their average annualized performance trailed the S&P index by 1.9 percent per year (8.8 percent for the funds and 10.7 percent for the index).
- Through the end of 2001, there were 623 actively managed stock funds with a ten-year record. Their average annualized performance trailed the S&P 500 by 1.7 percent per year (11.2 percent for the funds and 12.9 percent for the index).
- The figures above include the sales loads charged by many funds. Loads are akin to brokerage commissions, which come straight out of your returns. They're charged when you buy or sell shares of your fund. Even with these load funds excluded, the five-year average trailed the S&P 500 by 1.4 percent per year, and the ten-year average return trailed by 1.4 percent as well.
- None of these figures include discarded mutual funds, which would reflect poorer performance and bring these averages down significantly. The exclusion of these mutual funds is called "survivorship bias." With returns corrected for survivorship bias, average actively managed funds trail the market by about 3 percent per year.

Costs Drag Down Performance

Fund managers are supposed to be good, and some of them are; only we don't know which ones are good until the returns come in. Most managers, unfortunately, will only equal the market as a whole before costs. What drags performance down—and all investors should realize this—are the management fees, trading costs, sales loads, and other inci-

F*ace* **F***acts*

Mutual funds must disclose that past performance is not indicative of future results. Unfortunately, most investors and financial media use past performance as their primary mutual fund selection criterion. The truth is most mutual funds rarely outperform the markets for a significant period of time.

In fact, only one fund in the history of mutual funds has outperformed the S&P 500 for more than ten years straight.

dentals. To summarize, direct and indirect costs defeat the performance of mutual funds before you even get out of the starting gate.

Marketing Is in the Driver's Seat

For the first few decades after the inception of mutual funds, the emphasis was on enhancing shareholders' returns and protecting their principals. But at an accelerating rate during the last ten years a new strategy has emerged, moving from the management of funds to the marketing of funds. This trend has created havoc for lifetime mutual fund investors.

Think Taxes: Inside the Capital Gains Dilemma

There are no tax advantages to mutual funds, only disadvantages. If you pay taxes and own mutual funds, you have created a natural adversarial relationship. You will probably have to pay taxes when your stocks are sold in the portfolio. Not only that, you may also have to pay taxes when your stock fund loses money.

Here's a primer. Mutual fund companies during the tax year are required to distribute capital gains and/or dividends to their shareholders. Unless you own a nontaxable mutual fund (i.e., municipal bond fund, retirement account, etc.), you probably are going to have capital gains.

Mutual fund companies are not looking out for you when it comes to taxes. Shareholders pay capital gains taxes; mutual fund companies don't. Your capital gains are taxed at the standard tax rate: 28 percent to 35.6 percent (new tax law parameters), depending on your reported income, for stocks held for less than one year. If you hold funds for more than a year, it's 15 percent across the board.

As Sure as Death and Taxes

American households paid $345 billion in capital gains taxes on mutual funds in 2000. These gains had accumulated throughout the 1990s. When the air came out of technology stocks, portfolio managers began dumping them. But even if these stocks had lost their original value, they still accumulated capital gains. Remember, even if your stock fund loses money, you're still liable for capital gains because during the fund's history it made money, making its capital gains embedded.

Did we mention dividends? Even if you reinvest your dividends back into the fund, the IRS says you are still subject to tax on your dividends.

The Industry's Not Protecting Your Backside

There are ways to cut your tax bill with mutual funds if the companies were responsible. Critics charge that fund companies could lower capital gains distributions if they wished. One way is through improved bookkeeping. If fund companies were programmed to sell their highest-cost shares first when they reduce a large block of stock, it could result in a tax savings for investors. This is called HIFO (highest in, first out) accounting, and according to Vanguard, the low-cost index fund company, it could save investors as much as 1 percent of assets each year due to lower costs.

Trading less often would hinder the capital gains explosion, but because the average mutual fund turns over it stocks once in the course of a year (on which the commission costs average five cents a share every time a share is traded), this seems unlikely. "That's much higher than most investors pay for online brokerage," says *BusinessWeek*. The mutual fund structure prevents "tax harvesting," the timing of securities' buy-and-sell orders to utilize capital losses or defer capital gains.

The Short End of the Stick

Regardless of when you buy into a mutual fund, you become a proud owner of liabilities that were incurred before you even put your money down. Say you buy into a fund for $10,000 on December 12 at $10 a share. Shortly before the year ends, your mutual fund company calculates a yearly capital gain of $2 a share. Guess what? Because you have 1,000 shares, you shortly will receive a distribution of $2,000 all taxable to you. Even though you've only been in the fund for a couple weeks, you will have to pay the same amount of tax as the fellow who had been in it all year. Your original $10,000 investment may still be intact, but now you have a $2,000 tax bill.

Buyer Beware

Lesson learned? Never buy into a fund in December when mutual fund companies record end-of-year performance. Examine funds by their after-tax returns, rather than pretax. You won't find these figures in the fund advertisement or brochure. You can find the figures in the fund's prospectus—in very small print. Thanks to the SEC's February 2003 ruling requiring mutual fund companies to include pretax and post-tax information in their prospectuses, companies cannot conceal this information.

The only problem is that most investors don't read the prospectus.

Let's focus on what can and did happen in 2000. A lot of investors bought into a popular fund that year so the capital gains were spread among a lot of people. A bear market emerged because many investors rushed to liquidate that particular fund and its manager had no choice but to sell stocks, at possibly a gain, to raise enough capital for those redemptions. A huge capital distribution was left for the remaining stockholders.

There are examples of investors who put a few thousand dollars into a fund and later were hit by Uncle Sam for a five-figure tax bite. Was there a chance that the mutual fund managers could have foreseen the taxpayers' dilemma and altered their selling strategy? Not a chance. Mutual fund managers aren't paid to maximize tax efficiency, only to generate returns.

Figure 2.2 *Median Expense Ratio for Stock Funds*

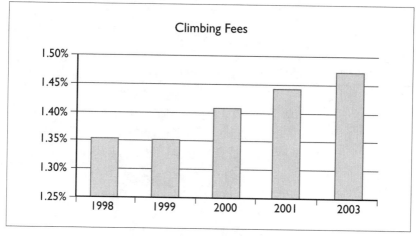

*The bedrock principle [is] that the interests of
mutual fund investors always come first.*

Paul G. Haaga, Jr., chairman of the mutual fund industry's Investment Company Institute

The Mutual Funds Billing Iceberg

Nine-tenths of an iceberg is unseen, under water. Mutual fund companies have become increasingly adept at applying extra hidden revenue streams to their funds, in addition to standard fees, which are climbing. In fact, as returns have diminished during the post-2000 period, mutual fund companies have actually been raising fees. (See Figure 2.2.)

Investors Share the Blame Too

The average mutual fund investor isn't even aware of the fees he's paying—disclosed or undisclosed. In fact, to add insult to injury, shareholders are paying for mutual fund advertising and promotion through 12b-1 fees. Unfortunately, as mentioned earlier, most investors don't read their mutual fund prospectus, where a lot of essential fee information can be found. All 93 million mutual fund investors reward mutual fund companies annually with about $70 billion in operating costs—and most don't realize they're paying it.

What does investing in funds really cost you?

Figure 2.3 *First-Year Load Fund*

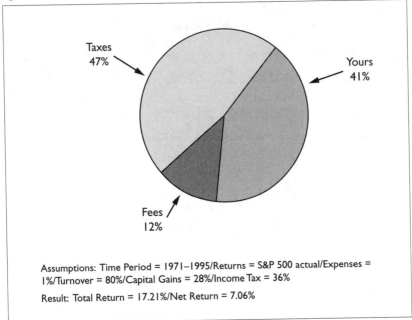

Taxes
47%

Yours
41%

Fees
12%

Assumptions: Time Period = 1971–1995/Returns = S&P 500 actual/Expenses = 1%/Turnover = 80%/Capital Gains = 28%/Income Tax = 36%

Result: Total Return = 17.21%/Net Return = 7.06%

You can expect to pay approximately 3 percent to 4 percent of your fund assets yearly in total costs (up-front or back-end costs) for a load fund. For a no-load fund, you'll still be paying about 3 percent to 3½ percent for your portfolio mutual funds. Check out these costs over the life of your portfolio and you'll see some serious money going into the coffers of the mutual fund companies. (See Figure 2.3.)

Unlike paying your electric bill or phone bill regularly, you hardly ever receive a bill from your mutual fund company. Your costs are simply deducted from your portfolio returns or off the top when a broker executes a trade. You may scream if your daughter makes an unauthorized long-distance phone call, but where are you when you pay a 5 percent load on a $25,000 mutual fund investment?

Reduce Fees? Don't Kid Yourself

During the bull market of the 1990s, the fund companies, with huge infusions of cash coming and internal expenses stabilizing, did nothing to reduce fees for their shareholders. In fact, because the fixed costs of fund companies (staffing, accounting, research, and so forth) became smaller, fees could have been reduced. Remember, fund companies increased revenues many times to over $7 trillion in 2000 from $371 billion in 1984. Instead, the internal fees these companies charged investors have risen by approximately 30 percent.

John Bogle, founder of the Vanguard Group, is critical of mutual funds. He says these hidden fees reduce the net rate of return of funds as a group. Over the long run, these funds tend to lag the market by 1½ percent to 2½ percent annually. These differences in annual returns, extended over long periods of time, make a dramatic difference in your final capital.

Bogle sums it up by saying, ". . . the drive to make money for others-the fund shareholders—may not be as powerful as the drive to make money for oneself through ownership participation in the management company."[5]

Bogle is saying that there are two sides pulling against each other in mutual fund companies: the shareholders (the investors in the mutual funds) and the stockholders (the investors in the mutual fund company).

Keeping You in the Dark

The mutual fund industry profits by keeping the lights off. As long as fund companies keep you in a sea of ignorance, the negative elements of mutual funds won't ever see the light of day. Most investors traditionally have to make do with dated semiannuals of their mutual fund holdings. That's the bare minimum as ruled by the SEC. Twice a year, you get to see what's going on in your account.

Investors today want financial information 24/7.

Even though the Internet has sped up the tracking of securities considerably, major fund companies have been painfully slow to keep investors current. This means that when you check your holdings on the Web, your figures are out-of-date, and possibly flat-out wrong or altogether missing because fund managers are changing your portfolio so rapidly.

I don't like funds. They lag market indexes, nick you with fees, and run up unnecessary tax bills.

Kenneth L. Fisher, columnist, *Forbes*, August 2001

That's not all. Arthur Levitt, former chairman of the SEC, in his revealing book *Take On the Street,* criticizes the highly profitable fund companies' reluctance to spend much money on educating investors. He quotes another SEC official as saying, "I think fund companies believe the underinformed investor is a more profitable investor." After a number of surveys and focus groups, the SEC determined that investors were even more uneducated on the way their money was being invested than anyone realized. It took years for the SEC to institute rules demanding clearer writing in fund literature and prospectuses.

Says Levitt:

> "Investors simply do not get what they pay for when they buy into a mutual fund; most investors don't even know what they're paying for. The industry often misleads investors into buying funds on the basis of past performance. Fees, along with the effect of annual expenses, sales loads, and trading costs, are hidden. Fund directors as a whole exercise scant oversight over management. The cumulative effect of this has manifested itself in the form of late trading, market timing, and other instances of preferential treatment that cut at the very heart of investor trust. It would be hard not to conclude that the way funds are sold and managed reveals a culture that thrives on hype, promotes short-term trading, and withholds important information."[6]

There you have it. These are some of the financial reasons you should get out of mutual funds. Go ahead and read the next chapter. A little more reinforcement might be in order to really get your attention.

3

THE FINAL STRAW: DECEIT, DECEPTION, AND FRAUD

It is discouraging how many people are shocked by honesty and how few by deceit.

Noel Coward

Unfortunately for investors, the story of the demise of mutual funds doesn't end with poor performance, high fees, and unfair tax burdens. The real plot of this chapter is today's climate of deceit, deception, and fraud that swirls around the financial industry in general and mutual fund companies in particular.

During the 1990s, mutual funds experienced rising markets and ten years of expansion. Investors were receiving double-digit returns. They were living the American dream. Along the way, American investors came to believe in that dream. They had faith in the system and became loyal to Wall Street. Any unexpected aberrations were short-lived and memories also were short.

Squeaky-Clean Industry Begins to Rust

Even though they increased in size and complexity over time, scandals were a mere hiccup among the mutual fund industry during the 1990s, and American investors returned to shareholder complacency. Mutual fund companies were, for the most part, squeaky-clean.

When the dot-com companies exploded onto the scene in 2000, and then imploded in 2001 carrying with them millions of Americans' in-

Speed Bumps

Despite being untainted by major scandal during their 63-year history, mutual fund companies have had many instances of fraud and corruption over the years. But these instances usually involved one company or a single individual or were too complicated for the individual investor to be concerned about. Investors considered these indiscretions merely inconvenient speed bumps and continued to pour millions of dollars into mutual funds. Investors could have taken these events as warnings:

- In the early 1970s, Bernard Cornfield's "funds of funds" collapse had investors suffering big losses amid fraud allegations.
- In 1988, the SEC charged the star manager of the Mutual Shares fund of taking a portion of brokerage fees paid by the fund. The firm, an advisory group, returned more than $1.1 million to fund shareholders by cutting its fees.
- In 1992, a Fidelity Investments manager was convicted of accepting a bribe from Michael Milken, former junk bond chief at Drexel Burnham Lambert Inc.
- In 2000, Dreyfus Corp. paid $3 million in restitution without admitting guilt on false disclosures about its Dreyfus Aggressive Growth Fund.
- More recently, the SEC has investigated numerous cases of investors suffering huge losses due to dubious promises made during the height of the dot-com tech bubble burst. In 2000, three Heartland bond funds were put into receivership after investors discovered that one fund's shares plunged 70 percent in value in a single day.
- In September 2003, the attorney of New York State accused a hedge fund—a largely unregulated investing pool for the wealthy and institutions—of trading certain mutual funds after the 4 PM close of stock trading. The hedge fund continued trading, earning profits on late-breaking news, something ordinary investors couldn't do. Further, the hedge fund was very deeply committed to market timing, moving large amounts of money in and out of funds to make short-term gains. While market timing isn't illegal, it's frowned upon by most legitimate fund companies. This process hurts the average investor because huge withdrawals of money drag down performance.

Source: Karen Damato.

vestment dollars, many shareholders took a reality check. The twin hammering of double-digit losses and huge capital gains taxes brought on a new awareness for the American mutual fund investor.

As of June 2001, investors were redeeming at unprecedented rates. Breaking all records, the year saw investors redeem a staggering $1.042 trillion from funds. This represented a 188 percent increase from the 1997 redemption level of $362 billion.

Then the seventh largest company in America, Enron, collapsed in the latter months of 2001, further disfranchising and disenchanting investors.

Following the Enron collapse were the bankruptcies of World Com and Global Crossing. Dozens of other corporate scandals suddenly emerged. Big Six accounting firms were accused of conspiring with bandit clients and their cooked books. Congress became incensed and made some midterm corrections with some new accounting laws.

In late April 2003, the SEC released hundreds of pages of internal e-mails detailing what securities regulators claim was an industrywide effort to dupe small investors during the dot-com boom. The report showed how research analysts hyped high-tech stocks to win investment bank business. Wall Street fought against the disclosures at a time when the industry was beset with massive layoffs and millions in lost revenues. Shareholders, angry at heavy stock market losses, won a $1.4 billion research settlement in a class-action lawsuit against the ten top brokerage houses.

Conflicts Abound in Mutual Funds

It appears that mutual funds even with their 60-year nearly tarnish-free reputation are every bit as peppered with conflicts of interest as the rest of Wall Street. A number of mutual fund firms are under the SEC's microscope to determine if they paid kickbacks to push their own funds with brokers.

A case in point, American Funds, the nation's third-largest mutual fund group, was charged in 2005 with paying out $100 million in preferential brokerage commissions to have brokers push its own funds with investors. This is a direct violation of industry rules, according to the National Association of Securities Dealers (NASD).

American Funds has been attracting more new money than almost any other competitor during the last few years because of its pristine reputation, while many firms throughout the rest of the industry have been racked by investment improprieties.

Specifically, the NASD charged that American Funds distributors gave out payments over a three-year period to about 50 brokerage firms that were top sellers of its funds. Such payments were done, says the NASD, to reward brokerages for past sales and to encourage future sales of American Funds' 29 fund groups.

"Prior cases in this area have focused on retail firms that received directed brokerage payments from mutual fund companies in exchange for giving preferential treatment to their funds," said Mary L. Schapiro, vice chairman of the NASD, in a statement. "This action makes it clear that it is just as impermissible to offer and make such payments as it is to receive them."[1]

The Beat Goes On . . .

In the past, Morgan Stanley has been accused of chiseling mutual fund investors out of millions of dollars utilizing high-pressure sales tactics.

Charles Schwab, which has the largest fund supermarket on the Internet, regularly recommends its list of best funds in which to invest. Unknown to investors is that Schwab has been recommending funds managed in a U.S. trust owned by—you guessed it—Charles Schwab.

Fidelity Investments, the largest mutual fund company, has long been known to tip the scales in favor of the marketing department. A recent Fidelity ad promoted four funds urging investors to invest for "the long term." Yet the advertising copy highlighting the success of the funds touted a six-month performance that was in double digits during a time when the market was doing extremely well. Three of the funds actually lost money over the full year.

The Straw That Broke It All

In 2003, investors' faith in mutual funds was shaken as never before. On September 4, New York State Attorney General Eliot Spitzer took

"The Mutual Fund Industry Is Scandal-Free No More"
(*USA TODAY,* September 4, 2003)

"Enron hit with federal lawsuit" (*USA TODAY,* July 20, 2003)
"Scandals run deep in the fund world" (*Investment News,* July 22, 2002)
"Funds sweating proxy policies" (*Investment News,* April 21, 2003)
"Buck passed on fund overcharges" (*Investment News,* April 7, 2003)
"Documents to detail dot-com accusations" (*USA TODAY,* April 28, 2003)
"Greed, upheaval testing wire houses" (*Investment News,* April 14, 2003)
"Mutual fund fee growth sowing investor discord" (*Investment News,* February 10, 2003)
"Now, mutual funds under fire" (*The Wall Street Journal,* September 4, 2003)

dead aim at the mutual fund industry after he received a ten-minute call from a Wall Street employee alerting Spitzer to a "late trading problem." The late trading charges he leveled against Canary Capital Partners, a loosely regulated hedge fund mostly for wealthy investors, implicated big names in the financial industry: Bank of America, Bank One, Janus Capital, and Strong Investments. Spitzer accused these companies of behavior so outrageous that it dwarfed the industry's earlier violations.

We're looking at the whole industry, top to bottom.
Sam Israel, NASD chief counsel for enforcement

Spitzer accused Canary Partners, run by Edward Stern, of arranging with Bank of America to buy mutual funds after the market had closed at 4 PM EST, but still receive the fund's pricing for that day. That gave Stern the opportunity to capitalize on any earning news that would influence the fund's price the next day. The hedge fund would have a sure, quick profit.

"It's like being permitted to bet on yesterday's horse races," said Spitzer.

Such late trading is illegal under New York's Martin Act and SEC regulations due to the unfair advantage the late trader gains over other investors.

Further, three mutual fund groups, Janus, Bank One, and Strong, allowed Canary to buy funds one day and sell them the next. Such excessive trading isn't illegal, but most fund companies consider it unethical. In fact, the February 2002 prospectus for Janus Income Funds says, "The funds are not intended for market timing or excessive trading."

The case's prosecutors claim that a fraud as simple as buying stocks after the market closed had to have the blessing of the bank and the mutual fund companies. They knew the scheme was illegal. In other words, some of the biggest players in the mutual fund world were blatantly involved in improper trading practices. This bombshell has marred the industry's reputation.

> *Small investors have been victimized for too long by unscrupulous behavior on the part of fund managers. The regulatory structure that should have picked that up didn't. We need to create a new regulatory environment that protects small investors against the games that have been played . . .*
>
> **Eliot L. Spitzer, attorney general of New York State**

> *If a fund company is cutting deals, it's obviously looking for an aggressive means to boost profits. It would certainly hurt my confidence in the company that they had to go out and play these games.*
>
> **Daniel Wirner, publisher of the *Independent Advisor for Vanguard Investors* newsletter**

More than that, in every instance, "The gains the hedge fund [was] earning came directly at the expense of the long-term shareholders," says Jason Greene, professor of finance at Georgia State University, Atlanta, who has studied the impact on fund performance of maneuvers such as these.[2]

Scandals Do Not Die

Spitzer continued to fire salvos at other fund companies for abuses. In fact, Spitzer's complaint alleged that Canary Capital Partners had engaged in market timing transactions with 30 mutual fund companies.

The SEC is investigating the entire mutual fund industry. The following firms have been the subject of more than normal scrutiny regarding their operations and products:

Alger	Evergreen	Legg Mason	Prudential
Alliance Bernstein	Excelsior	MFS	Putnam
American	Federated	Merrill Lynch	Raymond
American Express	Fidelity	Morgan Stanley	James
American Funds	Franklin	Nations	Scudder
Charles Schwab	Goldman Sachs	PBHG	Seligman
Citigroup	Heartland	Pimco	Strong
Columbia	Invesco	Pioneer	Wachovia
Ed Jones	Janus	Piper Jaffray	Waddell & Reed

Source: Jerry Wade

This is the biggest fraud in the fund industry since federal regulation began in 1940.

Mercer Bullard, chief executive of Fund Democracy, a shareholder advocacy group

As a result of the Spitzer investigation, Congress put together hearings on the matter and threatened to enact strong legislation that in the past with such scandals had been watered down after pressure was applied from industry lobbyists.

The SEC, somewhat lackluster and still removed from the problem, began a push to ignite old complaints on negligent boards, hidden fees, and conflicts between fund companies and investors. The agency began an investigation of over 80 of the largest mutual fund families, broker-dealers, and trading agents on their trading practices.

As long as the returns are there, the typical investor is very forgiving of the unethical conduct of a few bad apples . . .

Jeffrey Keil, vice president for Global Fiduciary Review, Inc.

We Didn't Do It and We Won't Do It Again

It's been more than two years since Attorney General Spitzer turned the mutual fund industry inside out upon his finding evidence of market timing and late trading by Canary Capital. Spitzer along with others who joined his cleanup campaign have forced some changes on the industry, removed some of the worst offenders, and even pressured some firms to reduce fees.

Improprieties continue to be uncovered, but the overall scandal has tempered the way many mutual fund companies conduct their business. For the common good, some of the fund companies are rediscovering their shareholders and recommitting to ethical behavior. Even firms like Putnam and Alliance Bernstein have cut fees.[3]

The SEC now has in place important new disclosure rules. Fund managers must divulge how much money they have in the funds they oversee. This also means revealing their bonus structure and compensation package.

The SEC also has mandated fund companies alter the makeup of their boards of directors by requiring that at least 75 percent of board members be independent.

The SEC has joined with the National Association of Securities Dealers (NASD) to reduce bad sales practices among brokerages.

More still has to be done. Most of the firms implicated in the scandal have reached agreements on settlements with regulators, but it's still a lengthy process to return those dollars lost to compensate shareholders. The fund companies for the most part admit no guilt but have to pay a hefty settlement. It's slow going because it's extremely difficult to track down all the investors, access the impact of the market timing on an individual investor basis, and find out precisely who was in that fund over a certain period during which the violations were committed.

Still, at this writing, the SEC has not finalized regulations to wipe out late trading and market timing that caused the investigations to be initiated in the first place. A "hard close" that bars trades by the end of trading on the New York Stock Exchange would go a long way in solving the problem. As for market timing, a solution is on the table to call for a redemption fee for short-term trading. The SEC is ready to adopt these proposals but is still working out the kinks with the financial services industry over their adoption.

Many other issues such as 12b-1 fees, which are basically a revenue-sharing process between the brokerage firms and the mutual fund companies, need to be regulated because the fees are used in ways very different from their intended purpose. Regulators are continuing to eye reform of mutual fund disclosure practices. The SEC expects new initiatives for mutual fund companies to better inform investors about mutual fund transaction costs. This effort could include a revamping of the mutual fund prospectus to make fees, investing risks, and other information clearer to investors.[4]

Are Investors Getting the Message?

If mutual funds are on the mend, what about the investors? It's true that just after the scandal broke investors withdrew their money in record numbers. Still, this was merely a small disturbance as investors' memories dim in spite of frequent stories of mutual fund misconduct.

As a result of the mutual fund industry going through its most distressing period in its six-decade history, a dozen fund companies tarnished by regulatory investigations into their trading practices, and long-standing chief executives of three companies made to depart along with other executives and managers, you would think investors would be exiting in droves. Not exactly.

A number of firms—notably Janus Capital and Putnam—that were implicated did fall from favor from investors for a while. Through the end of 2004, Janus Capital reported outflows of $15.6 billion and Putnam had outflows of $20.6 billion.

Most of the investor dollars it appears were shifted into stock funds managed by other big fund companies, like Fidelity Investments, Vanguard Group, and American Funds. It's apparent that investors did not redeem their holdings in huge amounts for long or put their money into bonds or individual stocks. There is no smoking gun that implied investors as a whole lost faith in managed stock funds.

In fact in 2004, the stock market posted a record $194.4 billion dollar flow into stock equity funds.[5]

What does it all mean? "It's not that individual investors never learn, it's just that they learn very, very slowly," said Hersh M. Shefrin, a professor of finance at Santa Clara University in California.[6]

During the months following the first revelations of the scandal that broke in September 2003, money has continued to pour into mutual funds. "The size of the flows as a whole tends to indicate that investors are not losing faith" in actively managed funds, said Don Cassidy, senior research analyst at Lipper, Inc.[7]

Investors are abandoning certain fund brands like Putnam and Janus, but there is no indication that investors are switching to other investment options, Cassidy said. He attributed the pattern to investor inertia, no perceived idea of viable alternatives, and fear of the unknown.

BEYOND MUTUAL FUNDS

Whatever the reason—inertia, no perceived options, or fear of change—if you have your wealth in mutual funds, this book pledges to offer you another, more viable asset management alternative. Before doing so, I want you to review two essential points from these initial chapters:

1. Mutual funds are investment vehicles possessing many trading practices not only widespread and improper but also harmful to your bottom line if you're an average long-term investor.
2. Mutual funds are unsuitable investment vehicles that are not practical for the investor interested in reducing taxes and improving return on investment.

If your portfolio has matured, you're ready to learn more about the most effective, personalized asset management alternative to mutual funds today: *separate account management.* But before we get to separate accounts, read the next chapter and get to know yourself a little better as I hold up the mirror of financial behavior to determine if you are a *rational investor.*

4

IF YOU DON'T KNOW WHERE YOU'RE GOING, ANY PORTFOLIO WILL TAKE YOU THERE

We have met the enemy and he is us . . .
Pogo

Although Pogo lives only as a fictional cartoon character in the "funnies," he was right. In a very few words, he summed up more about us than we know about ourselves. Nowhere is Pogo's wisdom so right as in the arena of investing.

The point of this chapter is not to poke fun (well, just a little) at you, the reader-investor, but to demonstrate how both the nature of the investment vehicle as well as human frailties can derail the path of wealth building. So if your portfolio performance is less than stellar, if your tax-man cometh with huge capital gains taxes, or if you're just plain losing your shirt in the market, whom do you blame? It's far easier to put your broker or advisor on the hot seat than coming to grips with where the real fault may lie: *you.*

EXAMINING YOUR FINANCIAL BRAIN MATTER

Because we just happen to be human beings, we have some strikes against us before we step up to the batter's box. Oh sure, we have good stuff between our ears. We can process huge amounts of information, recognize complex concepts, and even learn from our experience and the experiences of others. We do it much better than our feathered and furry friends from the animal world.

The human mind is like a superior computer that makes us human beings king of the hill. But this brain of ours also has limitations, specifically in the area of financial management. Researchers are learning that there are some funny mind quirks that program us to make poor financial decisions. These mental mistakes can result in costly errors, damping the performance of our portfolios.

The researchers even have a name for it: "behavioral finance." These new methods of looking at investor decision making links human psychology with the choices investors make—how frequently they trade, how they make buy-and-sell decisions, etc. In essence, the emotions we feel about our own money are very strong.

Before, we thought investors made decisions based on logic, rational thinking, weighing all available information before reaching a conclusion. If mistakes were made, other good decisions tended to cancel them out. Were we ever wrong!

The Old 80/20 Rule

There are some rational-thinking investors out there. The trouble is the irrational investors outnumber the rational investors five to one.

Out of 93 million American investors in mutual funds, recent studies tell us that only 20 percent are saving enough for retirement. These are the rational ones. The other 80 percent of this great land's 93 million mutual fund investors, according to studies, are at a standstill, achieving little or no savings, totally unprepared for retirement.

Irrational Investor: Take the Test

Are you one of the few rational investors out there? Let's take a test and see. Answer true or false to the following statements:

1. **You can beat the market indexes if you time your trades.** Researcher Brad Barber, referenced in other studies in this

chapter, concluded after studying over 60,000 investment accounts that passive investors beat active ones by 50 percent. In short, *the more you trade, the less you earn.*

2. **When the market's hot, you buy—when it cools down, that's the time to sell.** Morningstar research says that most investors can't time properly—jumping in too late and buying high. They panic sell when the market drops.

3. **We're in a new bull market.** Researchers in behavioral investor psychology say most people have an optimism bias of overconfidence. Learn more about *overconfidence* later in this chapter.

4. **I look at the numbers before I decide.** In spite of the wealth of information you can easily obtain from the media, your best friend, and your car repair guy, most tips still require due diligence research before taking action. In fact, did you know published stats are purely hypothetical? All of them assume you invest a lump sum once and hold it for a period of time. Most investors put their money in gradually over time, not all at once. Watch out for fancy ads with big performance numbers! They're not actually real.

5. **You know you're a rational investor.** Join the club. Seventy-five percent of you think you're an "above average" investor. Behavioral investor research says that the average investor's after-tax returns for 20 years haven't beaten the level of inflation.[1]

I guess you figured out by now the correct answers all are false. Could 75 million investors be wrong? Yes, most of the time.

Prime Example of Investor Greed: The Dot-com Disaster

During the buildup in dot-com stocks during the late 1990s, we saw investors ignore the rules of prudent investing. Did these firms have a real product to sell? In most cases, the only product of these firms was "information." The investors were true speculators (in a sense gambling). Researchers say gambling is a basic human trait motivated by entertainment pursuit and ego enhancement. Human nature being what it is, ignorance, greed, and hope determined how people invested during this time frame. Logic and due diligence never factored in to investment decisions. The dot-com implosion was a beautiful example of irrational market behavior that occurs time and time again.

It's not that investors are totally irrational, behavioral scientists argue, but their thinking is misguided by subtle biases and mental blind spots. According to Warren Buffett, we don't even have to be too smart. He has remarked, "Success in investing doesn't correlate with IQ once you're above the level of 25. If you have ordinary intelligence, what you need is the temperament to control the urges that get other people into trouble in investing."[2]

Overconfidence Will Put Your Portfolio in Trouble

Being overconfident is being unrealistic about expectations. In the financial world, investors habitually assume they know more than they do. All of us dwell on successes and forget failures. When you're successful, it's due to your superior wisdom and intellect. Failure is due to forces outside our control. Thus, people believe with a little luck and fine-tuning, the outcome will be better next time.

These little overconfident personality flaws can cause us to:

- **Trade excessively.** In one major study of 78,000 accounts at a discount brokerage from 1991 to1996, the average turnover was 86 percent. The investors that relied more on a buy-and-hold strategy (with a 1 percent turnover) had 17.5 percent annual returns beating the S&P (16.9 percent annually). However, the most active traders (with turnover of more than 9 percent monthly) had a pretax return of 10 percent. Conclusion: "Trading is hazardous to your health!"[3] The same researcher concluded in another study that individuals who switch to online trading have sufficiently lower returns. In this study, only two in ten day traders make money.[4]
- **Pick highfliers.** The market-trailing performance of mutual funds for years should be proof enough but investors still think they can pick the funds that can deliver superior future performance. Most investors fail. Still worse, investors trade in and out of mutual funds as they chase performance. From 1984 to 1995, the average stock mutual fund had a yearly return of 12.3 percent (15.4 percent for S&P 500). The average investor posted a return

of 6.3 percent. Result: Over that 12-year period, the mutual fund investor would have made twice as much money by simply buying and holding. Factoring in taxes would make these returns too embarrassing to print.

- **Make stock-pricing blunders.** We already know that investors pay too much to buy when funds or individual stocks are high and they lose when they sell stocks that are priced too low. So how do you know what a stock is really worth? Being a rational investor you would think a stock's price is determined by PE ratios, dividend pay out, growth states, past performance, etc. Not even close. Stocks are not priced on their earnings. They are priced on what investors can sell the stock to another for—nothing more. So the problem is when those funds and individual stock prices keep rising, overconfident investors think the sky's the limit and rising stock prices are never going to end. Eventually, the market realizes the price has gotten too outrageous and the balloon pops.

Still Shooting Ourselves in the Foot

Individual investor returns in mutual funds severely lag the performance of the funds themselves due to the "emotional behavior of the fund investor," according to the noted research firm DALBAR Financial Services, based in Boston. In essence, most fund investors are impatient, chase performance, are emotional, and buy funds high and sell low. This irrational behavior on the behalf of investors is astonishing.

The 2004 DALBAR study revealed that for the 20-year period ending December 31, 2003, fund investors earned 9.47 percent less than the actual performance of the funds. In a similar study conducted in 2001, the performance gap was 10.88 percent. To summarize, the stock market (the S&P Index) averaged 16.3 percent per year over this time period and the average investor earned *only 5.3 percent* per year![5]

Furthermore, the DALBAR report shows that because investors turn over their securities so often, their equity fund returns have been *lower than inflation*. The rate of inflation between 1982 and 2002 averaged 3.14 percent annually, while the average equity fund at that time only earned a measly 2.57 percent annually after taxes.

Bottom line: Your investment behavior and mutual fund expenses (expense ratios, 12b-1 fees, turnover costs, lack of tax control, etc.) affect

Face **F**acts

The Standard & Poor's (S&P) 500 Index from 1984 to 2000 realized an annual return of 16.29 percent each year. But during the same period, stock mutual fund investors on the average earned only 5.32 percent each year. Why? Investors refused to buy and hold. They moved in and out of the market regularly, hunting for big returns. These investors rode the emotional roller coaster, putting money in when prices rose, pulling it out when prices fell. The average hold period for mutual fund investors is around 30 months.

Source: DALBAR Research.

your returns more than the highs and lows of the market including the investment actions of your fund manager.

Feedback and Fallback Factor: Your Advisor

It is indeed difficult to be objective about our own strengths and weaknesses. If you can accept that, then, perhaps, utilizing advice from your own financial advisor may be a better path to travel than investing on your own. Certainly, there's research that bears this out. Remember your advisor is less emotional about your money.

DALBAR Financial Services produced a study in 1994 that demonstrated that do-it-yourself investors realize lower returns than investors using the services of financial advisors. The study concluded that for those investors lacking time, discipline, knowledge, and experience to maintain a portfolio over the long term, a financial advisor would make far more money than he would cost. The study also showed that when the client is paying the advisor for financial advice, the client is far more likely to follow through on that advice to get the maximum value for the service.

Some "Keepers"

While we have explored some of the mistakes of logic investors make when creating portfolios, it's important too that we highlight ten basic—but crucial—commonsense tips to keeping your portfolio intact and robust:

1. **Live under your means.** This is going to be really hard for most of us. It's easy to live beyond your means. Millions of us do it every day. This is the hard economic reality. Are you going to live as you're accustomed when the wheel of retirement kicks in? You're naive to believe Social Security and pensions are going to cover your expenses. The only thing left to do is save! Are you going to bed each night without a plan? If you don't plan where you're going, any road will . . . you know the rest. Figure out what you want: adequate retirement income, kid's college tuition, etc. Then determine your strategy. Say you want to retire in ten years and you need $20,000 a year to keep the wolves from the door. You will need $400,000 in assets to produce that cash flow. You need to save to get that $400,000 in the next ten years.

2. **Make risk a comfort factor, not a distress agent.** It may be an exaggeration to ask you to be comfortable with risk. But like stress, we all have it. The amount of stress makes the difference, and so does risk. Once you put your wealth to work, you will assume risk. If you feel more comfortable with minimum risk, put your money in Treasuries or in a bank savings account. Of course, inflation does threaten to erode your capital, rising faster than interest rates and reducing the purchasing power of your dollars. Investing in the market can be very risky on a short-term basis. Over the long term, however, with proper diversification, you should experience anticipated growth, plus the risk on your initial investment will become less each day the account grows.

3. **Divide and conquer.** Keep your portfolio protected by not investing in just a few stocks or one industry. The theory is to spread your securities across many different asset classes: small caps, large caps, international, etc. If one stock goes south, then you'll not be hurt as badly. Check your portfolio to see if you really are diversified. Though you may hold separate funds, you could still be too heavily invested in one sector, in

some cases even in the same companies! It's much better to spread your investments in different asset classes.

4. **Allocate your portfolio assets to the winner's circle.** There is no more important step you can make than allocating your assets in the right proportion to match your circumstances. Your plan should be to allocate your wealth between equities, fixed assets, and cash. Within the equity part of your portfolio, you should break down further between value and growth, and then divide more between large caps, small caps, international, etc.

5. **Hold tight after you buy right.** Your allocation of stocks for growth and value, and bonds for income and preservation of capital should be in balance. Once the balance is right according to your life's objectives hold on tight for the market ride of dips and drops, twists and turns, takeoffs and landings. Your advisor can help determine the proper allocation of the assets for your individual needs. Once the assets are placed, your advisor is there to hold your hand during the market highs and lows.

6. **Time is your ally, impulse your foe.** If you want to make money in the market, wait before making any changes in your portfolio. The impulse to act when the market is soaring or when the market is plummeting should be checked. Focus on the long-term horizon not the here and now.

7. **Pickpockets are picking your pocket now.** There're a lot of hands in your pockets when you play the market. The impact of all the financial pickpockets (commissions, management fees, marketing fees, taxes, etc.) picking at your returns can easily make investing a zero-sum game. It's up to you to minimize the pickpockets' returns. If your return on your investment is 10 percent before costs, and costs are 2 percent, $10,000 in 50 years will grow to $469,000. If you make 10 percent ROI without costs factored in, then you will have over a million dollars— by purging the pickpockets' purse.

8. **Mission impossible: Forget about timing the market.** "Buy and hold" is not about the latest stock tip from your brother-in-law. It's not about hunches and making quick profits. It's all about using a long-term proven strategy to accumulate wealth over time! The professionals use market timing daily to make minor profits taking advantage of foreseen price discrepancies

*F*ace *F*acts: *A*re *I*nvestors *R*eturning to *R*eality?

The equity fund retention rates set a new record in 2004. Retention was at the highest level since 1984 when tracking began. Investors held on to their mutual funds in spite of a weak market during the first three quarters. This contributed greatly to investors actually earning more than the S&P 500. This was not due to outstanding fund performance but to investor behavior. Investors wisely continued to plow money into their funds as the market declined, and kept it there until the postelection rally pushed real returns past the benchmark.

This desirable investment behavior in 2004 followed another year of good behavior (2003), which also set a record for retention.

Source: "Quantitative Analysis of Investor Behavior 2005," Annual DALBAR Study, DALBAR, Inc.

or receiving a favorable analyst report to buy low before the price shoots up. Most investors can't watch the market second by second to be able to react instantly to market changes. Don't even try! Buying and selling based on hunches is one of the fastest ways to lose money in the market. Instead, use fundamental analysis. Buy solid companies not hot stocks and hold them year after year in a diversified and balanced portfolio, hopefully, selected by you and your advisor.

9. **Write on.** If you want to succeed in the market, you have to write down your goals rather than just thinking casually about them. The investment policy statement (IPS) is a written plan set down by you to keep you from derailing yourself in the investment process. You write down your long-term financial goals specifying a target date you want to retire and determine how much income you will need to get there. If this sounds like work, it is. There's no free lunch for the successful investor. For your advisor, though, goal setting is an automatic process. That's what advisors do.

10. **Know that you're an irrational investor.** The best-kept secret of the rational investor is you are really an irrational investor.

20 Common Pitfalls Investors Routinely Commit to Shoot Themselves in the Foot

1. Herding behavior, driven by a desire to be part of the crowd or an assumption that the crowd is omniscient
2. Using mental accounting to treat some money (such as gambling winnings or an unexpected bonus) differently than other money
3. Excessive aversion to loss
4. Fear of change, resulting in an excessive bias for the status quo
5. Fear of making an incorrect decision and feeling stupid
6. Failing to act due to an abundance of attractive options
7. Ignoring important data points and focusing excessively on less important ones
8. "Anchoring" on irrelevant data
9. Overestimating the likelihood of certain events based on very memorable data or experiences
10. Overestimating the degree to which they would have predicted the correct outcome of an event after learning of the results of that event
11. Allowing an overabundance of short-term information to cloud long-term judgments
12. Drawing conclusions from a limited sample size
13. Reluctance to admit mistakes
14. Believing that their investment success is due to their wisdom rather than a rising market
15. Failing to accurately assess their investment time horizon
16. A tendency to seek only information that confirms their opinions or decisions
17. Failing to recognize the large cumulative impact of small amounts over time
18. Forgetting the powerful tendency of regression to the mean
19. Confusing familiarity with knowledge
20. *Overconfidence*

Source: Whitney Tilson.

To keep yourself in check, subscribe religiously to the first nine rules above.

Fortunes are being made and always will be made. It's the investing skills that make the difference. Here's some much-needed encouragement for you. With enough time, discipline, and understanding your brain's objection to objective thinking, you can make money in the market. With a financial advisor to guide you to a better financial investment strategy—**separate account management**—creating a balanced portfolio of securities tailored to your age and circumstances, you can take reasonable risks to earn steady rewards.

GAINING WEALTH
IN SEPARATE
ACCOUNTS

5

THE RISE OF SEPARATE ACCOUNTS

Two rules:
1. Preserve the principal.
2. When in doubt, see Rule #1.
Warren Buffett

MAKING THE CASE

One thing that Jason Mathews could take to the bank, literally, was the adage his father had embedded in his mind at an early age: Pay yourself first.

Since college, Jason, 42, had religiously put away $100 a month before he paid any of his bills. At first, he put all his money in savings accounts, and later CDs, as he moved regularly in search of older homes to fix up and convert to bed-and-breakfast facilities, which was the way he made his living.

During the late 1980s the idea of mutual funds appealed to Jason. His bank's CDs were making about 7 percent at the time. He knew he needed to start thinking long term—he needed an investment program with better returns to care for his wife and coming children.

In 1990, Jason and a friend got to talking about investments. His friend told him he was getting performance returns of around 12 percent a year in mutual funds thanks to his financial advisor's recommendations.

Jason called his friend's advisor the next day. He was somewhat apprehensive; he figured he had done pretty well on his father's advice by himself. He'd managed to grow his $100 a month into approximately

$100,000 just by harnessing the compounding value of money over the years.

Still, Jason decided to go with his new advisor's investment suggestions. The advisor put Jason into five mutual funds (large caps, small caps, growth, value, and aggressive) at $20,000 each. From the start, all of his mutual funds increased in value averaging 9 percent to14 percent. These returns continued for the next ten years. Jason let it ride, and his nest egg mushroomed to $200,000.

In January 2000, Jason got caught up in the dot-com excitement. Everything he saw in the media pumped up the investment opportunities in hot technology stocks. Other investors Jason talked to were making as much as 20 percent. Jason had his advisor sell all his funds to purchase high-technology mutual funds.

Then, in March 2000, Wall Street experienced a sellout larger than any since October 1998. Jason's funds lost 9 percent of their value almost overnight. Jason tried to recoup his falling funds by going online and trading. After jousting at windmills, it was all over. Jason still had his principal of $100,000, but by October, his earnings over the last ten years had disappeared.

Later, Jason received another crushing blow in the mail. In January, the tax incurred by his capital gains during the period he was invested exceeded $10,000, based on his 36 percent bracket.

Plainly upset, Jason called his financial advisor.

His advisor told him that he wanted to show him a new investment strategy that would give Jason tax relief that mutual funds couldn't provide, yet give him an opportunity for better returns because a top-gun money manager would service his account.

His advisor went on and told Jason with this new strategy, he would pay one flat fee based on the value of his portfolio with everything out in the open. Not only that, he would receive real-time reports on his account daily, not twice yearly like his mutual funds, and he would know exactly what stocks he was invested in.

Jason, who was always complaining to his advisor about his funds' fees and the fact that he didn't know which stocks were in his portfolio, asked about this new strategy.

"Its not new," said the advisor. "It's been around for years. It just hasn't been available to most investors, except ultrarich or institutions. It's called separate account management and it's the best investment strategy in the financial services industry today, for mid- to high-income investors like you."

SAMS: THE LEAP FORWARD IN 21ST CENTURY INVESTING

Separate account management is a tried-and-true investment strategy that's long been the tool of the superrich and institutions, now available to mid- to high-income investors. These accounts are also known as separate accounts, separately managed accounts, SAMs, managed accounts, individually managed accounts (IMAs), or "wrap" accounts. Whichever name it goes by, this investment strategy is the logical successor to mutual funds.

As a result, separate accounts (I use this term and SAMs interchangeably throughout the book) have recently become one of the most popular investment strategies in the history of the financial industry. So much so, that the mutual fund you know as the investment method of choice for 93 million American mutual fund investors will change considerably in the near future. (See Figure 5.1.) This will be due in a large part to the separate accounts revolution and increased government inquiry into the mutual fund industry for nefarious activities.

What's a SAM?

Separate account management (SAM) refers to a professionally managed group of securities owned by the individual investor. Separate accounts are portfolios of securities (stocks or bonds) selected by qualified money managers and held in an investor's own account. Unlike mutual funds, in which investors hold shares *representing* a stake in an overall portfolio but not the securities *themselves,* separate account holders actually own the securities in their accounts.

Because the investor owns his portfolio, he's able to tailor his holdings to be in line with his financial strategy and risk involvement. His ownership means a new approach to tax planning. For instance, he no longer needs to time the trades in the account to minimize his tax situation.

Figure 5.1 *Total Separate Accounts Industry Assets and Growth, Proprietary and Third-Party*

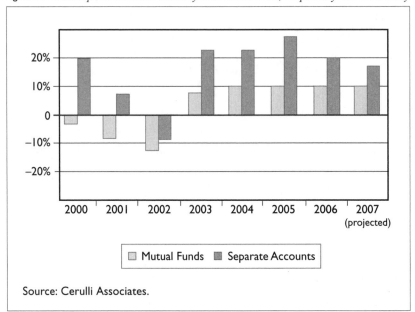

Source: Cerulli Associates.

A separate account offers a fee-based structure. This means brokers don't charge commissions or hidden charges as they do in mutual funds. The all-inclusive separate account fee covers the services of your professional money manager, the custodian of your account, your investment advisor, and all trading costs. Usually, the fee charged is around 2 percent of the yearly value of the account, depending on how much you invest. I'll discuss fees in detail in Chapter 11.

> *Separately managed accounts are encroaching on mutual fund assets due to their tax efficiency, customization potential, and cachet appeal. Ultimately, we'll see separately managed accounts service as the core investment in an investor's portfolio.*
>
> **Charlie Bevis, editor in chief of research studies, Financial Research Corp.**

With a separate account, you have at least one professional money manager working on your portfolio, the same as multimillionaires or large institutions. For a separate account, buy-and-sell decisions involve the investor. With his advisor, the investor selects teams of money managers who utilize different investment styles to enhance the portfolio, depending on the investor's strategy and level of risk.

A*re* Y*ou a* C*andidate for a* S*eparate* A*ccount?*

- **Do you have more than $100,000 in investable assets?** Separate accounts are especially appropriate for portfolios (including IRAs) above $100,000. But initial asset investments are dropping rapidly. Today, an investor can have a separate account for as little as $25,000, with much the same services as larger accounts.
- **Did you receive a tax bill from Uncle Sam for more than $10,000 during a recent tax year?** Separate accounts can be managed for tax efficiency. Additionally, taxes are incurred only on your investment gains not other investors in the pool.
- **Are you aware of the total fees and commissions you pay for a percentage of your assets in a mutual fund?** If not, better establish a separate account. Separate accounts are asset-based, rather than commission-based, giving your money manager special incentive to grow your assets. In addition, because fees are based on a percentage of your total assets, you can calculate at any time what your fees will be. Nothing is hidden the way fees are in mutual funds.
- **Are you receiving personalized counsel that helps match your investments to your goals and risk tolerance?** Separate accounts provide a customized investment strategy, developed by your independent advisor, based on your specific long-term investment.
- **Do you expect to receive a significant wealth transfer or pension rollover?** If so, separate accounts can provide personalized portfolio allocation of significant asset pools, taking into consideration tax consequences, immediate and long-term financial needs, etc.
- **Are you interested in exploring other asset management approaches besides mutual funds?** Separate accounts enable you to invest in a range of discreet investment vehicles beyond mutual funds, while maintaining a diversified portfolio.

Hiring top-gun institutional money managers to handle your assets together with other multimillion-dollar accounts is truly an extraordinary achievement. Technological advances (third-party platforms, computer interfaces, etc.) have made this possible. The high-net-income and

Top **T**en **R**easons to **P**ut **Y**our **M**oney in a **S**eparate **A**ccount

1. Access top money managers
2. Parallel your portfolio with your investment objectives
3. Expand asset control
4. Definite higher after-tax returns
5. Interact more with your independent advisor and money managers
6. Own fewer securities, which raises the possibility of increasing your short-term and long-term returns
7. Convert from ordinary income to long-term capital gains
8. Change your objectives, and change the makeup of your portfolio annually
9. View the status of your portfolio in real time (24/7)
10. Avoid securities for social, economic, political, or personal reasons (i.e., sin stocks)

Source: Cerulli Associates.

the "emerging affluent" investors, even with an investment as small as $25,000, can secure the services of these institutional-class money managers, and be treated the same as far as the management of their portfolio is concerned.

In short, what do you receive if you move your holdings out of mutual funds into a separate account? With a separate account, there is one flat fee for one or more professional money managers who will maintain your account with all services (trading, custody, management, and consulting), plus a fairer tax structure, improved performance, more control, and more clearly defined fees than with mutual funds.

Because many Americans have improved their financial picture over the last two decades, more investors have a greater interest in pursuing the kind of strategy the superrich and institutions have enjoyed all along.

THE VALUE OF ADVICE

Advice has been easy to find since Wall Street first opened its doors. Good, objective advice, on the other hand, has always been a much rarer commodity.

Even the earliest brokerage firms realized that investors would pay for advice, good or otherwise. In the early 1900s, after the telephone became an established staple across the country, brokers could communicate with prospects quickly for the first time. The fire of professional advice was ignited. Before the bubble burst in the 1920s, investment pools were formed to speculate in all sorts of enterprises—not all of them scrupulous—but all requiring the advice of someone. Fortunes were made and lost, and some made again, on investment advice.

THE INVESTMENT ACT SETS THINGS STRAIGHT

After the Depression, the interest in pooled investments rose again. Nothing was regulated, so some of these enterprises looked like the Wild West revisited. Stockbrokers provided advice to the middle class, but only the wealthy could afford professional expertise. It was a topsy-turvy world of buyer beware until the Investment Company Act of 1940 set the stage for the modern mutual fund.

Mutual funds didn't take off right away. It was much later before funds became a popular investment vehicle. There were only a dozen or so popular funds available in the early 1950s. But within a few decades, funds of all types (stock, bond, hedge, index, foreign, sector, and many more) proliferated. There were more than 5,000 funds in 2002. Mutual funds were originally sold only by brokers (load) for commission. When no-load funds came along, they were commission-free, but came with no advice. The advent of no-load funds stimulated further the interest in mutual funds. Along came 401(k)s and IRAs, and the rest is history. Americans put their assets into these programs in record numbers. The only problem was that the vast number of funds made it more difficult to make a rational buying decision.

Tool of the Rich

On a parallel track, fueled by advice-seeking wealthy investors, separate account management became the tool of the superrich and institutions. This process went smoothly for years—for the affluent. The process easily shut out the smaller investor, who had less than $500,000 to invest. So the average investor turned to mutual funds, as well as buying stocks and bonds directly.

Commissions Became Negotiable

Separate accounts became more popular with the affluent when commissions became negotiable for trades above $500,000. Later, the Securities and Exchange Commission (SEC) ruled the rates would no longer be fixed for any size trade. Next came a ruling in 1975, which allowed for discount brokerages to exist, like Schwab, Ameritrade, E*Trade, and others.

This gave rise to more imaginative billing procedures. E. F. Hutton began pricing fees as a percentage of client assets rather than a charge per trade. This gave more clients an opportunity to have their assets put into a separate account, rather than lumped into mutual funds. Account minimums were reduced to as low as $250,000 for a separate account program.

Costs to Maintain SAMs Drop

These changes by the SEC may have made it easier for new clients to secure a separate account, but few financial planners could afford to provide them because of the maintenance cost entailed in holding such portfolios. Throughout the 1980s, the cost of tracking labor-intensive portfolios remained high. In addition, portfolio managers had "a bird's nest on the ground" with the booming mutual fund business. From the beginning of the bull market in August 1982 through the 1990s, the mutual fund business went through the roof.

During this period on a parallel track, thanks to technology, the administrative cost of maintaining a separate account was reduced from approximately $1,000 yearly to $100 per portfolio. This allowed for sophisticated trading and tracking procedures and solutions. Today, these systems are so advanced that one person can reconcile up to 10,000 accounts. The computer revolution and commissions deregulation has made it possible for both manager and client to partake in the separate accounts revolution. It's truly a win-win situation.

SEVEN POSITIVE ADVANTAGES OF SEPARATE ACCOUNTS

1. Performance: A Return to Realistic Returns

Warning: Mutual funds may be hazardous to your financial health! Separate accounts offer potentially higher returns. Separate accounts can outperform mutual funds. This is especially true in the volatile down market we've experienced since March 2000. The average mutual fund lost value, and distributed a 9 percent average in capital gains—a double negative whammy.

This brought home to mid- to high-net-worth investors the message that mutual funds in a volatile market are less efficient because each fund is forced to carry high reserves, anticipating redemptions from other nervous investors. The fund manager has to juggle buying when the market is high and redeeming when the market is declining—a classic buy high and sell low situation. This asset flow affects all investors in the fund, and performance suffers. With the freedom from cash reserves, separate accounts have great potential to produce better post-tax returns than mutual funds. (See Figure 5.2.)

2. Tax Relief: Giving Uncle Sam His Due

The number one reason savvy investors are leaving mutual funds and turning to separate accounts is control over taxes. Reducing your taxes may be the strongest argument for establishing your own separate account.

It's no secret that mutual funds can be a tax nightmare. Investors with taxable fund assets were hammered twice in 2000—the average fund experienced performance losses and investors got hit with taxes on

Figure 5.2 *Performance Comparison*

Performance	Mutual Funds	Separate Accounts
Access to expertise of money managers	Yes	Yes
Provide higher after-tax returns	No, mutual funds penalize investors with capital gains taxes	Yes
Up-to-date performance reporting	No, usually semiannual; sometimes yearly.	Yes, viewable in hard copy and electronically on quarterly basis
Investor contact	No, most no-load mutual funds offer only an 800 phone number and a Web site	Yes, face-to-face discussions with an investment professional
Evaluate professional money managers	Yes	Yes, managers are evaluated and constantly screened by trained financial analysts
Determine investor's goals	No, typically with no-load mutual funds investors must determine their goals themselves.	Yes

Source: Stephen Gresham.

capital gains. This especially was a sore point in 2000, when the average stock fund lost 6 percent, and investors had to pay taxes on a record $345 billion in capital gains mutual fund distributions. In mutual funds, it doesn't matter if you invest with the pack early in the year or come in much later. A new shareholder has to pay the same capital gains as an investor who bought in on January 1. Each time a mutual fund manager

Figure 5.3 *Tax Planning Comparison*

Tax Relief	Mutual Funds	Separate Accounts
Hold securities individually	No, investors own the fund not individual stocks	Yes, investors own all the individual securities in their portfolios
Imbedded and unrealized gains	Yes, average mutual fund has a 15 percent to –20 percent imbedded unrealized capital gain	No, cost basis of each security in the portfolio is established at the time of purchase
Customized to control taxes	No, most funds are managed for pre-tax returns and investors pay a proportionate share of taxes on capital gains	Yes, investors can instruct money managers to take gains or losses as available to manage their tax liability
Tax-efficient handling of low-cost basis stocks	No, stocks cannot be held in an investors mutual fund account, so there is no opportunity to manage low-cost basis stocks	Yes, the handling of low-cost basis stocks can be customized to the client's situation, liquidating in concert with offsetting losses, etc.
Gain/loss distribution	Virtually all gains must be distributed; losses cannot be distributed	Realized gains and losses are reported in the year recorded

Source: Stephen Gresham.

decides to sell off stocks in the fund for a profit, you get hit with a taxable "element"—even if the fund lost money for the year. If you stay with the fund, you lose. (See Figure 5.3.)

Our research shows that concern over taxes is the number one reason investors turn to separate accounts . . . in separate accounts, tax planning should not take place just at year-end but losses harvested all year long.

Scott Dell'orfano, SEI Investments

A separate account manager, on the other hand, can do "tax harvesting"—offsetting gains with losses to deliver potentially higher after-tax returns.

As *The Wall Street Journal* noted: "Clearly, separate accounts have strong selling points. Unlike investing in a mutual fund and immediately being exposed to the fund's embedded capital gains, an investor has some say over stock purchases and sales in a separate account, giving him better control over his tax bills."[1]

Separate accounts can even go further in their capability to reduce taxes. These accounts can offset tax liabilities faced elsewhere in an investor portfolio or in a real estate transaction. In the next chapter, I'll go more in depth into the taxable implications of mutual funds and separate accounts.

3. Affordability: Getting What You Pay For

Once only available to the very rich, separate accounts are now within reach of the emerging affluent. As transaction costs have been forced down by the new technology of information management, increased marketing efforts, and the increase of competition in the 1990s, many more investors were able to join this exclusive process previously reserved for the DuPonts and Rockefellers.

The ticket to getting into a separate account is $25,000, down from a minimum $100,000 initial investment a few months ago. A lower investment minimum allows a new breed of investor—on average, younger and savvier—who expects to make money, demands excellent service, and understands the effect taxes and hidden costs have on her portfolio.

Stock mutual funds cost investors an average of 1.57 percent annually on total assets, according to Morningstar, the mutual fund research company. The investor with a separate account pays 1.77 percent, according to Cerulli Associates, the Boston-based research company that follows separate accounts. On the surface, it may appear that the investor pays more for the privilege of owning a separate account than a mutual fund. But hold on: Figures vary significantly for both separate accounts and mutual funds, and comparisons are complicated.

If you have the time to figure out the fees and expenses discreetly placed in a mutual fund prospectus, you'll find an array of distribution fees, sales charges, operating fees, and deferred charges that when totaled can often exceed the costs of owning a separate account.

Below the waterline are the real costs of mutual funds.

Ted Aronson, a principal of Aronson & Johnson & Ortiz

Mutual funds have significantly higher internal expenses, plus loads (commissions). Each time a broker transmits a buy-or-sell order on a fund, he can charge as much as 5.75 percent of assets. Of course, investors can skip the commissions by purchasing no-load funds, but these funds come with little or no financial advice. And don't forget the hidden fees that are taken directly out of your total returns from the fund.

A separate account, on the other hand, usually charges a flat fee for all services. This covers all account transaction charges and account maintenance costs.

Mutual funds charge more as assets increase in value. Separate accounts have one fee that can actually decrease as the investor increases the amount of money he puts into the account. For example, an investor with $1 million in assets in a separate account would probably pay only 1 percent to 1.5 percent of assets yearly. Take it to $5 million, and this investor would be paying around 0.5 percent annually. Investors also can often get their separate account fees reduced depending on the type of service and reporting process they request.

Further, brokerage firms offering separate accounts often negotiate fees off their marketing materials price list. These fees listed can be as much as 3 percent of assets. "The brokerages usually discount listed prices as much as 25 percent to 30 percent," says a researcher at Cerulli Associates. "Hardly any investor pays as high as 3 percent."[2]

Separate account fees are fast becoming a buyers' market, and the individual investor can better her fee arrangement by shopping around. (See Figure 5.4.) Chapter 11 is devoted to closely examining the fee structure of separate accounts compared to mutual funds.

Separately managed accounts will ultimately be [as] much a tool
in the future as mutual funds are today. Ten years from now there
will be supermarkets of separate accounts.

Scott A. MacKillop, president of Trivium Consulting

4. Transparency: The Cards Are on the Table

Performance reviews of your mutual funds are very slow. Separate accounts give the investor portfolio tracking 24/7. Most investors tradi-

Figure 5.4 *Affordable Comparison*

Affordability	Mutual Funds	Separate Accounts
Volume fee discounts	No.	Yes, larger asset allocations usually receive fee discounts, as much as 25 percent as account grows
Expenses without broker commissions	1.42 percent	1.00 percent
Expenses with broker expenses built in	1.56 percentage average	1.25 percent
Other costs	12b-1 fees, sales loads, redemption fees, etc.	None
Typical account minimum	$1,000	$100,000, but technology is increasing efficiency and driving cost down; minimum can be as low as $25,000.
Unlimited redemption/ withdraws	No, usually the fund carries restrictions	Yes

Source: Stephen Gresham.

tionally have to make do with semiannual disclosures of their mutual fund holdings. The SEC mandates mutual fund companies give summaries of their funds twice yearly but recommend quarterly.

Even though the Internet has sped up the tracking of securities considerably, the major fund companies have been painfully slow to keep investors informed in a timely manner. In fact, mutual fund investors can do little more than check daily prices and buy and sell. Investors can't even find out on the Internet what stocks are in their portfolio, let alone do anything meaningful, like tax liability monitoring. Moreover, you can't even check your fund prices accurately until after the market closes.

In fact, the mutual fund industry could compete with the Air Force's stealth bomber in its ability to stay below the radar. If investors don't ask, the companies are not inclined to tell. This has raised the interest in 2003 of security regulators and lawmakers determined to compel fund companies to disclose information on expenses, trading costs, brokerage incentives, and even manager compensation, director salaries, and fee disclosure. The SEC and NASD are addressing some of these problems as this book goes to print.

Contrast that with separate account holders who can view their positions almost on a daily basis. They're able to monitor their positions in their portfolios at any time, much as you do online with your bank statements. That also goes for access to experienced money managers handing your account, either through your financial advisor or, in many cases, through direct access, according to your level of investment.

Also, if a money manager needs to buy or sell a stock, he can do it early in the morning, instead of getting end-of-day prices as in mutual funds.

And best of all, the transparency of your portfolio is there for you to explore, examine, and make changes if need be because you own it. Restrictive disclosure policies and lack of control over money pooled with other investors more nervous than you is not good for your financial well-being. (See Figure 5.5.)

5. Customization: Packing Your Own Chute

The only money in your separate account is your own. After determining your investment strategy and risk level, and getting in sync with your investment advisor (if you have one) and your money manager(s), you choose a carefully crafted portfolio (i.e., large cap, small cap, growth, and so forth). Because you will own the securities in your separate account portfolio, you can choose to eliminate any security for any social, political, or personal reason. Say you work at IBM. You may not wish to have any of your own company's stock included in your portfolio because you already have stock options with the company or in your 401(k). You can choose not to put any IBM stock into your separate account portfolio.

Figure 5.5 *Transparency Comparison*

Transparency	Mutual Funds	Separate Accounts
Performance Reporting	Typically semi-annually; some more frequent	Quarterly performance rating
Customized performance reporting	Generally no, investors must calculate their own performance, which is problematic particularly for investors who use dollar cost averaging	Yes, automatically sent to investors every quarter; includes performance of individual portfolios and/or aggregate of multiple portfolios
Fees and charges readily available	Yes, but mutual fund companies make it difficult for investor to know what he is paying for	Yes, fee based—one flat fee for all services and full disclosure of those fees.
Online access to account	Yes	Yes
Transparency of portfolio	No, clients are not allowed to look up the securities in the fund	Yes, clients own their own portfolios and the right to know what stocks are in them
Quarterly performance reports customized to reflect actual activity and holdings	No, investors must calculate own performance of their portfolio	Yes, you can have reports electronically and in hard copy

Source: Stephen Gresham.

Try that with a mutual fund.

Customization of your portfolio goes even further. You have the right to impose your personal values on your portfolio. If you say no to tobacco stocks, then your money manager can eliminate these companies in your basket of securities. Needless to say, you couldn't specify specific securities in your portfolio with a mutual fund. With mutual funds, you might wait as long as six months to learn exactly what stocks are in your portfolio.

In essence, you have the right with a separate account to include or exclude securities based on your ethical, economic, or political views. (See Figure 5.6.)

Mutual funds are like taking your kids to a community pool and leaving them in the company of strangers. A separate account is like taking personal responsibility for watching your kids in your own backyard pool.

I'll discuss customization of your portfolio in greater detail in Chapter 8.

6. Asset Control: Taking Charge of Your Investments

With a mutual fund, one manager may watch as many as 150 stocks per fund. With a separate account portfolio up to three managers supervise approximately 50 securities. In today's market, investors have a better chance if more people are watching the henhouse.

A fund manager's span of control can be limited when he has scores of stocks to look after. In a separate account, each money manager, or team of managers, is responsible for fewer securities, and also usually has access to dozens of securities analysts to provide further backup monitoring. (See Figure 5.7.)

7. Prestige: Moving Uptown

Investors are outgrowing mutual funds. Sophisticated investors relish custom solutions that make them feel special and add wealth to their portfolios.

Many older Americans were weaned on mutual funds. But today, those in the emerging affluent generation are asking themselves

Figure 5.6 *Customization Comparison*

Customization	Mutual Funds	Separate Accounts
Ability to customize portfolio	No	Yes
Liquidity	Typically, the next day	Three-day statement of trades
Specify stocks to purchase	No	Yes, investor can instruct money manager(s) on what stocks to include or not include in portfolio
Tailor portfolio to investor's unique needs	No	Yes
Individual stock selection on economic, social, ethical, etc., preferences	No	Yes

Source: Stephen Gresham.

whether they should stay with the ultimate "retail" investment, one that is associated with mass market investing and now viewed by many as a commodity.

Having a private money manager servicing a major retirement fund or in the company of the superrich is a prestige factor with separate accounts that's difficult to ignore. "Some people just like to feel their investment program is a step above those investing in mutual funds," says one advisor who specializes in separate accounts.

Mutual fund managers don't differentiate between one investor and another. Their job is to get the numbers regardless of who is investing in the fund. Separate account investors receive asset management on an individual basis receiving custom solutions for the securities they own. (See Figure 5.8.)

Figure 5.7 *Asset Control Comparison*

Asset Control	Mutual Funds	Separate Accounts
Diversified portfolio	Yes	Yes
Manager independence from the "herd-instinct"	No, if clients want to redeem shares, fund managers must sell to raise the cash to do so	Yes, money managers can buy when the herd is selling and vice versa, customizing the decision to the client's objectives
Access to asset classes	Numerous	Somewhat more limited than funds
Unlimited withdrawals/ redemptions	No, most funds have restrictions	Yes
Asset control of account in and out flows	No, to refund investors department fund managers must raise money by selling securities	Yes
Ownership of securities	No, with a mutual fund the investor owns a share of the fund not individual securities	Yes

Source: Stephen Gresham.

SEPARATE ACCOUNT MANAGEMENT: WALK THE WALK

The bear market has done little to curb investors' enthusiasm for separate accounts. In fact, many investors are setting up their own separate accounts as never before. Since 2003, the number of separate accounts grew by roughly 500,000 to nearly 2.1 million.

Figure 5.8 *Prestige Comparison*

Prestige	Mutual Funds	Separate Accounts
Access to world-class money managers who service superrich and mega institutions/ foundations	No	Yes

Source: Stephen Gresham.

Taking a Bite Out of the Bear

Separate account management is here to stay. It continues to give the investor a more predictable and profitable say in his financial future. (See Figure 5.9.) Here's why: By now you know that a separate account is a group of stocks (and/or bonds) chosen by a professional money manager in close agreement with you and your financial advisor. All stock selections are based on your financial needs and goals, and your tolerance for risk.

As mentioned earlier, unlike a mutual fund, a separate account lets you directly own the stocks in your portfolio. This method of investing has been used for decades by only the wealthiest in this country. During the 1920s and 1930s, professional money managers were sought after to manage the fortunes of the very well-to-do. Later on, large institutional investors like pension plans employed these professional money managers to oversee their investments. The average investor was always excluded, because the money management firms sought accounts often as high as $20 million.

Again, new advances in tracking and maintenance technology have put separate accounts within reach for millions of Americans. Investment minimums are no longer in the millions, but viable for the emerging affluent investors. Now millions of new investors can increase net returns using positive tax strategies developed by high-grade money managers.

Figure 5.9 *SAM Total Assets, Actual and Projected*

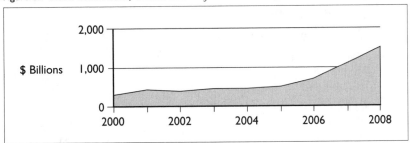

Your banker, stockbroker, or financial planner is not a money manager. These individuals assist you in making and defining financial strategy. They don't have the structure, research capability, and background to manage 50 stock/bonds in a portfolio in the unpredictable trading world of free markets as a money manager does.

Build Yourself a Financial Team

Usually the best arrangement for the average investor is a team effort that includes you, your financial advisor, and your money managers. Together, this team provides the best formula for probability of financial success.

A financial advisor with a large book of separately managed account assets is a more sophisticated advisor, and therefore takes a long-term outlook for his client.
Mike Evans, vice president, consultant, Financial Research Corp.

A Focused Approach Is Best

The separate account investing process works so well because of its consistency. The market, as we've seen, is volatile and chancy at best. The only way to achieve normalcy within the twists and turns of the market environment is a disciplined approach. The separate account allows investors to invest like successful investing institutions and multimillionaires, if they follow four essential steps:

1. Identify the goals.

2. Decide where your assets will go by building an investment policy statement (IPS).
3. Choose your financial advisor and money managers.
4. Monitor the plan in progress and rebalance as required.

Technology Has Made It Possible

Separate accounts began life as a financial strategy designed primarily for high-net-worth individuals and institutions. But it has become apparent that many more investors stand to benefit from the unique features of the separate account. Technology has leveled the playing field, and has opened up incredible opportunities for more investors to partake in the separate accounts revolution.

Investors have new choices that were not available even a year ago. The democratizing force behind the separate accounts revolution has been technology. Only with technology has it been possible to maintain separate account portfolios with adequate diversification, and to incorporate top-grade money managers and investment styles for a lower asset minimum entry fee. Fees are dropping in proportion to the number of firms offering separate accounts, improved and refined computer technology, and intense competition for the emerging affluent investor. This is making separate accounts a permanent part of the asset management landscape. (See Figure 5.10.)

SAM: THE BEST INVESTMENT FOR TODAY'S EMERGING AFFLUENT

The separate account is the most efficient and customizable investment vehicle available today. It's a system that enhances benefits for you and your advisor as your portfolio increases in value. And because you own your separate account, you're in on the decision-making process regarding the stocks you will own. Why would you invest your money in a system that refuses to consider your tax situation when it makes buying and selling decisions? Do you realize taxes could eat away as much as 40 percent of your gains, depending on your tax bracket? And manager compensation is not tied to more trading, as it is in mutual funds. In fact, just the opposite is true: Separate accounts give you one price for

Figure 5.10 *The Big Players in Separate Accounts*

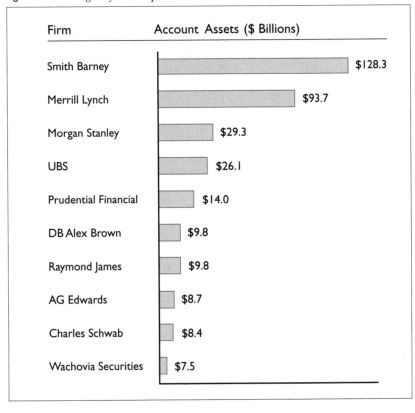

Firm	Account Assets ($ Billions)
Smith Barney	$128.3
Merrill Lynch	$93.7
Morgan Stanley	$29.3
UBS	$26.1
Prudential Financial	$14.0
DB Alex Brown	$9.8
Raymond James	$9.8
AG Edwards	$8.7
Charles Schwab	$8.4
Wachovia Securities	$7.5

the whole plate, not hidden fees and undisclosed charges under the fund companies' "don't ask, don't tell" policy.

Flexibility Is the Key to SAMs

With a separate account, you get the flexibility to include or exclude the specific securities you desire. You can limit your exposure to a security if you're already overloaded with that security in your 401(k), you get the flexibility to check your account whenever you wish, and you and your professional money manager can plan the management of your assets to minimize taxes. In fact, SAMs offer a level of flexibility that's superior to mutual funds in every aspect.

In the following chapters, you will learn how to set up your own separate account.

_c h a p t e r_

6

TAXES:
TAX PAIN OR
LESS TAX GAIN?

In this world nothing is certain but death and taxes.

Benjamin Franklin

You can't argue with Ben. He said
there are only two *sure* things life's journey offers. While death and taxes
will always remain two of life's certainties, you can control just how much
you owe in taxes and eliminate unnecessary fees and high tax penalties.

TAXES: REASON ONE FOR
LETTING GO OF MUTUAL FUNDS

Every year mutual fund investors are sent scrambling when they receive their end-of-year Form 1099s in the mailbox and discover a sizable
amount of their hard-earned cash going to Uncle Sam. Every dollar that
you pay in taxes is a dollar that can't grow for your tomorrow. It's a guaranteed loss!

Capital Gains: The Taxman's Best Friend

The mutual fund investor gets hit with a huge tax bill in addition to
the typically poor performance returns mutual funds generate. As for

Capital Gains Distribution

Distributions that are paid to an investment company's shareholders out of the capital gains of the company's investment portfolio. Capital gains distributions typically occur near the end of the calendar year and are taxable to the shareholder of the investment company.

This poses a problem for some mutual fund investors who purchase new mutual funds near the end of a calendar year. Because they receive a capital gains distribution, they immediately receive taxable income and face a mutual fund NAV, which is reduced from the distribution.

Source: Investopedia.com.

taxes, many taxable investors purchase a mutual fund after gains in that fund were already made. It doesn't matter to Uncle Sam when you came into the fund—at the beginning or at the end of the tax year. You're the owner. That's what counts to the IRS regarding capital gains. For sure, you and other numbed investors have to be asking yourselves: "How can I reduce these tax bills?"

Maybe a short primer on the taxation of mutual funds would be in order. Every time the mutual fund manager buys or sells a stock (or bond) the fund has a capital gain or loss. Investors are not without fault as they pump up taxes also by moving their funds from one fund to another (as mentioned in Chapter 4).

Yearly, the mutual fund company mails the results of short-term and/or long-term gains (held over a year) or losses to the shareholders. There is also an accounting of all net interest and dividends in a separate distribution.

50 Percent of Mutual Fund Investors Pay Capital Gains Taxes

So how large is the end-of-year taxable state that over 93 million American mutual funds investors find themselves in? According to the Investment Company Institute, the mutual fund trade group, at least 40 percent of stock-fund assets are held in tax-free accounts such as 401(k) plans and IRAs. A small number of the remaining 60 percent are institutional investors and trusts that are also tax-exempt. But the remaining group of investors—around 50 percent—own mutual funds that are taxable.[1]

How much of that tax money once belonged to you? The SEC says the average mutual fund investor loses 2.5 percent of their annual returns to taxes each year.[2] Other research puts the figure at 3 percent.

If you compound these percentages over a lifetime of investing, not even counting trading costs and commissions inherent in mutual funds, you can see how taxes can reduce the assets you will have when you reach retirement.

Don't Create Extra Taxes

To fully understand the implications of taxes dragging your mutual fund's performance ROI down, you need to recognize the inherent structure of the mutual fund's process and the philosophy of the fund company that markets it.

In short, if you have to live with taxes, why pay more than necessary? This is why you have to examine your mutual fund portfolio closely. You wouldn't overpay your income taxes, so why take on an investment vehicle that does.

Taxes Are Going to Get You

If you have a tax-deferred retirement account (401(k), IRA, etc.), capital gains taxes are no problem and you might regard this discussion as immaterial. In the end, however, you may have to take your tax-advantaged money and reinvest in taxable accounts at a later age (ages 59½ to 70) as deemed by your retirement plan. Lately, there have been more American households with large amounts of taxable assets that are being battered by the excessive trading of mutual funds. These funds are taxed at ordinary income rates that range from 28 percent to 39.6 percent (41 percent in California). (See Figure 6.1.)

SEC Now Requires New Disclosures on Taxes

In 2001, the SEC mandated fund companies to disclose standardized after-tax returns information. The amendment required break-

Figure 6.1 *Five-Year Average Tax Efficiency for Fund Groups*

Mutual Fund	Pretax Return	After-Tax Return	Tax Efficiency
AIM Weingarten	30.6 percent	26.6 percent	86.6 percent
Putnam G&I	13.4 percent	10.6 percent	78.3 percent
Vanguard	13.1 percent	9.2 percent	70.5 percent
Fidelity G&I	21.8 percent	19.7 percent	90.7 percent
AM Century Ultra	28.8 percent	25.9 percent	90.1 percent
Janus	31.3 percent	28.9 percent	89.0 percent
Average Fund			**84 percent**

downs of after-tax returns in every mutual fund for one-, five-, and ten-year periods. (See Figure 6.2.) This is mandatory information every mutual fund must publish in its prospectus. If the fund claims to be tax-efficient, tax data will be published in advertising and sales literature too.

The SEC ruling requires the funds present standardized after-tax returns in two ways: (1) "preliquidation" showing the effect of taxes on fund distributions only (this is for investors who buy and hold), and (2) "postdistribution," showing the effect of taxes on fund distributions when the shareholders redeem fund shares at the end of each period.

The SEC believes that requiring funds to disclose after-tax returns both ways will show shareholders the negative tax effect of the portfolio manager's buying and selling of portfolio securities, as well as the shareholder's individual decision to sell fund shares. The calculations assume the maximum individual federal income tax rate (currently 39.6 percent). The SEC believes that showing the worst-case scenario will wake up investors to begin thinking about taxes.[3]

We know poor performance of mutual funds is not new news. However, the proliferation of capital gains taxes has not received that much attention from investors. It was assumed that during 2000 and 2001, investors would become more sensitive to the negative effects mutual fund taxation plays on performance.

Figure 6.2 *Sample Disclosure for a Mutual Fund Showing Tax Expenses as Dictated by the SEC*

Average Total Return (During 2001)			
XYZ Fund	1 year	5 years	10 years
Return Before Taxes	– 16.8%	– 3.2%	– 4.5%
Return After Taxes on Distribution	– 17.7%	– 5.2%	1.3%
Return After Taxes on Distributions and Sale of Fund Shares	– 10.1%	– 3.3%	2.4%
S&P 500 Index	– 22.1%	– 0.6%	9.3%

They have not. According to one recent survey, what investors know about the impact of taxes on stock returns is very little. Further, the recent enactment by the SEC on keeping investors informed about taxable implications in the fund prospectus and sales promotions materials reveals only 30 percent of investors are aware of the new procedures.[4] One of the problems is that investors typically, as stated in earlier chapters, do not read their fund's prospectus.

High-Speed Turnover

What continues to burden taxable investors is the breakneck speed with which fund managers buy and sell stocks. The Strong Discovery Fund, one of the firms indicted by the SEC, has had an average turnover of stocks of 450 percent over a five-year period. This comes down to a stock being traded approximately every three months. Its five-year posttax return is 39 percent lower than its pretax annual gain.[5]

The average yearly turnover of a U.S. stock fund is around 90 percent.[6]

This makes it pretty difficult for the average taxable investor to beat the market. Most stocks that begin the year as part of a fund will not be there after the year is over. A fund with a 100 percent turnover trades all of its stocks in a year. It could trade a few stocks many times. But the higher the turnover, the more trading a fund does.

Fund managers have to beat the market by 2.5 percent to 3.5 percent yearly to beat the pretax return of a comparable index fund. Index funds

Index Fund

A portfolio of investments that are weighted the same as a stock exchange index in order to mirror its performance. This process is also referred to as indexing.

Investing in an index fund is known as passive investing. The primary advantages to such a strategy are the lower management expense ratios on index funds. Also, a majority of mutual funds fail to beat broad indexes such as the S&P 500.

Source: Investopedia.com.

are mutual funds designed to mirror the performance of a stock or bond index, such as the Standard & Poor 500 Index (S&P 500) or the Russell 2000 Index.

Turnover Equals Poor Performance

A significant study analyzing the ten-year cumulative performance records of open-end mutual funds in existence from December 1991 to December 2001 found a consistent negative relationship between fund turnover and performance on most sector funds. For example, in large-cap U.S. equity funds, the researchers observed that on the average, each 100 percent of turnover was expected to reduce the funds average annual pretax return by 124 bps (basis points) or 1.24 percent. Each 100 percent of turnover in small-cap I/S funds reduced the annual return by 255 bps. Other asset-class categories also demonstrated performance reductions resulting from increased trading.[7]

Turnover Averages 100 Percent Yearly

During the 1940s and up to the mid-1960s, only 17 percent of mutual fund stocks were traded annually. In 1997, the turnover rate was 85 percent—a fivefold increase. In 1999, the average turnover rate jumped to 103 percent.[8] Today the rate is around 90 percent, demonstrating investors have become more conservative in their trading during the last few years. But investors are still trading, frequently fueled by the industry's huge marketing machine constantly urging them to jump in and out of funds.[9]

Managers Turnover Too

When considering all aspects of mutual fund inequalities regarding taxes you can include constant manager turnover as another problem. Most new managers clean house with a newly inherited fund. Again, these actions generate unnecessary capital gains. A new manager might install a completely different strategy or significantly adjust the established approach. Whether or not he generates gains, you're going to generate taxes if you possess that mutual fund.

Applying the Quick Fix

There are alternative tax-avoidance strategies you can do to lessen your capital gains tax situation. For instance, if you wish to own over-traded stock funds, transfer them to your retirement account. No tax worries there.

You could also consider index funds for your taxable portfolio. Index funds tend to be more tax-efficient, but these vehicles set limits on higher performance returns.

Tax-efficient mutual funds do exist. Fidelity Investments, T. Rowe Price Associates, and the Vanguard Group offer such tax-efficient funds. Again, these are mutual funds, and even if a tax-efficient fund works for you, mutual funds still demonstrate other disadvantages that should cause you to seek an alternative investing solution.

You could dissolve your funds and invest exclusively in individual stocks. If you makeover your mutual funds portfolio to have only individual stocks you won't have to pay capital gains. Because the chief advantage of mutual funds is diversification, your diversification may suffer if you invest in individual stocks exclusively without adequate capital to reduce risk across asset classes.

All of these suggestions are temporary solutions for the high-net-income and the emerging-affluent investor. I suggest you consider another important option to reduce your taxes: Your own *separate account.*

THE SEPARATE ACCOUNT TAX REDUCTION SOLUTION

Investors are exiting mutual funds and turning to separate accounts for a very important reason: *control over taxes.* Relief from federal income taxes may be the main reason to set up a separate account but it's not the only reason, as the chapters that follow will reveal.

Nevertheless, separate accounts are able to capitalize on the sore spot of mutual funds—the tax bite that occurs most years when a fund distributes the capital gains it has made from securities sold during the year. Because separate account holders own their securities separately, they can buy and sell according to their taxable situation. As a holder of a separate account, you don't need to worry about "phantom gains." These are gains realized by mutual fund holders who enter a fund late and end up owing the IRS for capital gains before they even have the chance to participate in positive returns that were made before they purchased the fund. Because all capital gains in a mutual fund are distributed proportionately on the shares you own, you get to be taxed before you benefit from the increase in the value of the holding.

In a separate account, you are not tied to losses that may result when investors pull the plug on a mutual fund that has lost value.

Are You a Tax Reduction Candidate for a SAM?

As a tax rule of thumb, if the IRS took more than $10,000 from you during the last tax year, you would probably benefit from the increased tax efficiency of a SAM.

Here's another way of looking at your tax situation: Mutual funds record yearly short-term gains and losses. If you have a gain during your taxable year, and, say, you are in a 39.6 percent tax bracket, your mutual fund portfolio has to have a gross of 16.56 percent to net 10 percent. A SAM investor would have to only gross 12.5 percent to net the same 10 percent return. (See Figure 6.3.)

Exploring more tax benefits of separate accounts, if you itemize your tax return with a Schedule A, a client can deduct all fees paid into his separate account. The IRS does not allow for fees to be deducted with mutual funds.

Jim Dew, Dew Wealth Management, Scottsdale, Arizona

Figure 6.3 *Pretax Returns Necessary to Achieve 10 Percent Return after Taxes*

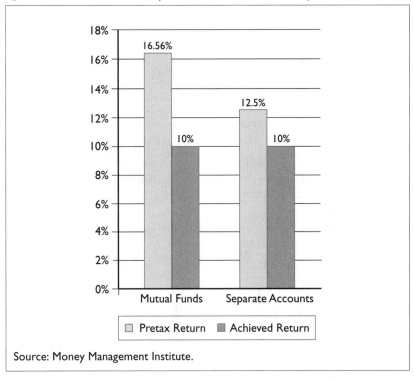

Source: Money Management Institute.

There are other advantages of making the commitment to a separate account for tax reduction.

As soon as you activate your account with your advisor, you begin your relationship with your SAM. Unlike mutual funds, you are not burdened with capital gains from past and present trading within the fund.

Your manager along with your advisor's input should offer a direct hand in helping you develop an individualized tax strategy.

Let's look at a second tax reduction benefit of your new separate account. You own your account. You are the only shareholder. If you are immersed in mutual funds, there're many others just like you. The actions of other shareholders can adversely affect you, such as when a fund manager has to sell early to satisfy new redemptions coming in.

With a separate account, you're in control. You have achieved power over taxable events. Whereas a mutual fund manager makes trades routinely creating taxable events, your separate account manager will now take your tax reduction needs into consideration before trading actions.

The high turnover of mutual funds kills any opportunity for tax harvesting
for our clients. That's why we recommend separate accounts,
because they are more tax-efficient.

David Robinson, president, Robinson, Tigue, Sponcil & Associates, Phoenix, Arizona

Tax Harvesting Is Key

"Tax harvesting" is when you realize a gain and then take a loss within your portfolio. This action eliminates the capital gains you built up during the year by selling securities as a capital loss. You would use this same process if you're owned the securities directly.

The whittled-down, after-tax returns that can be generated for you, the client, depend on three factors:

1. Your financial advisor's skill in devising for you a strong asset-allocation strategy
2. Your financial advisor's skill in selecting separate account managers who are sensitive to developing strong tax strategies
3. The amount of tax harvesting accomplished in a taxable year

Tax harvesting is the key to saving on your taxes. Tax harvesting is taken throughout the year but becomes especially important during the fourth quarter. These events are predetermined according to your asset-allocation strategy.

What You Need to Watch For

If this were a perfect world, then our SAM theory of dodging an unnecessary tax burden would work like the atomic clock.

But it takes you, the investor, to set the clock.

You need to be aware that not all money managers are the same. Some are sensitive to tax reduction; some are not. You need to recognize the difference. That's where your advisor comes in and why he or she is on your team. In the development of your asset-allocation strategy, a key to the success of your portfolio, selection of the right managers, has to be accomplished.

Your advisor will pay careful attention to the tax-saving performance of your money managers. It is most important that your advisor

Tax Gain/Loss Harvesting

Tax gain/loss harvesting is a process of selling securities at a loss to offset a capital gains tax liability. It is typically used to limit the recognition of short-term capital gains, which are normally taxed at higher federal income tax rates than long-term capital gains. This process is also known as "tax-loss selling."

For many investors, tax gain/loss harvesting is the single most important area for reducing taxes now and in the future. If properly applied, it can save you from paying higher taxes and help you diversify your portfolio in ways you may not have considered. Although it can't restore your losses, it can certainly soften the blow. For example, a loss in the value of Security A could be sold to offset the increase in value of Security B, thus eliminating the capital gains tax liability of Security B.

Source: Investopedia.com.

examine the past performance of the managers and make certain they mirror your tax-saving agenda. Exemplary return performance is not enough if you're also seeking tax savings. Returns can be misleading in the larger scheme of tax reduction.

A manager could be a star on a pretax basis but fall on his face once the tax bill has arrived in your mailbox.

> *As the high net worth demographic grows, more and more people want the tax advantages you can receive from a separate account.*
> **Cerulli Associates**

Tax Reduction Revisited

If I have convinced you to make tax reduction as much a part of your life as brushing your teeth, then you need to be sure your advisor and money manager are in harmony. Make sure

- your portfolio is lined up with your financial objectives, your level of risk acceptance, and your individual tax circumstances (I

Think Taxes When You Invest in a Mutual Fund

Keep these three questions in mind:

1. **Has the mutual fund recently changed managers?** New managers like to clear the decks of stocks chosen by their predecessors. This generates unnecessary capital gains.
2. **What is the fund's tax overhang?** This is the amount of capital gains embedded in the fund that will inevitably have to be paid.
3. **What is the fund's turnover rate?** A fund with a higher turnover rate will have a high tax burden.

Source: Richard Rutner.

will go into more detail regarding your portfolio in the following chapters);

- you agree to a definite schedule of making decisions on capital gains and losses; and
- you recognize the importance of the dividend and manage its stream during the course of the year.

Remember skilled trading, not excessive trading, keeps costs low. Excessive trading generates high trading costs and capital gains. This, in turn, saps after-tax returns in mutual funds. By establishing a separate account, excessive trading that causes bounce-back tax bills will no longer be a concern. You own the stocks in your portfolio and you're in sync with your financial advisor and money manager who can sell underperforming stocks on a systematic basis to offset capital gains.

Fundamentally:

Less turnover = Fewer costs + Lower taxes

Fewer costs + Lower taxes = Higher returns

Isn't that really what you want from your portfolio?

The Bottom Line: Taxes

Mutual Funds:

- Most mutual funds are not tax-efficient.
- Limited tax-efficient mutual funds are marketed heavily by some fund companies.
- Mutual funds have embedded capital gains by their nature.

Separate Accounts:

- Separate accounts allow the investor the opportunity for maximum control over his tax situation.
- Minimizing taxes means higher returns.
- You own the stocks in your portfolio.

7

PERFORMANCE: QUESTIONABLE RETURNS OR UNQUESTIONABLY BETTER RETURNS?

Remind people that profit is the difference between revenue and expense.
This makes you look smart.

Scott Adams

More than 93 million Americans own mutual funds. During the early years of our millennium, most of those Americans lost money owning mutual funds. Double-digit returns were not there as they were during the 1980s and 1990s when the investment of choice—mutual funds—helped millions of Americans buy homes, educate children, and fuel retirements.

In today's market environment, mutual funds with built-in tax inefficiencies and downward spiraling returns have investors clambering to discover alternate asset-management options. Separate accounts, a respected financial strategy, traditionally utilized by the ultrarich and big institutions, promises a more stabilized ROI (return on investment) than mutual funds can deliver.

MUTUAL FUNDS: SO RIGHT FOR THE TIMES, JUST NOT THIS TIME

Of some 5,000 mutual funds during the years 2000 to 2003, only 20 percent performed well enough for investors to pay for their fees and loads.

Most mutual funds have been sputtering, delivering returns on the average 2 percent less per year than the stock market returns in general. In good times, this is no call to arms. It's the cost of doing business. But in bear times, the inadequacies (lately, deception too) of the mutual fund investment vehicle has come home to roost.

To hear the fund companies tell it, with billions of promotional dollars touting their products, they say they produce results, positive performance results.

Most Mutual Funds Are Underperformers

The simple fact: More than 90 percent of mutual funds have underperformed the stock market as a whole for the past five years.[1]

It's easy to dislike funds for the simple reason you don't have any say in how profits are made or determined in your fund. If you hold Coca-Cola stock for ten years, never dreaming of selling, chances are you're going to rack up some healthy annualized gains. Here's Wall Street at its best—compounded returns unsoiled by capital gains taxes.

With mutual funds, you're at the mercy of the commonplace overtrading by the funds' managers. On average in today's investment climate, these managers turn over all their assets at least once a year. This leads to those negative distributions we have been talking about when you file with Uncle Sam on April 15.

Investors Fight Back: Redemptions

Investors were mad and outflows from mutual funds were very much evident during the years 2000 to 2003. Stock funds lost 9 percent of their assets—something that hasn't happened in this manner since the Great Depression, the fall of 1998, the dot-com implosion of 2000. With investors voting with their feet and pocketbooks, redemption levels escalated at unprecedented rates. Breaking all records, the year 2000 saw investors redeem a staggering $1.042 trillion from funds. The $1 trillion of redemptions in 2000 represented a 188 percent increase from the 1997 level of $362 billion.[2]

It was easy to blame such a huge loss on the bear market. For a time, American investors bought that story. Few mutual fund investors realize even today that poor returns may come from something other than a bad choice of funds or the down economy. They even came back into the market in 2003 and plowed good money after bad. Eventually, it became evident; the 60-year investment vehicle Americans came to depend on as their investment of choice is no longer a viable option.

Of course, during the go-go years of the 1980s and 1990s while making those double-digit returns, most investors did not raise a whimper. Why should they? Americans were enjoying great returns and who cared if the expenses of owning mutual funds could be higher than the investors cared to know.

Today the tune has changed. Investors are frustrated and mad. Compounding the performance losses is the revelation of misconduct throughout the industry first revealed by the attorney general of New York State in September 2003.

As Americans redeemed millions of dollars from the fund companies' coffers, typical investors began looking for alternative ways to invest their wealth.

Separate account management, an asset management concept long cherished by the likes of the Fords and Rockefellers, was rediscovered. As noted in earlier chapters, separate accounts became more accessible as an investment platform because of software and computer application breakthroughs. The very same professional money managers who serviced the asset wealth of the ultrarich and institutions became available as an asset for new clients. Initial investment for setting up a separate account went from millions to even as low as $25,000. This afforded a new opportunity for the new "emerging affluent" as well as the high-net-worth individual to merge their portfolios into a more performance-oriented and tax-friendly vehicle than offered by mutual funds.

MUTUAL FUNDS MAY BE HAZARDOUS TO YOUR FINANCIAL HEALTH

I have addressed the points of mutual funds performance weaknesses throughout the book. The structure of the mutual fund investment vehicle itself inherently causes poor performance. If you as a mutual fund investor realize that, then you can move to a new plateau of investing, set up a separate account as your portfolio strategy, and begin making sense of your returns.

Setting up a separate account is paramount to improving the performance over your old mutual fund portfolio. How can I say this? Isn't a stock, a stock? If both a separate account and a defined mutual fund could possess the same group of stocks, then, at the end of the reporting period, should not their gains and losses be the same? Yes, but . . .

Here is the difference: The mutual fund with higher trading costs and built-in high tax limitations creates a post-tax return that potentially delivers less performance than a similar separate account. This is what it's all about: your take-home pay at the end. Let's summarize some of these built-in limitations to the performance of mutual funds. Doing so, the separate account concept becomes more lucid as a performance enhancer.

Mutual funds kill their potential for becoming performance superstars by their high volume of trading. Too much trading causes increased taxes and reduces performance. Period.

If these limitations to mutual funds hinder performance, then the unbridled aspects of separate accounts should improve performance.

Achieve Higher Returns: Mutual Funds or Separate Accounts?

Some late-breaking research has reached that same conclusion. Separate accounts can deliver higher returns to investors than mutual funds or exchange-traded funds, according to a study conducted by David Stein, chief investment officer of Parametric Portfolio Associates, a Seattle-based investment firm specializing in customized separate accounts. (See Figure 7.1.)

Exchange-traded funds (ETFs) are listed on a stock exchange and trade like stocks. You can use traditional stock-trading techniques, such

Figure 7.1 *Less Tax Pain, More Gain*

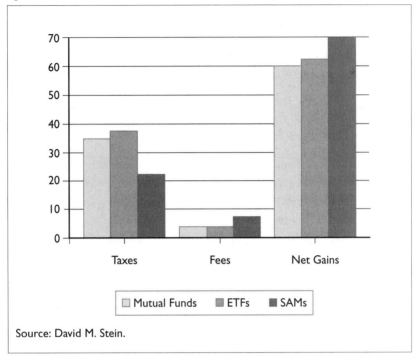

Source: David M. Stein.

as stop orders, limit orders, margin purchases, and short sales. But ETFs resemble mutual funds as a basket of stocks.

There's a belief out there among certain financial professionals that performance is about equal between separate accounts and mutual funds.

The research proves this to be untrue. To make a fair comparison, Stein utilized passive index-based strategies with mutual funds, ETFs, and separate accounts. The result is based on after-tax wealth accumulation.

The assumption is the return on three investment strategies with a $100 investment, managed for 25 years, and then redeemed.

Further, Stein gave each vehicle a yearly return of 10 percent with an 8 percent capital appreciation and 2 percent awarded dividend. The tax rate was determined to be 20 percent on capital gains and 40 percent on dividends.

As a benchmark, the initial $100 was determined to be worth **$1,083** after 25 years minus taxes and fees.

The performance of the index mutual fund with a 0.2 percent annual fee and a 5 percent annual gain realization (it distributes 5 percent unrealized capital gains to investors each year) rewarded the investor with **$590 or 60 percent of the total pretax increase.**

This was after taxes and fees were taken out.

Next, the ETF showed its performance utilizing the same criteria: 0.2 percent annual fee and a 1 percent annual gain realization. What did the investor reap after 25 years? The investor would receive **$617 or 63 percent of pretax potential.**

Taking a look now at the after-tax return of a similar investment with a separate account, a higher fee of 0.3 percent and a 1 percent annual gain was assumed. Tax loss harvesting, a major investor benefit of separate accounts, was added.

The result: The investor came out ahead receiving **$692 or 70 percent of the pretax increase.** This performance in the study conducted years earlier was higher for separate accounts in spite of the researcher setting the fee structure higher than SAM fees are running today for the most part.[3]

Your Loss, Your Gain

So what's the best strategy? Without a doubt, a separate account plays its trump cards with risk, return, and tax decisions all secure and customized for the individual investor. As mentioned earlier in Chapter 6, the key to bettering your returns when capital losses are realized is to use them to erase the gains accrued from other investments. In addition, short-term gains can be offset against long-term losses also.

In contrast, mutual funds and ETFs are commingled, causing lack of control with other investors in the pool gains and losses.

In the end it comes back to taxes—*the largest single cost for the taxable investor.* If you get on board with your advisor and institutional money manager(s) with a clearly defined tax strategy, then your returns performance will surely improve.

> **Redemption:** The return of an investor's principal in a security, such as a stock, bond, or mutual fund.
>
> Redemption of mutual fund shares from a mutual fund company must occur within seven days of receiving a request for redemption from the investor.
>
> Source: Investopedia.com.

THE PERFORMANCE-CUTTING SINS OF MUTUAL FUNDS

Redemptions

The cash you put into your mutual fund is utilized in two ways. A portion is used to outfit you as a player—buying, selling, and making a return for your cash participation. The other is keeping your cash on the sidelines not as a player but as a bank to pay off those investors who want to redeem and move on. It's difficult to impossible to find out how much of your wealth is working and how much is unemployable, sitting in the tank waiting to pay off other unhappy investors like yourself.

Then, what happens during a down market when a huge number of investors cut and run from the fund? Anticipating redemptions, the fund manager usually holds back from finding good buys for the fund. Instead, he is unloading his stocks to raise cash. The fund's performance is beaten up and, of course, everyone in the fund suffers with the capital gains tax. The SEC says that 15 percent of all mutual fund gains are lost due to capital gains. During 2000, a really bad year for Wall Street, the tax bill for Americans holding mutual funds was 19.8 billion.[4]

Diversification

What's this? Diversification is a good thing. Doesn't it spread your risk across asset classes to prevent you from having too much of your wealth in one basket? Mutual fund policy law from 60 years ago says that a fund manager may not have more than 5 percent of his more produc-

> **Diversification:** A risk management technique that mixes a wide variety of investments within a portfolio. It is designed to minimize the impact of any one security on overall portfolio performance.
> Diversification is possibly the greatest way to reduce the risk.
>
> Source: Investopedia.com.

tive stocks in his fund at one time. In essence, the managers have to sell their best highfliers when they begin to fly too high.

By selling off the best stocks boosting returns for the total fund, the rest of the stocks can become also-rans flattening the ROI (return on investment).

Diversification becomes asset dilution. It affects the investor not only in poorer performance minus the higher returns but also in producing stocks sold prematurely which increases trading costs. Yes, again I mention that taxes are awarded indiscriminately to all investors no matter when they came into the fund.

Selling the Perception of Great Performance

The great temptation for a fund manager responsible for a lackluster fund is to inflate end-of-year performance results by increasing the amount of stocks the fund holds. This stock ballooning drives up the price of the stocks inflating the value of the fund portfolio. This makes the manager happy because it normally affects his bonus if he presents positive year-end gains. It makes the marketing department happy because it has another fund to tout as a performance superstar to continue its role as an asset gatherer.

This fraudulent action known as "portfolio pumping" is among many such maneuvers designed to sell the perception of great mutual fund performance. The fund manager creates an impression of an upward trend in the fund's value by putting a vast amount of dollars into a particular security at the end of a reporting period in order to drive up the value of the fund.

In fact, the last day of the year is seen as especially critical for losing funds to make managers look better. In fact, research showed the 62 percent of funds lagging the S&P 500 by as much as 25 basis points still managed to beat the market index based solely on the performance of the fund *during the last day of the year*.[5]

Research shows that such misdeeds occur more often than one might think. Portfolio manipulation is an ongoing problem with mutual funds. Lori Richards, head of the SEC's inspection program, even has assigned a task force to investigate the increase in portfolio fraud. "We are looking for signs that a particular mutual fund may be pumping up its performance at the end of a reporting period."[6] The task force has discovered at least 40 funds from 2000 to 2004 that have increased performance returns from 3 percent to 5 percent on the last day of the quarter.

It's not what you make; it's what you take . . . to the bank!

Peter F. Tedstrom, Brown & Tedstrom, Denver

SAMS: ASSET MANAGEMENT WITH BETTER PERFORMANCE

With excessive costs in the front end, excessive costs in the back end, and open/hidden costs in the middle, mutual funds hit you coming and going. These costs slice into your ROI in both the bear years and the bull years. Again, I must tell you that when added to the mix, capital gains taxes potentially can slice off as much as 50 percent of your gains. No only that, who can you trust when mutual fund companies routinely pump up performance figures to portray hot, action funds to stimulate more investors jumping into their funds? Do market timing and late trading scandals leave you cold regarding mutual funds?

Barron's reports that equity separate accounts have returned 10.96 percent over the past ten years, whereas mutual funds returned 7.78 percent. According to *Barron's:* "Separate accounts have good hands-on involvement with advisors and brokers and have the ability to rotate among asset classes. These programs can also minimize income-producing parts of a portfolio for tax savings."[7]

Separate accounts possess financial principals that allow them to outperform mutual funds theoretically. Again, that's theoretically; but many financial experts believe that SAM investment returns are clearly higher than comparable mutual funds. Some preliminary research shows this. In any event, with no redemption reserves, no built-in tax inefficiencies, and no causal relationship from other investors in the mutual fund pool, separate accounts unquestionably are better structured to produce better returns.

The Bottom Line: Performance

Mutual Funds:

- Funds usually underperform the market.
- High fees hinder performance returns.
- Built-in capital gains reduce performance returns.

Separate Accounts:

- There is no unnecessary tax burden.
- Investor has hands-on security maneuverability.
- Structure potentially allows better ROI.

8

CUSTOMIZATION: OFF THE RACK OR TAILOR-MADE?

We are continually faced by great opportunities brilliantly disguised as insoluble problems.

Lee Iacocca

Investing with mutual funds is like getting on a Greyhound bus in Dallas and traveling to Memphis. You'll get there all right—after suffering through about 50 stops and 50 kids with runny noses. Is that the way to travel? Wouldn't you rather ride in a private limo with your own driver, without any stops or hassles along the way?

Investing in mutual funds is like traveling on Greyhound. You are thrown in with investors who are more neurotic about investing than you are. You're investing, but you're subject to the whims of other investors and the fund manager.

With a separate account, control of your journey is left to you and your advisor.

MUTUAL FUNDS: HERD MENTALITY

Earlier we touched on the fact that you and other investors in mutual funds don't actually own any of the stocks in your portfolio. You own shares of stocks. That's a big difference. It means you have no control over which securities fund managers buy and sell. You can't buy more or less of one particular type of stock to balance out your other investments and you can't opt out of any particular asset class or company.

THE JOY OF OWNING YOUR OWN PORTFOLIO

The only money in a separate account is your own. You're the boss!

For people who would rather own than rent, SAMs offer controls that are not available in mutual funds.

With a SAM, you can custom design your portfolio to suit your individual needs. Usually, you work with your financial advisor to hammer out a customized portfolio based on the many choices of portfolios the institutional money manager(s) and sponsoring broker-dealer(s) have to offer. You develop your investment policy statement (see sample statement in Appendix).

Some restrictions do apply with separate accounts, particularly those with entry investment input of less than $100,000. Most have some structure, for instance, giving you a choice of a "packaged" separate account based on asset classes, degrees of risk, investment style, and domestic, global, or social/political issues. The selection of the money manager or managers can be a customized process. Some managers specialize in large caps, tax reduction, mid-caps, etc. Again, it's what you feel comfortable with in accordance with your advisor's input and advice based on his or her evaluation of your goals.

The investors who have established separate accounts like the customization process. Having a separate account says you and your advisor are in charge. You set the strategy. You decide what stocks or bonds make up your portfolio. You have access to top money managers, and can even change a manager if you wish, if and when the time arises.

The mix-and-match appeal of separate accounts makes SAMs attractive to the new breed of investor who wants more control and input in this portfolio.

Asset class: Different categories of investments are sometimes described as asset classes. The major ones are stocks, bonds, and cash or cash equivalents. When you allocate the assets in your investment portfolio, you decide what proportion of the total value will be invested in each of the different asset classes. Investments such as real estate, collectibles, and precious metals are generally considered separate asset classes. So are futures contracts, options, and mutual funds that follow certain alternative investment strategies, such as market neutral investing, more typically associated with hedge funds.

Source: Investopedia.com.

BUILDING A PERSONALIZED PORTFOLIO

If you don't smoke or gamble and don't wish to have a stake in any stock that economically supports either of these "sins," then you can exclude these type of stocks from your portfolio entirely. If you believe sinning is winning, then you can include them in your portfolio at will.

If you have a problem with the big pharmaceutical companies that allegedly marketed drugs to the American public potentially accelerating heart conditions, you may eliminate them from your portfolio. You instruct your advisor/money manager not to put these types of stocks in your portfolio, mentioning them by name if desired.

Having the capability to define who you are within an economic, political, and/or social context—an advantage of separate accounts—is becoming more appealing to a large number of investors.

Social responsibility has trickled into investing decisions. American investors can utilize their stock portfolios to make a statement socially or politically. America is the most caring country in the Western world, so why shouldn't our positive values be manifested into the asset management process?

With a separate account, such social responsibility investing can be accomplished by:

- **Avoidance**—Refusing to invest in any company contrary to your views

Customization: You can customize your portfolio by having your money manager buy or sell certain securities. You might choose to:

- Exclude certain securities of which you feel you have a sufficient number in other portfolios
- Exclude certain securities you have a moral objection to such as tobacco industry stocks
- Incorporate securities you already own into your professionally managed separate account

Source: Vivian Marino.

- **Being proactive**—Investing in a company in sync with your values system

For example, say you were troubled when you received a listing of stocks from your money manager from a customized separate account with investing emphasis on large caps. You noticed your portfolio contained the stock of a major apparel manufacturer that is currently in court answering to charges of violating child labor laws right here in the United States. Because children are a big priority in your life and you work in a childhood center for abused children on a part-time basis, you don't wish to invest in this company. You call your financial advisor and address the problem with him. "We will take that stock out and replace it with a company more to your liking," he says.

Try and do that with a mutual fund.

One other thing to note: Research into comparisons between socially responsible investing and regular investing reflects some improvement of returns with the right selection of socially responsible stocks.

PROFESSIONAL MANAGEMENT IN YOUR CORNER

What the Money Manager Does for You

Owning a separate account is like a membership in an exclusive club where everyone gets the same preferential treatment. Whether it's a $5 million portfolio or a $50,000 initial capital input, the concept is the same. You go into a separate account with a customized portfolio tailored to your unique needs. Then, with the help of your financial advisor, you are exposed to some of the best professional money management minds on the planet.

> *Baby boomers are coming into retirement with IRA money to roll over into an investment vehicle that allows for more customization of the total wealth management process . . . that's what separate accounts can deliver.*
>
> **Lars Schuster, director of separately managed accounts, Financial Research Corp.**

Usually your financial manager works with a major brokerage firm that either offers its own proprietary management programs and/or third-party management programs in which the broker-dealer has an arrangement with an outside money management firm.

Broker or independent advisor firms decide which third-party managers to offer you, and your advisor reviews the managers' performance and performs due diligence. Even after broker-dealers pick the managers they want to carry, individual brokers often cull the choices further.

Professional money managers on the broker-dealer roster make decisions based on years of experience serving the needs of exacting clients. They have the high caliber support of research analysts, traders, and portfolio managers all prepared to maximize your overall return while reducing the risk, costs, and the taxes you pay.

You do allow discretionary responsibility of your portfolio to the money manager. He or she has been brought into focus regarding your financial goals through you or your financial advisor. Think of your money manager as a running back in position to score touchdowns with your financial advisor as quarterback calling the winning plays. You, the investor, are the coach.

Broker-dealer: A person or firm in the business of buying and selling securities operating as both a broker and dealer depending on the transaction.

Technically, a broker is only an agent who executes orders on behalf of clients, whereas a dealer acts as a principal and trades for his or her own account. Because most brokerages act as both brokers and principals, the term broker-dealer is commonly used to describe them.

Source: Investopedia.com

We're on the cusp of the SAM revolution, and it's not that people are going to take all their money out of mutual funds; it's where the new money is going to go.

Marcia Selz, PhD, president of Marketing Matrix, International

PROLOGUE: PACKING YOUR OWN CHUTE

As I discussed earlier, most money managers will allow customization to accommodate the investor. The most common customization is the elimination of "sin" stocks (gambling, tobacco, liquor, etc.) from the portfolio.

This is not to say that no mutual funds exist with a socially responsible slant as a part of their investment strategy. There are a few, but none offer the flexibility of a separate account's customization. In a separate account, it's not unheard of for money managers to allow investors to grandfather in securities already held by the investor and make them part of the account. This eliminates delays of the investor's positions and avoids excess taxes for the short term.

Hire the Can-Do Manager

Does every manager give the investor this kind of service? The answer is no. The willingness to respond with this kind of service differs. If you're a client, you need to explore this issue when you are considering hiring money managers through your advisor.

Overall, the separate account does offer a means by which a client can modify her portfolio. If you wish to exclude certain stocks because you already own stocks of the same companies in other investments, then you can work with your money manager to discard them.

Within Reason

There are limitations on how much customization is possible in a separate account. If you are participating in a separate account that is committed to a specific investment objective, be aware that the customization of your account should track that objective. To be sure, query your advisor on any separate account plan under review on how much customization within the SAM is allowed. While customization affords you greater freedom, it must be used judiciously. Trying to customize the portfolio too much can handcuff the professional money managers who are pursuing the objectives of the account.

Customization Is Not Yet a Household Word

The majority of separate account investors presently are not utilizing customization, a big benefit of separate accounts. In fact, only about a quarter of clients today have an active customization feature that is being applied to their account, according to Chris Davis, the executive director of the Money Management Institute. However, Davis expects the use of the benefit option to increase. "It's a feature that will grow in use as a portfolio grows in size and the client's needs also grow," Davis said.[1]

Davis compared the customization element with a four-wheel-drive SUV. You don't use the off-road feature all the time, he said, "But when you do get off the road, you're sure glad that you have the feature."

Having the option of customization of your securities in your portfolio is an important benefit that will become more of value as you discover this aspect of the separate account platform. The separate account investor no longer has his hands tied when it comes to making investment decisions with his account. The separate account puts the investor in control. This will probably make many on Wall Street wary, but during these days with the market more sensitive to the ups and downs of a roller-coaster economy, the investor needs to seize control of his wealth.

The Bottom Line: Customization

Mutual Funds:

- Investor does not own stocks.
- Investment is pooled with other investors.
- Investor has no say in fund's holdings.

Separate Accounts:

- Investor owns stocks.
- Money managers buy and sell securities in portfolio.
- Investor has the option to include or exclude stocks in portfolio.

9

ASSET CONTROL: MANAGER IN CONTROL OR INVESTOR IN CONTROL?

*You cannot control what happens to you, but you can control
your attitude toward what happens to you, and in that, you will be
mastering change rather than allowing it to master you.*

Brian Tracy

Think about span of control. The U.S. Army says the ratio of span of control should be no more than one noncommissioned officer (NCO) to seven enlisted men. More than that and management gets a little unwieldy.

The same shaky situation exists in the mutual fund world. Who do you think has a better handle on things in these circumstances: One mutual fund manager responsible for overseeing about 150 stocks in a fund, or six to ten separate account managers watching over one account with 100 securities or less?

The answer is obvious even for the few of us who are multitaskers. It's a fact that the span of control of a manager in charge of a mutual fund can be overwhelming with scores of securities to look after and be responsible for.

In a separate account, each money manager or managers advise on usually fewer than 50 securities in each client's portfolio. Further, these managers (as do mutual fund companies) usually have access to dozens of securities analysts and researchers to provide additional reinforcement.

This brings us to the subject of asset control.

Asset control refers to who has control over your portfolio. In mutual funds, the fund's manager does, not you. In a separate account, you have control and your advisor and the manager(s) of your account receive their marching orders from you.

WHO'S WATCHING YOUR MONEY?

In today's market, investors have better prospects if more experts are keeping a careful eye on the actual business practices and bottom lines of funds and managers. It's a fact. A mutual fund manager's span of control can be extremely limited if he is tasked with dozens, sometimes hundreds, of stocks residing within one fund. That is exactly the situation in many of the 8,000 or more funds out there on the market.

Fidelity's Puritan Fund has as many as 1,000 separate stocks on any trading day supervised by one manager. Another large Fidelity fund, Growth & Income, has some 172 securities handled by one manager. Fidelity's Contra Fund has 521 stocks, again with one manager in charge.

Giving Up Asset Control with Mutual Funds

Recognizing that you do not own the stocks in your portfolio but merely shares of stocks along with a large pool of people like yourself, what do you give up when you invest in mutual funds? Control. In mutual funds, you give up control.

Marketing is dictating your fund's direction. One thing you won't give up with a mutual fund is a marketing machine. Your fund company's objective is achieving profitability. Forget those ideas about investing "the old-fashioned way." The fund companies earn their money increasing their profits not making profits for the investor.

The fund companies gather assets by creating favorable perceptions of their products. Without addressing the tawdry actions of deception uncovered in September 2003 by the New York State attorney general (see Chapter 3), the usual modus operandi is spinning the perception of performance at the expense of the investor. The fund companies do this in a number of ways:

- Creating new funds to sell, not creating new investments
- Hyping the records of the smallest funds even though evidence shows that the funds' performance will shrink as the funds grow
- Siphoning dollars from portfolios to provide capital for massive marketing campaigns to attract new investors
- Giving lukewarm warning to their shareholders regarding the inherent risks of investing[1]

While pumping up funds' perceptions does exist throughout the industry, know also that the fund companies employ hundreds of professional, honest managers who dedicate themselves to doing the best for their investors day in and day out. However, as the examples above suggest, the intense environment of maximizing profitability fuels the funds' marketing machine.

One Example of Lack of Investor Control: Style Drift

Say you choose a large-cap income mutual fund to expand your wealth. You determined this fund would include big capitalization companies such as IBM, AT&T, GM, etc. At a later date, you discover the fund is now chock-full of small company securities, even international stocks. This is called "style drift" because the fund manager decided to invest in different asset classes instead of sticking to the prospectus's main objectives. It happens all the time. Needless to say, a manager's change of investment strategy leads to fluctuating risk control in your asset allocation plan. It's all legal because it is outlined in the prospectus, but how many shareholders really read the prospectus?

Is There Board of Director Protection?

It should be one of the more solid methods of monitoring control of your stock funds, but it isn't. The board of directors of your fund company is appointed to oversee the actions of the fund managers to make sure they are acting in the best interest of the investors. This group is supposed to act as a watchdog, fighting for investors' rights.

Too often, however, these boards function as extensions of the marketing department. The board members usually command big salaries

and therefore rubber-stamp the investment actions of the fund managers, knowing full well that their salaries are riding on the success of the
buying power of those stock funds.

New rules released in 2004 will help close the "good old boy" mischief of director abuse. The chairman of every mutual fund board must
now be independent. That is, the chairman must have no ties to the company. Research has shown that 80 percent of fund company board members are insiders. Further, the new ruling says that 75 percent of all
board members must be "independents."

A SEPARATE ACCOUNT: HANDS-ON CONTROL

As an astute investor in today's market, you need hands-on control
of your assets under management. It is evident that the separate account
platform offers more in the way of investor participation. Separate accounts deliver you the control over investing your wealth. An investor
who has the control has the power.

The Bottom Line: Asset Control

Mutual Funds:
- Fund managers my be responsible for hundreds of securities.
- Investor is cuffed to the whims of fund managers.
- Investor has no say in stock selection.

Separate Accounts:
- Money managers are responsible for 30 to 80 securities.
- Investor is in control of his portfolio.
- Investor suffers no impact from other investor actions.

10

PRESTIGE FACTOR: INVEST WITH THE REST OR INVEST WITH THE BEST?

Who decides when the applause should die down? It seems like it's a group decision; everyone begins to say to themselves at the same time, "Well, okay, that's enough of that."

George Carlin

Never underestimate snob appeal.

Many older and wealthier Americans who were weaned on mutual funds are comfortable with the investment process that has been around for some 60 years.

That feeling is disappearing. Today's investors are more comfortable with change. Today, those with "emerging affluence" are asking themselves if they should stay with the ultimate retail investment—one that is associated with mass market investing, and that is now viewed by many as a commodity.

A private money manager servicing your separate account alongside a Ford Foundation or a Bill Gates is a prestige factor a separate account carries that is hard to ignore.

Mutual fund managers don't differentiate between one investor or another. Their job is to boost the inflow from the account and to get the numbers regardless of who's investing in the fund.

Separate account investors receive asset management on an individual basis and custom solutions for securities they own. Bill Gates gets the same treatment.

Don't ever underestimate snob appeal.

OUTGROWING MUTUAL FUNDS

Unless you thrive as a hermit on a mountaintop, you have, like most of us, regular contact with people. Family and friends are a given. You like human contact and feel goodwill toward folks most of the time.

The downside of human contact is when you find yourself in an overstuffed elevator that gets stuck between floors. It's uncomfortable, stressful, intimidating, and even scary.

The same can be said of mutual funds. You don't have belly-to-back elevator contact but you still have contact with people. Dealing with other investors in your mutual fund can invoke feelings similar to the overcrowded elevator—stress and intimidation.

The inflows and outflows caused by human nature may be some of the more subtle difficulties with mutual funds. Fellow investors panic when markets fall and become greedy as market rise. This, of course, causes cash to depart in the form of redemptions when your fund bottoms out; conversely, it causes excess cash to pipeline in when your fund is peaking.

Instead of following the traditional words of investor wisdom—buy low and sell high—just the opposite occurs.

Who feels the impact of human nature? Every investor in the fund suffers the consequences of a bloated fund with too much cash. It becomes too unwieldy for good management control. This causes funds to grow too quickly, turning good performing funds into bad performers from one year to the next.

"One advantage of mutual funds that's really a disadvantage is it's easy to get out [of them]," remarked Peter F. Tedstrom, of Brown & Tedstrom, Inc., in Denver. "This makes it simple for an investor to call in a sell order as soon as the market dips," said Tedstrom, "Consequently, in the end, the investor suffers poor performance returns by frequent trading in and out of his/her portfolio."[1]

ASSET MANAGEMENT
ON AN INDIVIDUAL BASIS

Unlike the crowded mutual fund elevator, a separate account lets you invest as an individual. Yet, you are not alone. You have in your corner a support staff, usually a financial advisor and a selected money manager, or sometimes more than one manager due to the platform selection complexity and breadth of your account portfolio. No matter how many managers you employ, you and your advisor call the shots. You no longer are vulnerable to the whims of the masses of the mutual fund. What you put down in your investment policy statement (IPS) sets the asset management strategy and risk tolerance for your separate account team to follow.

This sets the stage for you as client to make contact with highly professional institutional-style money managers. This usually occurs through your financial advisor. A private money manager services your separate account—no mutual fund can touch that level of personalized attention.

That becomes important to a separate account holder as a member of a new breed of investor who demands the personalized attention that these portfolio money managers have lavished on ultrarich clients and institutions for decades. You can now play in the league where the price of admission once was $1 million or more.

Are You Like the Superrich?

A recent study of ultrahigh-net-worth individuals—those Americans worth $5 million or more in assets—found that these very rich people wish to be richer.

Return on investment (ROI) is important to the ultrarich, but so is capital preservation. What's most important to them over trust, advisor relationship, or communication is investment performance. "They still put a high value on growing their wealth," says David Thompson, vice president at Rhinebeck, New York–based Phoenix Marketing International.[2]

Both groups, the emerging affluent and the ultrahigh-net-worth investors, rate risk as one of their most important concerns.

"Ultimately the management of risk is more important than returns," says Troy Daum, a Certified Financial Planner at Wealth Analytics in San Diego. "If you lost money, that's far more devastating than outperforming the market by 'X' amount."

He went on to say if he had a client who wanted a target rate of return of 7 percent and he could secure 9 percent with a risky investment, he would advise the client to stay with the 7 percent goal in an investment with less risk.[3]

Ride with a Winner

With $8 trillion in assets, mutual funds are not chopped liver. They will be an investable vehicle now and in the future for millions of Americans with restricted investing resources.

Mutual funds are one of the few investment vehicles that provide sufficient diversification for a limited resource investor in the market. Purchasing individual stocks with little capital exposes many investors to unnecessary risk.

The separate account investment strategy is definitely the better vehicle for larger accounts, those with $25,000 or more to invest. More of the rising affluent also are realizing this and the growth of separate accounts has been mushrooming in the marketplace. The Money Management Institute estimates SAM assets could be $1.3 trillion by 2008. Since 1990, we have seen average growth of 30 percent yearly in separate accounts.

In other words, separate accounts are not a fad hyped by investment marketers. The growth I have detailed in previous chapters reflects the moods and desires of mutual fund investors to establish a financial strategy that gives more control, better performance returns, a realistic tax structure, positive transparency, and lower fees.

The prestige factor of being a separate account owner is also a viable and important motivation for many investors. High-net-worth clients are driven to achieve perfection in their financial lives and their personal lives. They want an investment program that separates them from "retail" mutual fund investing. With a separate account you possess asset management on an individual basis, receiving custom solutions for the securities you own. You receive personalized attention—an upscale alternative to mutual funds.

T*he* B*ottom* L*ine:* P*restige*

Mutual Funds:

- You are investing with the masses.
- You are looked upon as a commodity.
- The actions of other investors affect everyone in the fund.

Separate Accounts:

- You follow the same strategy utilized by the ultrarich and institutions.
- You receive more personalized service.
- It's your account!

11

FEES:
LARGER, HIDDEN FEES
OR FLAT FEES?

Experience is a good school. But the fees are high.

Heinrich Heine

Mutual fund fees are fast increasing. And did I mention that mutual fund *returns* are decreasing?

If a tire company raises prices on a set of tires, barring inflation, you'd expect a better tire, a better warranty, a better something—not a tire that blows out easier than before. Higher prices shouldn't make for a shoddier product.

Tell that to the mutual fund companies. Performance is lower; your price for that performance is higher. Does that make any sense?

In a separate account, you pay one flat fee for all services rendered. It's out in the open.

And did I mention that *fees* for a separate account are decreasing?

WHAT IT COSTS YOU TO
OWN A MUTUAL FUND

The mutual fund companies carefully cloak information and spin their marketing pitches to prevent investors from figuring out exactly what they are paying to own a mutual fund.

Let's get the pricing structure of the mutual fund business out in the open, because in many cases the fund companies are reluctant to do so unless prodded by SEC regulations or investor outcry.

Ways You Pay for Mutual Funds . . . And May Not Understand Why

The management fee. The management fee comes packaged with every mutual fund. You'll find out all about it if you read the fund's prospectus, which in reality most investors don't. The management fee pays the expenses of running the business—salaries of the managers, rent, accounting, lights, telephones, office machines, etc. Be cautious of management fees because they can be excessive in some funds. You will pay somewhere in the neighborhood of 1 percent to 1.5 percent yearly.

Distribution or service fees (12b-1 fees). This fee sends a red flag to both regulators and investors alike. This fee that most but not all funds charge is to promote the sale of more shares of the fund to other investors. The fund can use these proceeds to pay for advertising, salespeople's commissions, or service fees to a broker. The initial idea behind this fee was for it to be used to educate the investor on investing. Now, however, it seems to pay for everything except education. You may or may not find these expenses broken out in the prospectus. You may find the 12b-1 fee under promotional expenses or some such. The fee ranges from 0.25 percent to 1 percent per year and it is to be spent to cover "sales and marketing" costs. The 12b-1 fee can pay for some questionable items. Be wary.

Other expenses. These are expenses not included under "management fees" or service fees (12b-1). These could be custodial expenses, legal and accounting expenses, transfer agent expenses, and other administration expenses.

Expense ratio. The management fees and the 12b-1 fees are posted in the fund's expense ratio. The expense ratio should be very important to you. Again, it's in the prospectus. There's a relationship existing between cost and investor return. If your fund has a low expense ratio, that's good for you. A high ratio is not good. The ratio can vary from

Load/No-load fund: Some mutual funds charge a load, or sales commission, when you buy or sell shares or, in some cases, each year you own the fund. The charge is generally figured as a percentage of your investment amount. Brokers, financial planners, and other advisors sell most load funds. In contrast, no-load funds, which don't have sales charges (but may levy other fees), are usually sold directly to the public by the investment company that offers the fund. Some companies offer both load and no-load versions of the same fund.

Source: Investopedia.com.

0.25 percent to over 3 percent annually. One poll found that due to investor apathy or ignorance, 75 percent of investors did not realize that the expense ratio is an annual fee deducted from the fund's earnings, thus lowering shareholders' returns.

Trading costs. Trading costs are not disclosed. We can surmise from portfolio turnover what it costs the shareholder. Some funds never trade, others in the norm, turn all the stocks in the fund at least one time a year, maybe more. Buying and selling generates extra costs for you that vary according to the markets in which the fund is traded. NYSE trading costs are less than the costs of foreign or emerging market stocks or bonds. In any case, frequent trading costs eat up the profits of the fund. Remember, the higher the turnover rate of a fund, the higher the costs.

Commissions. Mutual funds are marketed to the public as load or no-load funds. In a no-load fund, you don't have to pay a commission to own the fund. But you don't receive any investment advice from a broker either.

A load fund comes with advice from a broker and a commission. After a rocky history of charging exceedingly high commissions, the industry has settled down to an average of 5 percent to 6 percent in front-loaded funds.

That doesn't mean they don't want to charge more. We are led to believe that no load means no commission, right? But consider this: The broker sells a fund to you as a no-load fund, gives you advice, and puts

Net asset value (NAV): In the context of mutual funds, this is the total value of the fund's portfolio less liabilities. The NAV is usually calculated on a daily basis.

Source: Investopedia.com.

your money to work in the fund that day. That broker collects his 5 percent or 6 percent commission from the sponsoring mutual fund (for the recommendation). The fund company recovers the commission by charging you about 1.5 percent a year as a hidden cost. In the event you bail out before the fund company regains the broker's commission, they simply charge you a "back-end surrender fee." Did anyone tell you to expect this charge if you redeemed your fund "early"? I doubt it.

If the investor keeps this fund for years, that 1.5 percent hidden back-end surrender fee keeps rewarding the broker with more commissions than if he sold you a straight front-load fund in the first place.

The whole idea of back-end commissions, says Max Rottersman, founder of FundForensics.com, which examines funds' costs, "is to mislead investors into thinking they are not paying commissions."[1] They are sometimes called B shares and you stay away from them.

Let's forget the price of the fund in the first place. You will probably notice the acronym NAV being used. It stands for net asset value. This is the price you pay for one share of the fund. If you divide the amount of assets in the fund by the number of shares outstanding, you will have your NAV per share. If a fund has $1 million under management and 100,000 shares outstanding, then its NAV would be $10.

Purchase fee. A purchase fee is another type of fee that some funds charge their shareholders when they buy shares. Unlike a front-load sale, a purchase fee is paid to the fund (not to a broker) and is typically imposed to defray some of the fund's cost associated with the purchase.

Mutual funds are very profitable because technology has made them cheap but they still charge yesterday's prices. If you divide up the $70 or so billion dollars the industry charges each year in shareholder advisory and servicing, you end up with an average of $700 paid by each investor.

Max Rottersman, Fundforensics.com

Redemption fee. This is another type of fee that some funds charge their shareholders when they sell or redeem shares. Unlike a deferred sales load, a redemption fee is paid to the fund (not to a broker) and is typically used to defray fund costs associated with a shareholder's redemption.

Exchange fee. This is a fee that some funds impose on shareholders if they exchange (transfer) to another fund within the same fund group or "family of funds."

Account fee. This is a fee that some funds separately impose on investors in connection with the maintenance of their accounts. For example, some funds impose an account maintenance fee on accounts whose value is less than a certain dollar amount.

WHAT IT COSTS TO STAY IN MUTUAL FUNDS

Hidden trading costs, bloated commission structures, sales charges both seen and unseen, and pumped-up expense ratios all drive up profitability for the fund company at the expense of individual investors.

Are you willing to pay all this just to beat your bank's interest on a CD? In the average fund, the expense ratio averages 1.6 percent per year; sales charges, 0.5 percent; turnover-generated portfolio transaction costs, 0.7 percent; and opportunity costs—when funds hold cash rather than remain fully invested in stock—0.3 percent. The average mutual fund investor loses 3.1 percent of his investment returns to these costs yearly.[2]

In 1950, the average mutual fund charged around 0.75 percent. In January 2003, that figure more than doubled to over 1.5 percent.

This does not include the hidden trading costs that add another 1.2 percent on average depending on what expert you talk to. Today, the total cost to own an average fund is 2.7 percent. This still does not include sales charges if you purchase through a broker. Remember, 70 percent to 80 percent of all mutual funds underperform the Standard & Poor's 500 Index year in and year out.[3]

This underperformance is caused by average-performing funds having assets withdrawn to pay managers, marketing tabs, office rents—all operating costs. All these expenses are capsulated under the total expense ratio, which is a percentage of total assets of the fund. The industry sells funds that duplicate the market's returns but because the funds must pay their annual expenses with your money, the average fund's performance *loses* when compared to the market.

Hidden Trading Costs Abound

Investors can live with the missteps of soft dollar arrangements, late trading, and timing mischief by the mutual fund companies, but the industry's method of pricing its products has the full attention of the average investor. Not only are the costs of mutual funds higher than they have to be but mounting evidence points to the industry misrepresenting and understating their fees.

Consider a recent study by the Zero Alpha Group (ZAG), which concluded that in the pricing structure of mutual funds, including expense ratios and 12b-1 fees, distortion is standard operating procedure among the fund companies. The study found that U.S. investors are paying $17.3 billion in "hidden" trading costs not reported openly in the stated expense ratios of the funds.

An earlier analysis conducted in January 2004 by ZAG examined 30 top domestic equity mutual funds representing roughly $750 billion in investor assets through the end of calendar year 2001. The study found that 43 percent of the funds' expenses were omitted from their expense ratios and that the transaction costs of some funds exceed 400 percent of their expense ratios.[4]

"Mutual fund companies still lack giving investors full disclosure of fees. Real trading costs can run well over what is being published as the cost of investing in mutual funds," said Bob Enright, partner in the Burton/Enright Group in San Francisco. "Even if you go to a mutual fund prospectus and read it thoroughly, you still can't find out the full nature of what you're paying unless you order an additional statement to find out really what the trading costs are."[5]

These undisclosed costs referred to by Enright would never be accepted by consumers if they were buying a home mortgage or an automobile.

Mutual funds are the cornerstone of retirement planning for millions of Americans. This makes it even more imperative that investors get clear and complete information about what they are really paying to own a mutual fund. The mutual fund companies are working hard to see that you don't.

WHAT IT COSTS TO OWN A SEPARATE ACCOUNT

The Advantages of Flat Fee Pricing

If you wish to eliminate the loads, redemption fees, 12b-1 marketing fees, trading commissions, and soft dollars that proliferate among the mutual fund industry driving your fund expenses higher than is disclosed, consider flat fee pricing. If nothing else, this method of pricing cuts through the clutter of confusion connected to every mutual fund investment vehicle.

In a separate account, one yearly fee covers management fees, trading costs, and incidentals. Further, it includes fees for the money manager as well as the financial advisor. All other administrative functions necessary to service the account are also included.

The fee ranges between 1.5 percent and 3 percent of assets. Why the large spread? Separate account fees are based on a sliding scale. The more money you initially put in the pot, the lower the fee percentage. With mutual funds, the annual expenses remain constant no matter how much cash you invest. In any event, the separate account offers a much clearer, less deceptive form of fee structure.

So much so that, unlike those of mutual funds, separate account fees are fully disclosed. They are required by law to be fully disclosed in an all-inclusive form or as "unbundled" individual segments. Cutting through the legalese, that means the investor in a separate account is going to know what he or she is paying for.

Costs of Having a Separate Account Are Decreasing

For the customized service you receive from a separate account, the fees are quite reasonable and are cheaper than mutual funds. This comparison is after you subtract the poor returns and tack on the capital gains present in mutual funds.

While mutual fund fees are increasing, separate account fees are decreasing. One way this is being accomplished is cost cutting. McKinsey, a New York consulting firm, says the annual cost to a client of a SAM fell to 1.69 percent in 2004 from 2.1 percent in 1999.

We are seeing more independent advisors begin to offer their clients SAMs. Most enthusiastically endorse the SAM concept when they discover these accounts are reasonable for clients and offer greater tax efficiency.[6]

Not everyone agrees that separate accounts are the more economical investment vehicle. Mutual funds may or may not be as expensive as a separate account. However, with a separate account it's a lot easier to see what you are getting: a professional money manager versus inflated expense ratios. Which seems to be a better value to you?

MINIMUMS: THE COST OF MEMBERSHIP

Your Name No Longer Has to Be Getty

Once upon a time you had to be a Vanderbilt or a Getty to qualify for a separate account. Just as we have seen plasma TVs and Apple iPods become more affordable, so have separate accounts. When products flourish, the price comes down.

Traditionally, your ticket to a separate account with a professional money manager investing your wealth was $1 million or more up front. It's still this way with many firms. T. Rowe Price requires $2 million to get into one of its separate accounts.

Minimums Are Dropping

The wire houses (Smith Barney, Merrill Lynch, and others) and even Bank of America are signing up investors for separate accounts with $100,000 minimums.

Some investment firms have lowered the minimum entry fee to $25,000 by utilizing sophisticated software that allows their separate account portfolios of stocks to be purchased in fractions of shares.

Most advisors will tell you at this juncture of the separate accounts revolution that investors should be able to open an account with at least $250,000 to be able to safely spread risk by diversification over asset classes. That's not an insignificant amount. But for many of today's investors, it is a realistic figure.

The present average account size for a typical separate account is $250,000 compared to the average account size for a mutual fund of $36,000 industrywide. As costs for membership in separate accounts are decreasing, membership is expected to increase for the 37 million Americans who have household investable assets of $100,000 or more. Experts predict the average separate account size to drop from $230,238 in 2005, $222,785 in 2008, and $217, 043 in 2011.[7]

What Are You Getting for Your Money?

Clear fees and no hidden ballooning costs make the personalized portion of a separate account more investor-friendly than ever.

With the mushrooming growth in the business, separate accounts would seem a match for any investor who has the ticket to get in (from $25,000 to millions) and who is disappointed with the performance and deception of mutual funds.

The growth of separate accounts is no paper tiger. The numerous advantages of separate accounts are pushing sales percentages and thus exceeding hedge funds, mutual funds, and standard brokerage accounts.

If you pride yourself as a buy-and-hold investor who doesn't require a lot of hand-holding, a separate account probably wouldn't be for you, especially if you like to trade stocks and bonds on your own. But for investors who thrive on the expertise and feedback of professional investment guidance, a separate account wins hands down over a basket of mutual funds. The initial ticket of membership is high but decreasing. More Americans are becoming the generation of the emerging affluent. These Americans are able to afford a more refined method of accumulating wealth: *the separate account.*

T*he* B*ottom* L*ine:* F*ees*

Mutual Funds:
- Eighty percent of funds yearly fail to match the S&P.
- High and myriad fees confuse investors.
- Fund companies keep investors in the dark.

Separate Accounts:
- Fee-based accounts let investors know exactly what they are paying.
- SAMs cost less than funds.
- Costs are decreasing and negotiable.

12

TRANSPARENCY: DELAYED REPORTING OR NEAR REAL-TIME REPORTING?

I get no respect. The way my luck is running,
if I was a politician I would be honest.
Rodney Dangerfield

MUTUAL FUNDS PROVIDE NOTORIOUSLY SLOW REPORTING

The SEC wants every investor to be fully equipped to make informed decisions beforehand. Transparency is important. It refers to the information you have to work with about the markets you invest in and the corporations whose stocks or bonds you buy. The SEC is there to help. The SEC requires all corporations to disclose any and all information impacting their financial positions so investors like you can make prudent decisions.

Unfortunately, mutual fund companies like to delay when information is available to investors.

Do Other Products Keep You in the Dark?

Say you are shopping for a new refrigerator. You can go to Sears or Best Buy to check out the different models and compare prices. If you're more diligent, you can go online, find every refrigerator made, and compare before finally deciding which one is best for you and your family.

In any event, everything you need to know about the model of refrigerator you're interested in is out there.

Contrast the buying experience of a refrigerator or any other product for that matter with purchasing a mutual fund. It's most difficult to find out about all the real nuts and bolts (specific equities, bonds, or cash holdings) of a mutual fund. A mutual fund gives you data twice yearly, sometimes quarterly, which is out-of-date long before you receive it.

Out-of-Date Before Printing

Financial experts reason that by the time the report is published (usually in four-color, glossy stock), the portfolio holdings will most likely have changed. In fact, the fund companies have been known to "window-dress" a semiannual or annual report by pumping up some stocks, then selling them off after the report is published. These actions are not only unethical, but also illegal under SEC guidelines.

It was only a few years ago that the fund companies published performance data on an annual basis. If the fund companies had their way, that's the way it still would be today. An SEC ruling came along and reversed the process, instructing the companies to inform their shareholders at the very least twice yearly or more appropriately quarterly.

Even then it's not enough. Little-useful, easily-readable information exists on mutual funds. Don't expect to see a fund's current holdings unless you open a prospectus.

If you do manage to get hold of a mutual fund semiannual or quarterly report, which is outdated the same day it is printed, sit down with it in a comfortable chair under a strong reading light. Undoubtedly, it will be riddled with generic terms (growth and income, balanced), with an overall assessment of the past ten years looking spectacular. If only you got in ten years ago! The one-year and six-month performances usually look a little less promising. You don't know if the stated objective of the fund is still viable or not. Is the fund still behaving as it states? The mutual fund name sounds stable but it is more a creation of marketing than of the finance department. Fund companies love to fluff up the fund name. Can you imagine a fund being named ABC High Risk Fund? No, ABC Balanced Growth has a better ring to it. In the end, with a little time spent with your mutual fund's six-month or quarterly report, you

Figure 12.1 *SEC Does the Right Thing*

Here are some recent rulings by the SEC in an effort to regulate mutual funds:

- Required new reporting procedures of portfolio manager's compensation and potential conflicts of interest
- Improved disclosure of market timing
- Boosted disclosures regarding the "fair valuation" of securities in portfolios
- Adopted a new code of ethics
- Instituted a new process on how mutual fund boards of directors evaluate and approve investment-advisory contracts
- Required 75 percent of fund board members and its chairman to be "independent"
- Made more information available to investors on break-point discounts on front-end loads
- Adopted a new, tougher compliance program
- Disclosed a mutual fund's proxy voting record for stocks in the portfolio

still won't have any indication of where the fund manager sees the future performance of your fund.

Even with the introduction of the Internet, which has sped up the tracking of securities immensely, the major fund companies have been painfully slow to keep investors current to what stocks the shareholders own and when and if those stocks are being traded.

Will the mutual fund scandals alter the closed-door attitude of the fund company toward its investors? With the new rulings coming from the SEC and Congress, there should be more positive transparency by the fund companies.

Some of the new procedures recently instituted and that are ongoing are highlighted in Figure 12.1.

It's one small step for investors with many more steps to go. If the SEC plays it too close to the vest, we have Congress waiting in the wings to bring in firepower that was put on hold when the SEC jumped to the fracas with guns blazing in 2003. Don't count Congress out. If investor complaints and media reports keep coming, expect renewed interest in additional stricter rules on mutual funds.

Major Mutual Fund Shortcoming: Lack of Transparency

True transparency in costs and fees is lacking in mutual funds. The investor pays in numerous ways. Some are open and known by the investor like management fees and commissions. Others like 12b-1 and trading fees are sublimated. Other fees are hidden, keeping investors completely in the dark as to what they are paying.

"Mutual fund investors can find information on annual fees that mutual funds openly charge investors. However, that transparency only goes so far; it doesn't get at another cost of mutual fund investing: the cost inherent in portfolio trades directed by fund advisors," says Scott Sarber, vice president, Petersen Hastings Investment Management of Kennewick, Washington. "Only a part of that extra cost is detectable through publicly available documents and that's only if you dig into mutual fund documents that very few investors know anything about."

When you add on top of that the completely unreported implicit costs of trading, you are left with a big credibility gap in mutual fund reporting to the investor.

The absence of transparency is a major shortcoming of mutual funds. There's little information forthcoming to let the investor know how her mutual fund is run. This is also detected by the way fund companies levy their fee structure, keeping the investor in the dark on how she pays for the product.

There are other examples of how this lack of transparency impacts your mutual fund investment:

- Fund family simply closes down a poorly performing fund
- One fund may be merged with another fund within the same fund company
- Merging of two mutual fund companies
- Advertently shifting out of the stipulated fund to a more successful and advertised fund
- Changing the investment strategy of a fund (i.e., from small cap to a larger cap)
- Fund manager of fund team is changed[1]

How do these actions affect your visibility of what is going on with your fund? The fund companies do not always tell you that they are taking some of these actions. A fund company has been known often to shift the investment style of a fund without advising the shareholder it has done so. Some shareholders are astounded to find that a fund they own no longer matches the holdings stated in the original objective. An extreme example was a bond fund that at close analysis contained 20 percent high-tech growth equity stocks.

How prevalent is this problem that the industry calls "tracking error." In 2002, the SEC required at least 80 percent of a fund's assets be in sync with its name and stated objective. If a fund is in violation, it must change the name or the assets in the portfolio.

We are a long way away today from achieving genuine transparency in terms of revealing the real costs associated with these mutual funds.

Gregory Carlson, president, Carlson Capital Management, Northfield, Minnesota

SEPARATE ACCOUNTS: PORTFOLIO TRACKING IN ALMOST REAL TIME

Contrast the transparency of mutual funds to SAMs. Separate account holders can review their accounts almost on a daily basis. Their stock performance review is readily available on close to a real-time basis.

Compare your SAM account to banking online. A few years ago, it was unheard of to be able to view your bank accounts immediately each morning, determine the amount of cash in the checking and savings accounts, transfer funds if need be in real time, and even, lately, view the image of a check you wrote but forgot to include in your check register.

Viewing your separate account information online is similar. Your account is there in black-and-white (also color). You can quickly grasp the status of your account: performance, trades, research data, and tax information.

Regular Reporting

Separate accounts also issue printed reports. Most often the client reports are published quarterly, sometimes monthly. You can expect to receive the following information:

- A list of securities in your account
- The number of shares you hold
- What each share is worth and the total value of your shares
- Each security's cost basis (the price you originally paid for the stock)
- All activity during the reporting period (sales, purchases, dividends paid, etc.)
- Asset allocation of your portfolio (the allocation you agreed to with your advisor to maximize performance while minimizing risk)
- Information that compares your SAM performance with a benchmark (to give you a report card that indicates how your portfolio is doing; for example, a comparison to the S&P 500)

The Paper Trail

With a separate account, you will never have an empty mailbox or computer screen. Because you have separate securities, expect to receive all the stock paperwork that each company can grind out. Every time a trade is made, an e-mail or letter or both is sent to notify you. Of course, it also goes into your company statement. Another reason to choose a separate account with a money manager is that most trade infrequently. That's a good thing. Frequent trading can cause unwelcomed tax penalties for certain investors.

"I think from a transparency point of view, separate accounts definitely have an advantage," says Scott MacKillop of Trivium Consulting in Evergreen, Colorado. "As a person who owns separate accounts, I can attest to the number of confirms I get in our mailbox every week. You definitely know what you're holding."

Some third-party platforms may suppress confirms or trades and report them all at once on a quarterly statement sent to the clients. Check with your financial advisor(s) on what type of reporting is available.[2]

Money Manager Access

Can you really call your money manager anytime to find out how your stock scores are doing? The reality is, probably not. But again, maybe you can. You set up your account to have direct access so that is what's written down in the plan. On the other hand, a better approach would be to contact your financial advisor. Tell him or her what's on your mind and you should have answers back in short order.

Actually, if you are in a separate account, you probably wanted peace of mind in knowing that your wealth is being actually managed in a thoroughly professional manner. Let the advisor and money manager manage your money, leaving you free to manage and enjoy your life.

TRANSPARENCY CAN MAKE A DIFFERENCE TO YOUR BOTTOM LINE

No style drift. I referred to style drift in Chapter 9. Mutual fund managers have been known to drift from their original fund prospectus and trade stocks not sanctioned but based on whimsical investment opportunities in the marketplace apparent at the moment. Because of the clearer transparency built into the separate account strategy, money managers maintain investment discipline. In reality, you know as an investor in your separate account that your asset class stocks are the same ones with which you originally opened your account.

Also, at today's lower minimums, you can select along with your advisor only those institutional money managers that manage assets by a certain asset class (i.e., large-cap growth stocks or small-cap value stocks, etc.). This stops style drift immediately and exhibits another advantage over mutual funds.

No diversification redundancy. If your separate account is invested across a number of asset categories (large caps, small caps, etc.), your money manager retains a controllable number of stocks to be able to determine if adequate diversification is being realized. In other words, he can see if he has overlapping securities in the portfolio. Redundancy of holdings does not become a problem that weakens diversification. In a mutual fund, a manager might have hundreds of stocks in his account and be unable to provide adequate supervisory control over that many stocks. Duplication of stocks is a common problem in mutual funds.

No closet indexing. Many of the biggest fund companies have the same stocks in similar amounts in different funds. A recent study found that Fidelity had 65 percent of its Magellan stock holdings identical to those of the S&P 500. There were S&P stocks in Fidelity's Growth & Income Fund (63 percent) and Blue Chip Growth Fund (58 percent). This is called "closet indexing." This process exposes investors to unfavorable concentrations of risk because they may be duplicating their stocks if they are invested in more than one of the above-mentioned funds.[3]

Transparency is not always forefront in a client's mind as a major benefit for separate accounts. Yet the value of having up-to-date information about your portfolio at your disposal is your secret weapon. Armed with information, you are in the driver's seat. Making minor adjustments to your account is possible, along with the capability to hire and fire money managers based on the results of your readily available SAM reports. Don't forget, with a separate account you know exactly what you are being charged and what you are paying for. It makes sense.

The Bottom Line: Transparency

Mutual Funds:
- Fund companies are slow on reporting results.
- Investor never knows in real time what stocks are in his account.
- Fund companies can hype performance results.

Separate Accounts:
- Investor can receive SAM account information in real time.
- Reporting is quarterly, monthly, and even daily (trades).
- Investor can hold advisor and money manager(s) accountable.

PLANNING WEALTH WITH SEPARATE ACCOUNTS

13

SETTING UP YOUR SEPARATE ACCOUNT

When it comes to the future, there are three kinds of people: those who let it happen, those who make it happen, and those who wonder what happened.

John M. Richardson, Jr.

Congratulations, you're coming closer to making a decision to set up your separate account. By doing so, you may have the distinction of being a member of the *early growth* group—those people who commit to a product or process in the early years of its life stage cycle.

Not that separate accounts are new like plasma TVs. They have been available for the superrich for over 30 years. It's only in the last five years during the massive bear market and the 2003 mutual fund scandal that this investment process long embraced by the superwealthy began to catch on with the more mainstream investor.

By now, you know setting up a separate account will make you a bona fide member of the *separate accounts revolution*—the most significant asset management strategy stimulating the financial business today.

Hype? No, this revolution presently in the growth stage has been increasing assets by around 30 percent for the last five years—about 18 percent in 2004 alone. The separate account phenomenon promises to be a $2 trillion business by 2010, according to one of the major research organizations that monitors the business, Cerulli Associates.[1]

Let's get started. We have a lot of ground to cover. This is a long chapter, but by the end you'll have established a solid foundation for your separate account.

FIRST THINGS FIRST:
STUDY THE PLAY BOOK

Learn the Lingo

Commingling *separate accounts* and SAMs throughout the book has been my way to describe *separate account management.*

Right off, you'll begin hearing other terms—*managed accounts, individually managed accounts (IMAs), separately managed accounts, wraps,* etc. All mean essentially the same thing: separate account management.

Wrap accounts should be explained. Coined by Jim Lockwood, one of the developers of the modern separate account as we know it, the term refers to the fact that the fee is "wrapped" around the account charges. This was a new concept at the time in the 1970s. A straight fee percentage of the client's assets was unique at the time. The usual process of billing the client involved a commission on transactions. Commissions were the preferred method by which brokers were being compensated at the time and still are today. In essence, the original *wrap account* consisted of individual securities run by a professional money manager for a client. Lockwood put together the first separate account, or wrap account, in 1975 for the Hutton Investment Management Company.

Hence, the separate account also became known as the wrap-fee account because the total fee wrapped all the costs of the account. The name stuck in the financial media.

I will post unique terms and their definitions throughout the book. In the glossary at the back of this book, you will find other terms that you may encounter from time to time. I will continue to use the terms *separate accounts* and *SAMs* throughout the remainder of the book.

One more time, what's a *separate account?* If there's still any confusion in your mind, I am going to clear it up right now.

A **separate account** is a method of investing in which a client assigns a portion of his wealth to a professional money management firm to invest *according to his or her wishes.* Sounds like a mutual fund, doesn't it?

> **Wrap account:** A wrap account is a professionally managed investment plan in which all expenses, including brokerage commissions, management fees, and administrative costs, are "wrapped" into a single annual charge, usually amounting to 2 percent to 3 percent of the value of the assets in the account.
>
> Wrap accounts combine the services of a professional money manager, who chooses a personalized portfolio of stocks, bonds, mutual funds, and other investments, and a brokerage firm, which takes care of the trading and recordkeeping on the account.
> Source: Investopedia.com.

Both separate accounts and mutual funds do have professional management, diversification interests, and liquidity.

However, in a mutual fund your investment is commingled with that of other investors who own shares of the same securities. In a separate account, you *own* your individual securities. By having that ownership, you have much more control over your investments.

Elements of Separate Accounts

Part Two describes in detail the vital differences between separate accounts and mutual funds. There is still more you need to know about how you and your family can benefit from one of the most investor-friendly strategies in the financial industry today.

First, not that many investors, or independent advisors for that matter, know much about separate accounts. Investors, who are less informed, do not know how separate accounts work. They are not aware of the key separate account benefits. They are naive to who the supporting members of the account-building team are. Most investors probably don't know where to go to set up a separate account.

Advisors, although knowledgeable of the rising popularity of separate accounts, are taking a wait-and-see attitude before jumping in and offering them to clients. Meanwhile, the major wire houses are prospering with separate accounts; they now own almost 80 percent of the business.

Where Do You Find an Investor Advisor?

- The free, independent directory provided by Paladin Registry matches you to five-star advisors in your area (http://www.paladinregistry.com).
- National Association of Personal Financial Advisors (NAPFA) is the professional association of fee-only financial advisors (http://www.napfa.org).
- The Wise Advisor's Web site matching system is designed to objectively pair individuals quickly and easily with the ideal advisor based on the individual's unique needs. It's free and confidential (http://www.wiseadvisor.com).
- Financial Planners Association assists individuals in finding a Certified Financial Planner (CFP) (http://www.fpanet.org).
- MSN Money's Web site let's you find an advisor not only for investments but for other areas too. Due diligence is provided by DALBAR Research, a respected research firm (http://moneycentral.msn.com/investor/dalbar/main.asp).

"As the high-net-worth demographic grows, more and more people want the tax advantages and customization you can get with a separate account," said a researcher at Cerulli Associates.[2]

Things will change as technology reduces the complexity of the administrative end of separate accounts and the minimum investment continues to drop for investor entry. Separate accounts are now offered not only by the major wire houses but also by regional brokers, banks, insurance companies, independent financial advisors, and mutual fund companies.

Even 401(k)s will also offer SAMs as an investment option. "We are seeing more and more persons getting their money out of their 401(k)s upon their retirement [and] rolling their nest egg into an IRA with a separate account," said Chris Consentino, communications director for Money Management Institute. "These retirees want someone to manage their wealth for them so they can enjoy life. A separate account is superior to mutual funds in this regard."[3]

The Value of Financial Advice

According to a 1998 survey:

- 85 percent of those who use paid financial advisors say using an advisor is worthwhile.
- Planners (35 percent) and brokers (33 percent) are the most frequently used paid financial professionals.
- Nearly all consumers (92 percent) who use financial professionals are comfortable with their finances. Only 76 percent of those who do not use professionals make this claim.
- Financial comfort comes from long-term relationships. Clients who have used their professionals for less than one year are least comfortable with their finances. Clients with relationships of more than ten years have a comfort index of 3.54 out of 4.
- Brokers and accountants have the longest relationships with clients (8.0 and 7.8 years, respectively), while financial planners have the shortest (6.4 years).
- High-net-worth individuals (over $500,000) make the best clients. They
  - pay the highest fees,
  - are more likely to use professionals (70 percent versus 48 percent with a $25,000 net worth), and
  - consider professionals worthwhile (92 percent versus an average of 85 percent).

Source: Financial Planning Association.

Know the Players

The key players to be chosen for your separate account team will be detailed in Chapter 14. For now, though, knowing who's going to be in your corner when you set up your separate account is necessary for you to understand the scheme of things.

Top Ten Questions to Ask Your Financial Advisor

1. Have you handled separate accounts in the past?
2. What's the profile of your practice?
3. What's your current client profile?
4. What's your client load?
5. What's your typical client allocation?
6. How long have your been an advisor?
7. How many assets do you have under management?
8. What are your fee structure and other account expenses?
9. What is your procedure in selecting money managers?
10. Can you supply me with your ADV*?

*A financial advisor who manages more than $25 million in assets is required to file Form ADV with the SEC. Form ADV includes information about the advisor's operations, discloses any problems with regulators (such as SEC and NASD) or clients, and describes the advisor's services, fees, and approach to financial planning. Form ADV is not a riveting read, but it's a smart idea to go through it before you select an advisor.

Client. You, as the client, are perhaps the most important player in your separate account. It's your portfolio comprised of stocks chosen by your managers, and, most important, it's your money.

Financial advisor. Next to you, the most essential team member is your financial advisor. His or her expertise is financial planning, a skill you will surely require in setting up your separate account.

If you don't have a financial advisor, I strongly suggest you get one. The reasons to do so will be covered in more detail in Chapter 14.

Nationwide, there are about 45,000 Registered Independent Advisors (RIAs). That number narrows by eliminating the nonactive, institutional manager and commission-only type, leaving approximately 15,000 RIAs working as fee-based or fee-only advisors. Those are the ones you want to hire.

You don't want an advisor who sells a separate account like a mutual fund. The ideal financial advisor is one who is prepared to cultivate the full separate account potential and tailor its benefits to your personal in-

Top **T**en **Q**uestions *to* **A**sk **Y**ourself **B**efore
Going **I**t **A**lone

1. How will I protect the portfolio if the market drops 10 percent? 20 percent? 30 percent?
2. If I die, who will take care of the day-to-day decisions regarding the portfolio?
3. How will I select the money managers?
4. What are the most important criteria of a money manager: Return? Expenses? Taxes?
5. How much should I allocate to each money manager?
6. Where do I go to find a money manager?
7. Whom do I talk to if there's a problem?
8. What is the best asset to be in in the domestic market? Internationally?
9. When do I cut my losses?
10. Who will control my emotions?

vestment situation and explain the differences properly between mutual funds and SAMs.

The independent advisor remains indispensable in the separate accounts selection and monitoring process for the foreseeable future. An advisor is worth the extra 1 percent you pay yearly on your assets in a separate account.

Money manager. The services and financial expertise of a top institutional money manager will probably not be available to most investors in a lifetime of stock market investing. However, a key feature of the separate accounts process is professional portfolio management. The investor delegates the authority to the money manager who makes the daily investment decisions. Working with your financial advisor, the selection of money managers to service your separate account falls on both of your shoulders. When choosing money managers, you want one who has professionalism, experience, a reliable personality, and a good track record.

Who are these professional money managers? Just because they have not been in your frame of reference in earlier investment strategies, doesn't mean they're not there in every variety. There's a lot of money

---

Sources of Money Managers

- Money Manager Review's Web site can locate, research, compare, rank, track, and even contact any one of 800 money managers the site follows; fee charged (http://www. managerreview.com).
- WrapManager lists over 125 money managers. This site can build separate account programs from scratch and help you select a money manager; fee charged (http://www.wrapmanager.com).
- Dmoz's Open Directory lists in alphabetical order hundreds of money management firms (http://www.dmoz.org/Business/Investing/Money_Managers/).
- Looking for a money manager with an emphasis on social investing? You can find one at http://www.business-ethics.com/PrivateMoney Mgrs.htm.
- The Web site of the American Institute of Certified Public Accountants contains good information on the selection of money managers and provides links to good sources elsewhere online (http://www.aic pa.org/index.htm).

---

manager talent out there. You could choose as many as 10 to 20 money managers for one separate account program!

Program sponsor. Your separate account portfolio is usually assigned to a program sponsor who takes responsibility for administration, recordkeeping, and trading stocks/bonds assigned to you. The major brokerages houses usually handle this responsibility but turnkey asset management programs (TAMPs) also allow independent advisors, broker-dealers, insurance companies, CPAs, and banks to handle the administrative side of a client's portfolio.

Can You Do It Yourself?

You can travel the road to a separate account without the services of a financial advisor; however, I do not recommend this course. If you are prepared to put down a fair share of your personal wealth for asset management, you should take steps to reassure yourself that your wealth will

Top Ten Questions to Ask Your Financial Advisor When Selecting a Money Manager

1. How would you define his or her investing style?
2. How long has this individual been with the company? What is his or her experience level?
3. What is his or her education? Is he or she certified in the field?
4. What sectors does this money manager specialize in?
5. What is the research process within the management company?
6. Is the research readily available, useful, and does the money manager make use of it?
7. What is the average turnover ratio in the accounts he or she holds?
8. What is the first consideration the money manager has in structuring a portfolio?
9. How important are my goals in the money manager's mind when he or she structures a portfolio?
10. How does the money manager get paid?

be protected in the very best manner possible. However, if you want to do it yourself and save the 1 percent usually billed to your account by an independent advisor, here's how.

If you are choosing this route, you must be deft at the investing process. Crunching the numbers or performing a daily review of the newspaper stock columns is a regular part of your routine. You're very comfortable with allocating a portion of your wealth to domestic growth equities or international stocks and bonds. Routinely, yearly, you love to rebalance your portfolio. You are quite proficient with the Internet, finding and acting on the wealth of information available on your holdings. And you have the time to invest to make it all happen. Remember, a major benefit you're receiving from your advisor is *time*—the time it takes to set up the account, select all the players, allocate the resources, monitor the progress, and perform all the administrative tasks.

If all of this appeals to you and sleeping comes easy knowing you're handling your separate account portfolio by yourself, by all means, go ahead and set up your own separate account.

GETTING COMFORTABLE WITH SEPARATE ACCOUNTS

A Separate Account Primer

To grasp the big picture, clients with investable assets of as little as $25,000 can get into a separate account serviced by a professional money manager. These money managers make key trading decisions based on directions handed to them by the combined forces of the client and the client's investment advisor. Routinely, these money managers handle multimillion-dollar accounts for very-high-net-worth clients and/or institutions. The client's financial advisor serves as the point person assisting in developing the investor's short-term and long-term investment objectives. The advisor is there to coordinate the asset allocation breakdowns within the client's portfolio. The advisor is paramount in selecting the money managers and the specific separate account investment package in sync with the client's investment policy statement (IPS).

After establishing the portfolio in the market, the advisor is responsible for monitoring the client's portfolio to ensure the IPS is being accomplished according to the plan.

After selecting a money manager and a program sponsor (a brokerage firm or other financial institution), the advisor, with your approval, places your money with a money manager who is an expert in specific asset classes. The three general overall categories are **growth, value, and core** (a blend of growth and value). Most money managers narrow their specialty focus down to either growth or value. When searching for the ideal match between client and money manager, you will encounter these sectors of money manager specialty:

- Large-cap growth
- Mid-cap growth
- Small-cap growth
- Large-cap value
- Mid-cap value
- Small-cap value
- Core
- International growth and value
- Emerging markets
- Global
- Fixed income

The advisor is there to place your money with the right money manager who specializes in those asset classes carefully laid out in your original IPS. The money manager may receive the money directly or through a sponsoring brokerage company, such as Smith Barney or other firms.

In the end, the portfolio should contain a manageable number of individual securities numbering between 50 and 120, with 75 being the average. You will see your holdings online almost immediately. If you don't like the stocks that were selected, then adjustments usually can be made. Managers offer basic portfolios built around sector specialties. Portfolios can be individually customized to the needs of the client.

Funding Your Account

In general, the new separate account investor should have at least $100,000 to invest. However, newer programs being developed as this book goes to press have account minimums in the $25,000 to $50,000 range. I will review in detail some examples of these lower minimum requirements later in the book.

Internet-based financial firms are offering even lower minimums and lower fees for separate accounts without investment consulting. These are called folios that offer a basket of stocks in which to invest. More on folios is found in Chapter 16.

More financial firms are reducing minimums to compete with the online service companies. Offering lower minimums can allow high-net-worth customers with larger accounts to divide into smaller separate accounts, and even to set up individual accounts for family members.

Depending on your initial investment, the operating fee can drop through negotiating. In fact, separate accounts are always negotiable, unlike mutual funds that have hard and fast pricing—open and hidden. Keep in mind, the more money you invest to open a separate account, the better you can spread your wealth across more asset-class portfolios to create the diversification you need to reduce risk. When you do put the money up front to fund a separate account, what will be the ongoing costs? As I covered earlier, a separate account usually has a total cost between **1.8 to 3 percent** of assets managed on an annual basis.

Say you make an initial investment of $100,000, you'll usually pay a higher percentage of assets than another investor with a separate account investment of $500,000.

Reductions of 25 percent are not unheard of simply by meeting a financial advisor's minimum asset requirements. If the investor opened an account with $100,000 at a 3 percent fee, he might actually pay only 2.25 percent due to a 25 percent reduction. The more money you put in, the lower the fees.

Where Do You Go to Open a SAM?

Your independent financial advisor is the best source for locating the optimum separate account package for you because he or she will be familiar with your financial history and asset management objectives.

That being said, if you still choose to create a SAM yourself, let's explore where the separate accounts can be found.

Currently, the brokerage industry owns most of the separate account management business. The large wire houses (Salomon Smith Barney, Merrill Lynch, Morgan Stanley, Paine Webber, and Prudential) offer the most separate account portfolios. In total, these firms managed around 70 percent of the business at the end of 2004.[4] (See Figure 13.1.)

In the years to come there will be less dominance by the wire houses as the infusion of more regional brokerage houses (e.g., Raymond James) and third-party providers begin to offer separate accounts within the framework of their business.

Who else is claiming a share in the separate accounts market? The mutual fund companies have or are establishing their own separate ac-

Figure 13.1 *Wire Houses Dominate the Separate Accounts Business Presently but SAM Providers Are Expanding the Market*

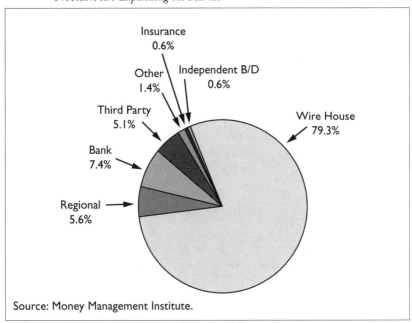

Insurance
0.6%

Other
1.4%

Independent B/D
0.6%

Third Party
5.1%

Wire House
79.3%

Bank
7.4%

Regional
5.6%

Source: Money Management Institute.

counts programs to take advantage of a business opportunity. As investors are deserting the ranks of mutual funds, these companies don't want to be left behind. It is likely fund companies will gain ground in separate accounts because the mutual fund investor can easily make the transition to a separate account if one is offered by his current fund company. Fund companies currently offering separate account programs are Invesco, Fidelity Investments, and Oppenheimer.

Independent financial advisors are also joining the separate account revolution. Though few in number so far—approximately 7 percent had separate account business in 2004—the number of advisors offering separate account services is expected to swell.

Comparison Shop

Just as with any major purchase, comparison shopping is important before you decide on the best separate account for you. By now, you should realize you could get a separate account with or without a financial advisor from places ranging from the largest brokerage firm to a mutual fund firm. Separate accounts are also available from broker-dealers representing independent financial advisors, banks, insurance companies, and regional brokers. You can even go online and find companies selling folios (customized stock baskets) at very low minimums.

To succeed without the aid of a professional advisor, however, you must invest a significant amount of time in due diligence before making any investment. As the business is rapidly changing—lower fees, reduced minimums, choices between different money managers, more SAM portfolios among sectors, etc.—it is crucial that you have the most up-to-date and thorough information when creating a portfolio.

SETTING UP THE ACCOUNT

Let's go through the process of opening a separate account. First, sit down with your investment advisor. For the purpose of this example, I'm going to assume you have an investment advisor on your team. (If you choose to set up a separate account on your own, you can meet directly with your money manager.) For the initial meeting with your financial advisor, arm yourself with all your current account statements and other financial records. Be prepared to discuss your financial goals and the lifestyle you would like to have for you and your family in the future.

Plan to invest some time in this meeting because it is crucial that you and your financial advisor be on the same page from the beginning. This can only happen if the advisor has a thorough understanding of your financial history and future goals. You will need to fill out some paperwork including a risk profile questionnaire. Your advisor can help you complete the paperwork.

Blueprint for Success: The Investment Policy Statement

You know the old adage: If you fail to plan, plan to fail. Hopefully, the information presented thus far has prepared you to launch your investment policy statement.

The importance of the IPS to the success of your financial future should be underscored. In fact, as a mature, established investor in mutual funds and/or stocks/bonds you may have created an IPS before.

If you've been investing for years and have never been asked to develop an IPS by your broker/advisors, don't panic. Robert B. Jorgensen, financial consultant and author, says he has been working with clients for 15 years with hundreds of portfolios and substantial retirement plans, and found that only about 10 percent had an effective IPS that was being utilized and followed properly.[5]

The IPS Makes You Think

To develop an IPS for the first time is not a painless exercise. The IPS makes you think. This is a highly charged creative process stimulating you to consider how you will attain your retirement goals, generate funds for a new boat, pay for your daughter's college education, etc. Your goal is financial freedom and this document will be one of the major catalysts to propel you and your family there. It's much easier to go through this process with a financial advisor, even if you hire one for this project alone.

Elements of the IPS

Let's review the major elements that compose the IPS to help you get an overview of this important document. A sample IPS is found in the Appendix.

This document can be the perfect road map to direct you toward your financial future. The IPS ensures you and your financial advisor and money manager(s) stay on track. It details your financial goals and aspirations with a built-in triggering device to make sure you don't deviate from the path of capital preservation, capital acceleration, or both. With a baseline established, you could keep your objectives secure in spite of short-term swings in the market. Look at your IPS as a warning system that will alert you to make changes in your portfolio should your investments get off course. It will also help you stay on course by reminding you to ignore temporary downturns in the market. Depending on your risk tolerance (already defined in your IPS), this document will allow you to weather the short-term swings in the market by keeping your focus strategically on longer-term portfolio performance. Your IPS also will measure the success of your financial advisor and money manager(s). The information in your carefully crafted IPS will clearly determine whether or not you're meeting measured goals and objectives based on your time line.

It's Your Game Playbook

The IPS is a playbook that will help you determine which moves to make and when. This will take emotions out of the game and put logic in control of your investment. For instance, if a group of stocks plummet as the market closes on Friday, you might be inclined to tell your advisor to sell all the stocks on Monday. Of course, the downturn could be for myriad reasons: new product announcement delay, cyclical activity, analyst reporting that could be in error, etc. Whatever the reason, that's the nature of the market. Your IPS saves you from falling victim to short-term volatility. Long-term performance counts. Reducing your emotions increases your performance.

On the other hand, if a goal in your IPS states that your diversified stocks must be above a certain level and your portfolio is underperforming according to this criterion, the guidelines are set for you to take action.

You can identify benchmarks to measure your stock's performance such as the S&P 500 Index. You can even set up your risk tolerance level with each manager in your portfolio so that alarm bells sound when that index is exceeded. All this information can be secured by your financial advisor or set up on a Web site for even more real-time security.

Every Journey Begins with the First Step

The process of putting together your IPS begins with your initial meeting with your investment advisor. My best advice for creating an IPS is don't do it by yourself. Set up a separate account with an advisor. I believe that having a financial advisor assist you in preparing your IPS is essential for long-term success. Unless, of course, you are not emotional about your money.

Objectives

Your financial objectives form the linchpin holding your portfolio together. Know that your risk tolerance is an important variable in setting your financial objectives; I address this in more detail below. Your risk tolerance, age, resources, income requirements now and later, liquidity demands, tax reduction concerns, income streams you desire, time goals, etc., are essential elements that contribute to your IPS objectives. Yes, your health and longevity assumptions need to be factored in. If a major change occurs in the future, alert your advisor and he can make a change in your portfolio.

For example, say you are 60, want to retire, and would like to have about $100,000 yearly on which to live. You also have to finish paying off your house as well as a vacation home in North Carolina. You also would like to leave the kids some inheritance when you pass on.

When you discuss this with your advisor, he or she will factor in elements like your age, financial resources, inflation, risk tolerance, and other factors. All of these elements will be incorporated into your IPS.

Risk Tolerance

One thing is a given: You can't eliminate risk. Even a U.S. Treasury note, long known as the safest investment vehicle on the planet, has a degree of risk.

Knowing that you'll have risk with a separate account portfolio is essential for you to venture to the next plateau. How much risk will you accept? You must determine the trade-off between risk and reward, which is a challenge. In short, you understand this already whether you're a neophyte investor or one with 30 years equity trading under your belt: The more reward you want, the more risk you'll have to accept. The less risk you take, the less money you'll make.

Say you invest $100,000. In the first month, your investment goes up 3 percent. You feel pretty good right? During the next month, it goes up 2 percent. You're feeling even better.

But what happens if your money declines? What percentage decline could you withstand?

What if, on your next quarterly statement, you see that your $100,000 has become $97,000? Would you sell? The next quarter, you're

Figure 13.2 *The Lifeboat Drill—When Will You Jump Ship?*

Potential Quarterly Decline	Original Investment— $100,000	Check the box where you would take actions
(3%)	$97,000	❏
(6%)	$94,000	❏
(8%)	$92,000	❏
(10%)	$90,000	❏
(15%)	$80,000	❏
(23%)	$77,000	❏
(35%)	$65,000	❏
(50%)	$50,000	❏

Source: Larry Chambers; by permission of John Wiley & Sons.

down to $94,000; then it drops to $92,000. How are you feeling now? Are you still OK with doing nothing or are you anxious to get out of this investment at any cost? The quarter after that, it drops to $90,000. Then it goes down further to $85,000, then $77,000, $65,000, and eventually $50,000. (See Figure 13.2.)

At what point do you jump out? At a 15 percent drop, most investors want out, but when it isn't related to a specific dollar amount, almost all investors will say they are willing to accept a greater percentage.[6]

As the investor, you need to understand the risks. Only you know how much market volatility you are willing to withstand. Once you understand risk tolerance, you will understand how investment performance is directly linked to it. Take the quiz in the box on pages 154 to 156 to determine your tolerance for risk.

Your IPS Is a Life-Changing Document

Your IPS is not a tattoo. It can be altered. Your life's circumstances do change. At any time you may need more or less cash to live on. As you age, you may become more conservative, requiring less risky equity positions. Or, maybe, you get a second wind, want to buy a Ferrari, and have the urge to chuck it all. That too is possible with the document called your IPS. Feel free to amend your IPS. Tell your advisor about the Ferrari, but tell your spouse first.

Remember, your IPS is your global positioning device. It defines your financial objectives, establishing the strategy necessary for you to achieve those objectives. Don't forget, it keeps you on the straight and narrow by restricting you from second-guessing your investment decisions. The IPS can drain some of the emotions out of the daily dips of the market protecting you from unnecessary anxiety and giving you a good night's sleep.

BUILDING YOUR PORTFOLIO

Controlling Your SAM Assets

Asset allocation. Asset allocation is the core of your separate account development. It's how you put the puzzle together. You have already played with the individual pieces—your net worth, tolerance for risk, time frame, and other variables. Now you and your financial advisor decide how the pieces fit together. This is the fun part; but keep in mind that the real reason you're doing this exercise is to build a protective shield around your portfolio to make sure all its elements don't go up (not likely) or down too quickly. You are looking for your portfolio to provide a consistent return over a long time frame, from 5 to 20 years.

The first thing you must do is determine how much of your investment dollars go into cash accounts, fixed income, and equities. Cash is money in the bank. Fixed-income investments are, for the most part, low-interest-paying vehicles such as CDs, bonds, and guaranteed investment certificates. Equities are market investments such as stocks and bonds. For the point of this book, we are leaving other investments that might be a part of your portfolio out of the picture (e.g., real estate).

Your risk considerations are a factor in selecting each asset class. Your tolerance for risk is one of the important variables in selecting any allocation of your wealth.

The time horizon details where you want your portfolio to be at different increments of time throughout your life. You should consider all factors that come into play at different times of your life that will affect

Investment Risk Tolerance Quiz

1. In general, how would your best friend describe you as a risk taker?
   A. A real gambler
   B. Willing to take risks after completing adequate research
   C. Cautious
   D. A real risk avoider

2. You are on a TV game show and can choose one of the following. Which would you take?
   A. $1,000 in cash
   B. 50 percent chance at winning $5,000
   C. 25 percent chance at winning $10,000
   D. 5 percent chance at winning $100,000

3. You have just finished saving for a "once-in-a-lifetime" vacation. Three weeks before you plan to leave, you lose your job. You would:
   A. Cancel the vacation
   B. Take a much more modest vacation
   C. Go as scheduled, reasoning that you need the time to prepare for a job search
   D. Extend your vacation, because this might be your last chance to go first class

4. If you unexpectedly received $20,000 to invest, what would you do?
   A. Deposit it in a bank account, money market account, or an insured CD
   B. Invest it in safe high-quality bonds or bond mutual funds
   C. Invest it in stocks or stock mutual funds

5. In terms of experience, how comfortable are you investing in stocks or stock mutual funds?
   A. Not at all comfortable
   B. Somewhat comfortable
   C. Very comfortable

6. When you think of the word *risk* which of the following words comes to mind first?

   A. Loss

   B. Uncertainty

   C. Opportunity

   D. Thrill

7. Some experts are predicting prices of assets such as gold, jewels, collectibles, and real estate (hard assets) to increase in value; bond prices may fall, however experts tend to agree that government bonds are relatively safe. Most of your investment assets are now in high-interest government bonds. What would you do?

   A. Hold the bonds

   B. Sell the bonds, put half the proceeds into money market accounts and the other half into hard assets

   C. Sell the bonds and put the total proceeds into hard assets

   D. Sell the bonds, put all the money into hard assets, and borrow additional money to buy more

8. Given the best-case and worst-case returns of the four investment choices below, which would you prefer?

   A. $200 gain best case; $0 gain/loss worst case

   B. $800 gain best case; $200 loss worst case

   C. $2,600 gain best case; $800 loss worst case

   D. $4,800 gain best case; $2,400 loss worst case

9. In addition to whatever you own, you have been given $1,000. You are now asked to choose between:

   A. A sure gain of $500

   B. A 50 percent chance to gain $1,000 and a 50 percent chance to gain nothing

10. In addition to whatever you own, you have been given $2,000. You are now asked to choose between:

    A. A sure loss of $500

    B. A 50 percent chance to lose $1,000 and a 50 percent chance to lose nothing

11. Suppose a relative left you an inheritance of $100,000, stipulating in the will that you invest ALL the money in ONE of the following choices. Which one would you select?

A. A savings account or money market mutual fund
B. A mutual fund that owns stocks and bonds
C. A portfolio of 15 common stocks
D. Commodities like gold, silver, and oil

12. If you had to invest $20,000, which of the following investment choices would you find most appealing?

A. 60 percent in low-risk investments, 30 percent in medium-risk investments, and 10 percent in high-risk investments
B. 30 percent in low-risk investments, 40 percent in medium-risk investments, and 30 percent in high-risk investments
C. 10 percent in low-risk investments, 40 percent in medium-risk investments, and 50 percent in high-risk investments

13. Your trusted friend and neighbor, an experienced geologist, is putting together a group of investors to fund an exploratory gold mining venture. The venture could pay back 50 to 100 times the investment if successful. If the mine is a bust, the entire investment is worthless. Your friend estimates the chance of success is only 20 percent. If you had the money, how much would you invest?

A. Nothing
B. One month's salary
C. Three months' salary
D. Six months' salary

Note to reader: Go to http//:www.rcre.rutgers.edu/money/riskquiz/ and take the test online. You will discover your tolerance for risk and what type of investments would be best for you according to your risk score.[7]

The Four Factors for Determining the Asset Allocation of Your Wealth

1. Your risk tolerance
2. Your expected rate of return before and after taxes
3. Your projected time frame of your portfolio (remember people are living longer)
4. Your selection of assets and classes of assets

your portfolio (e.g., college for children, big purchases—home, car, travel, etc., retirement income, etc.).

The next element of your asset allocation is determining the rate of return you would like to achieve factoring in your risk tolerance and time horizon. All this together must mesh with a "comfort" factor that satisfies your financial objectives and goals.

The last step is assigning the dollar amounts to each of the asset groups. For instance, stocks are broken down in two broad groups: value and growth. Stocks are subdivided further into styles like small cap (companies under $500 million in assets), international, and so forth.

To allocate your assets, you need to decide for all the sectors and groups *what* percentage of your wealth would go *where*. *Why* is also going to be a factor according to your financial objectives, risk comfort level, time horizon, etc. This is where your advisor proves his mettle.

The idea of asset allocation, or diversification, is that most investments across different asset groups do not rise and fall at the same rate or at the same time. You know that money market accounts pay smaller returns but carry relatively less risk. More volatile aggressive growth stocks carry much more risk but the potential for reward is higher. With asset allocation comes the natural process of diversification that reduces risk across the board.

You will encounter changes in your life and as those changes come into play, you will need to change your financial goals from time to time. It's called rebalancing and it is very important in the process of utilizing your IPS as a lifelong tool.

In many research studies, asset allocation is most important in allowing the investor to position his wealth in different sectors. The industry has fine-tuned these sectors of cash, fixed income, and equities further into very fine asset classes. This makes it possible for the most aggressive growth investor to coexist with the most conservative investor in each other's quest for high-performance returns.

Experts say that picking the right sectors can increase your performance success more than individual securities. So now the right direction for the investor is to pick the best-performing sectors that will determine what your allocation mix should be.

The easy way to do this is to look at your time lines. If you are just starting an investment program early in life, you need to develop a long-term strategy that emphasizes a high percentage of stock equities to

Figure 13.3 *Allocation for an Aggressive Portfolio*

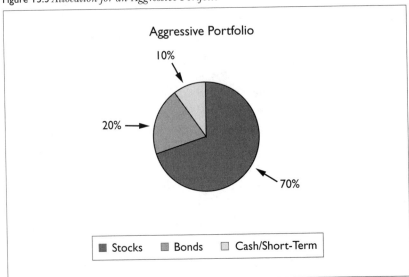

build growth. Thus, you can invest more aggressively. For the individual who has a long investment future ahead of her, a sample allocation would be 70 percent equities, 20 percent bonds, and 10 percent cash. (See Figure 13.3.)

If you're in the peak earning years (ages 30 to 50), then it's recommended you fashion your portfolio into a more balanced approach with

Figure 13.4 *Allocation for a Balanced Portfolio*

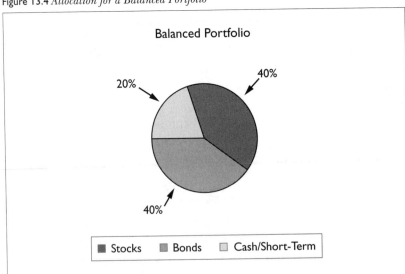

Figure 13.5 *Allocation for a Conservative Portfolio*

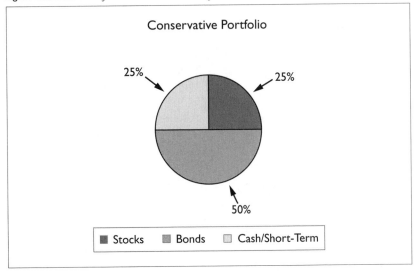

equal investments in both equities and bonds. Such a strategy could be 40 percent stocks, 40 percent bonds, and 20 percent cash. (See Figure 13.4.)

If you're in retirement, most advisors would recommend capital preservation by investing in more bonds than equities. Such a breakdown might include 50 percent bonds, 25 percent stocks, and 25 percent short-term instruments or cash. (See Figure 13.5.)

These asset allocations are just guides as an individual's risk tolerance and performance return objectives will dominate the breakdown of assets within the three categories of cash, fixed income, and equities.

Determining your rate of return. Once more, asset allocation is reducing risk while achieving the best possible rate of return. With risk tolerance in mind, you should set the rate of return you require to increase the wealth for you and your family. Your rate of return is directly related to your willingness to take risk. You should realize that over a longer time horizon, risk will drop and returns will be less volatile, and what you really want is a buildup of capital in your portfolio.

What is a comfortable return? Based on your risk tolerance, you need to accept a percentage of decline. How much decline would you accept to keep your portfolio intact? Say you can put up with a 10 percent decline quarterly. Divide that decline in half (5 percent) and add 3 to 4 percent. That gives you 8 to 9 percent rate of return over a three- to five-year time line with a well-structured investment portfolio.

Figure 13.6 *The Case of Diversification*

1. A $100,000 investment with a fixed rate of return of 8 percent will grow to $684,850 after 25 years.
2. The same $100,000 could be evenly diversified between five separate investments each with a different degree of risk.

The net result of option 2 could be an accumulation value of $962,800 after 25 years or $277,950 more than the guaranteed investment option 1. Although three of the five investments performed less than the fixed rate investment, the diversification into other assets that did perform well provided a greater long-term total return.

SINGLE FIXED-RATE INVESTMENT
$100,000 at 8 percent for 25 years $684,850

DIVERSIFIED INVESTMENT

$100,000		
	$20,000 at Total Loss	$ - 0 -
	$20,000 at 0 percent return	$ 20,000
	$20,000 at 5 percent return	$ 67,730
	$20,000 at 10 percent return	$216,690
	$20,000 at 15 percent return	$658,380
TOTAL		$962,800

Source: Erick H. Davidson and Kevin D. Freeman.

Diversification. To determine the best way to protect your portfolio from the seesaw of the market, diversify your holdings. You're in a good position with a separate account because your portfolio will contain an average of around 75 separate securities. If one declines, then another stock could pick up the slack. One warning: To protect yourself, don't choose stocks from only one or two sectors. This makes you vulnerable. Instead, concentrate on buying stocks in different industries. You could also diversify by investing in bonds, real estate, and cash money markets, in addition to equity stocks. (See Figure 13.6.) Your financial advisor will assist you in diversifying your wealth according to your desired rate of return and risk tolerance.

The time line. In general, the more time that goes by, the better the chance you won't incur a loss. How much are you going to need to maintain the lifestyle you desire for the rest of your life? Based on the objectives you outlined in your IPS, you now know how much you will need to maintain that lifestyle. For instance, say you want to have $1 million in cash in the bank when you retire in ten years. How much risk do you have to accept and what rate of return do you need to secure that $1 million? If you can achieve that amount with a low rate of risk and moderate return, fine. If you cannot, then you will have to readjust your tolerance for risk and go for a higher return.

Keep in mind, people are retiring sooner and living longer. This requires a greater dependence on their portfolios. Clients who are baby boomers are moving into retirement age. They do not wish to alter their standard of living or change their lifestyle. They seek the ideal portfolio—generated income, reduced taxes, returns that exceed inflation, and low volatility in the stock market.

Tax-proofing your SAM. I have mentioned previously that by having a separate account and having direct ownership in your portfolio, you have control over your taxes. By working together with your advisor, you will figure out your rate of return versus risk tolerance. Then you need to figure out the impact of taxes on your portfolio. If you want a 10 percent return after taxes, then by deferring all the gains to make them long-term gains rather than short-term gains, you might have to achieve at least a 12.5 percent rate of return depending on your tax bracket. If you are turning the stocks in your portfolio around 100 percent yearly and you're in the top tax bracket, then you might have to achieve over 16.5 percent to realize a 10 percent return.

By always tax-proofing your portfolio, you can invest with less risk and expect higher after-tax returns. You can probably anticipate the tax savings to pay your fees for the money management of your nest egg.

Getting SAM feedback. In most cases, you will not be able to speak directly with your money manager on a regular basis. His firm is there to make you money, not to chat. That's another reason you have a financial advisor acting as a liaison between you and the program sponsor. Your financial advisor, in most cases, will have frequent communication directly with the sponsoring firm.

You will, however, have more opportunity to access your money than was possible with mutual funds. You will be able to access your securities and track their performance in almost real time with a few mouse clicks on your home or office computer.

MAKE IT HAPPEN

At this point, you have the basic knowledge to proceed in setting up your separate account. The following chapters will highlight the more important factors like hiring (or firing) the support staff, getting comfortable with the SAM fee structure, and even altering the makeup of your separate account to better fit your investment objectives.

SELECTING YOUR BOAT
HANDLERS

It's easy to make a buck. It's a lot tougher to make a difference.

Tom Brokaw

Just as important as deciding to set up your own separate account will be selecting the people who will help you obtain optimum portfolio performance and monitor your portfolio's progress. By now, you should have a good idea what roles these individuals play and how they will affect one of the most important aspects of your life: *your wealth.*

Let's cover in more detail exactly who will be there to handle your "boat" (your separate account) in the choppy waters of the market.

THE BOAT HANDLERS

The Big Boys of Separate Accounts:
The Wire House Broker-Dealers

Today, after some 60 years in existence, most of the separate account investment business is concentrated in the brokerage industry. SAMs can trace their beginnings back to the big brokerage firms. It was natural the houses would develop and refine the concept.

Wire house: In the early days of investment management, national brokerage firms were linked to their multiple branches by telephone lines to be able to transmit financial news almost instantaneously giving them an edge on the competition. Because of the communication links by telephone lines, these firms became known as wire houses.

Source: Investopedia.com.

Today, the concentration of separate account business is divided among five major wire houses: Merrill Lynch, Morgan Stanley Dean Witter, Paine Webber, Prudential, and Salomon Smith Barney. In total, these wire houses controlled a 79 percent share of the overall market at the end of 2004.[1]

Regional Brokers/Venders

Other providers in the separate account business are the national full-service brokerages such as AG Edwards, Raymond James, Wheat First Union, Everen, and Deutsche Banc Alex Brown. These regional brokers have approximately 14 percent of the business.

There are third-party venders also in this group such as Lockwood Financial and SEI that set up separate accounts with their clients but sometimes utilize the technical/administrative services of the brokerage houses.

Not Just Credit Cards: Independent Brokers and Dealers

Linsco/Private Ledger (LPL) and Financial Services Corporation (FSC) are leading players in this category. These big companies have the wherewithal to establish separate account programs.

New Money to Be Made: Banks

Not to be left out, the big banks are getting into separate accounts too. Major banks such as Wells Fargo and Chase Manhattan are leaders here presently. Although the big brokerage houses dominate the business, bank-owned brokerages are moving into separate accounts.

Wells Fargo Securities, Inc., owned by Wells Fargo Bank, has a separate account program that has access to dozens of top money managers. This program is a fully coordinated separate account program with a full wrap fee around all services. Initial minimum is $100,000, which gives investors access to money managers that usually require an investment of over $1 million.

A New Career: Accountants/CPAs/Insurance Agents?

CPAs and insurance agents backed by their companies are getting on the separate account bandwagon. Sometimes the last person in the office gets the business, so it is with these professionals who have access to suitable clients needing investment advice.

The insurance industry, for instance, is responding to market demand to support its agents to become fee-based investment advisors. There is ample evidence that insurance agents have the marketing expertise and contacts among high-net-worth individuals to build substantial investment advisory business rather rapidly.

CPAs too, usually rated the most trusted advisors of business owners and professionals, are finding they can be in the financial advisory business too, instead of referring clients to outside investment advisors. This is accomplished by the ready availability of turnkey asset management programs (TAMPs). These programs manage all components of the asset management process. This gives the CPA and others command over the separate account (or mutual fund) process to concentrate on developing an investment business with their clients.

Thus, we are seeing accounting and insurance professionals who want to enter the world of financial management and utilize the separate account concept as a springboard. This means investors have additional options when seeking a financial advisor.

Large-capitalization (large-cap) stock: Companies that have a market capitalization of between $10 billion and $200 billion are considered large cap. These are the big kahunas of the financial world. Examples include Wal-Mart, Microsoft, and Exxon. Sometimes these stocks are called megacaps. Keep in mind that classifications such as large cap or small cap are only approximations that change over time. Also, the exact definition can vary between brokerage houses.

Source: Investopedia.com.

Pardon Our Dust: Mutual Fund Companies

With vast net withdrawals raising the attention of the mutual fund companies after the 2003 scandal, the major fund companies in the industry are adding and/or beefing up their separate account programs.

Fidelity Investments, MFS, and Oppenheimer have made a major commitment to separate accounts. Oppenheimer introduced new SAM programs in 2004. Fidelity is offering numerous separate account programs now. MFS is offering as many as seven separate account programs in the sectors of large-cap, mid-cap, and international portfolios.

Another way the fund companies are establishing themselves with separate accounts is through outsourcing, that is, acquiring or developing business relationships with firms that are experienced with separate accounts. One example is Alliance Capital Management, which purchased Regent Investors Services, a firm heavily involved in separate accounts.

One of the companies that is a pioneer in the separate account business is Franklin-Templeton of San Francisco. This company has been offering separate accounts since 1991. One of the authors of the first major book on separate accounts, Kevin Freeman, was named to run the first separate account program at Franklin-Templeton. With its separate account group, the company has around $4 billion under management today.

Four larger fund companies all have established separate account programs at present: Fidelity Investments, Putnam Investments, American Funds, and the Vanguard Group.

Registered investment advisor (RIA): An investment advisor who registers with the Securities and Exchange Commission (SEC) and agrees to be regulated by SEC rules is known as a registered investment advisor.

Only a small percentage of all investment advisors register. And while the designation doesn't mean that the SEC vouches for their effectiveness, being registered is often interpreted as a sign that the advisor meets a higher standard.

Source: Investopedia.com.

Make no mistake about it, the fund companies have no intention of losing business in the new bustling separate account industry. They will be strong contenders in the years ahead. For their present client base, which is invested in mutual funds, the transition to a separate account will be as simple as filling out new paperwork. Keep in mind, the same mutual fund managers will most likely be servicing their own separate account programs within most of the fund companies.

One on One: The Independent Advisor

Perhaps having the most to gain and presently the slowest to respond to the new concept of separate accounts is the independent advisor. Today, it is estimated that 15,000 registered investment advisors (RIAs) are offering separate accounts to their client base.

This is a broad-brush group. They can be brokers at the big firms who are charging fees instead of commissions. They can be independent advisors with a single shingle on their office door.

As more advisors become fee-based, it will be natural for them to service clients with separate accounts. Because the very concept of the separate account creates more individual servicing of the client's goals and needs, the advisor moves to the same side of the desk as the client. No longer selling a selection of mutual funds, the advisor becomes truer to his nomenclature and helps to advise the client. It becomes a win-win situation for both the client and the advisor.

THE SHIFT IN THE BUSINESS

Today, the separate account industry is a $752 billion business demonstrating a five-year growth rate of 32.1 percent.[2] Shortly, the separate account business will pass from its growth phase to the maturity phase. By that time, separate accounts will be a $2 trillion business during the years leading up to 2010.

> *Separately managed accounts are the wave of the future. . . .*
> *Clients like the idea of owning their own customized account and*
> *having their own portfolio manager handle the day-to-day decisions.*
> **Keith Tigue, Robinson, Tigue, Sponcil and Associates, Phoenix, Arizona**

What Does It Mean for You?

As you can see, there are myriad choices confronting you in selecting where to place your separate account. I recommend you first consider an independent advisor who receives separate account administrative support from broker-dealers and/or a total turnkey approach through a third-party platform provider.

Further, there's the option of setting up and maintaining a separate account on your own.

In any event, you will need to conduct due diligence to determine the best choice to service your separate account.

The separate account revolution propelled by technology and spurred by competition gives the investor more choices, better fee structures, and more control than ever before.

YOUR FIRST TEAM

Let me explain in more detail the roles the independent advisor and money manager(s) play in putting your portfolio in operating mode. I have addressed the issue of setting up a separate account on your own. This will save you the annual 1 percent of assets fee, but I urge you to proceed with caution. Hiring a competent professional to manage your wealth is, I believe, your best course of action.

Benchmark: A standard against which the performance of a security, index, or investor can be measured. Most equity mutual funds and portfolio managers use the S&P 500 Index as the benchmark to beat.

When evaluating the performance of any investment, it's important to compare against the right benchmark. For example, comparing a bond fund to the Russell 2000 (which is an index of small caps) is not meaningful.

Source: Investopedia.com.

The Independent Advisor Role

The financial advisor is the gatekeeper of your separate account. You purchase the account upon his recommendations and you own the separate account as a fee-based brokerage account.

Your advisor's job is to comprehend fully your present and future financial situation. He is there to help you work out your short-term and long-term goals. Your advisor draws out your feelings about investment risk and your view of your time horizons. Out of this comes an investment policy statement (IPS) that will help structure an appropriate asset allocation, as we covered in detail in Chapter 13.

After your IPS is formulated, your investment advisor will suggest one or more managed accounts for your portfolio. He will also recommend money managers for those accounts.

Advisors and the firms they work for constantly evaluate money managers with due diligence. They look for managers whose track records of performance meet or exceed their performance and risk benchmarks.

Your advisor will generally have established preferences of money managers his firm has utilized or approved. Usually, this is based on good working relationships he has had previously with individual managers or management firms.

Advisors also gravitate to money managers who are responsive in providing customer support, insightful analysis, and efficient record-keeping, because easily accessible, high-quality information improves the advisor's relationship with you and other clients.

Once you've invested in a separate account, your financial advisor's role is to monitor the performance of your account and to act as a liaison and coordinator between you and the money manager you've chosen together.

Setting Benchmarks

It's important to establish benchmarks against which you and your advisor can measure the progress you're making toward the goals you've defined. Those benchmarks can be public ones, such as the Standard & Poor 500 Index for a separate account investing in large-cap stocks, or a more personal standard.

Evaluating current performance against your expectations will help you judge whether you've made the right investment decisions. You can always change managers or asset allocations if you're disappointed with the results, though most experts suggest that you don't act too hastily.

Measuring against well-chosen benchmarks, which your advisor can help you identify, may also help clarify whether your expectations are reasonable; if not, you may have to adjust them to be more in line with market realities.

Using TAMPs

Most independent advisors along with banks, insurance agents, CPAs, etc., utilize turnkey asset management programs (TAMPs) to compete against the resources of the big brokerage wire houses. TAMPs allow the members of this independent group to vie for the separate account business. These fee-based programs (which include both separate account and mutual fund programs) allow the advisors and others to compete by providing four services:

1. Technology (client profiling, asset allocation, IPS creation, and proposal generalization)
2. Type and nature of asset class selection
3. Management of rebalancing and reallocation
4. Performance measurement and reporting/billing services[3]

TAMPs are able to manage all aspects of the separate account process for the client. TAMPs can develop the IPS, create a portfolio, manage asset allocations, and perform all administrative functions.

Selecting an Advisor

It's no secret and most clients know this: You as a client desire to work with a trusted, high-integrity, knowledgeable investment professional who is sincerely interested in preserving and expanding your wealth.

However, you don't like to pay extra for this. To you, it's part of the ongoing relationship with a financial advisor. That's why selecting a financial advisor who is fee-based and proficient in the separate account process is not as difficult as it might seem. It's uncomplicated because you know you're going to select an advisor skilled in handling the separate account management process. The amount of her fee is directly linked to the successful performance of your portfolio. These types of advisors are not mere asset gatherers. They retain a full circle, offering planning services that not only include building your portfolio but understanding your lifestyle and life goals.

What will be more difficult for you is finding this individual.

Finding an Independent Advisor

I would like to think this book has triggered your interest in securing a financial advisor to handle your separate account. Just as meaningful, perhaps, has been the lackluster performance of your mutual funds during these years of the bear market. Maybe it's the disappointment you had in 2000 with low performance returns and high capital gains taxes. Or maybe you just don't like the way mutual fund companies are doing business. Whatever the reason or reasons, you have decided you might require some financial advice.

By now you have learned two things about finding a financial advisor to handle your wealth:

1. Select a fee-based advisor.
2. Select an advisor experienced in separate accounts.

There's much more to explore before you actually sit down and interview prospective advisors.

There are Web sites that can direct you to independent advisors in your geographic area including http://www.fpanet.org and http://www.napfa.org. You can ask friends and relatives if they know of financial advisors that come with high recommendations. Better yet, your CPA, lawyer, and other business associates can probably come up with some referrals. You could even take in a free meal at numerous financial seminars given by financial advisors routinely in your area. Besides the meal, you can get a feel for their expertise and the chemistry these presenters have with you. Watch for a caring attitude.

Before you venture out there, arm yourself with knowledge. When evaluating an advisor, look for:

- An advisor who is experienced handling separate accounts
- An advisor who is fee-based. Why? It means his advice is based on what's best for you, not on pushing products and padding his pockets with commissions.
- An advisor who has been in business at least five years for compensation
- An advisor with certification
- An advisor who is highly regarded by peers in the business
- An advisor who has at least 100 clients and/or $25 million in assets under management
- An advisor who does not have regulatory problems (see the box on the following page)
- An advisor who has clients similar to you and in your financial situation
- An advisor who takes time to listen to your needs before making recommendations
- An advisor who talks about taxes and their implications
- An advisor who does not talk badly about his competition
- An advisor who has a quality roster of money managers to service your portfolio
- An advisor who considers all aspects of your financial life (assets, insurance, taxes, real estate, college expenses, retirement issues, estate planning, employer benefit plans, etc.)

How to **C**heck the **D**isciplinary **H**istory of a **F**inancial **P**lanner or **A**dvisor

You can contact any of the agencies or associations below to acquire information about a financial advisor's disciplinary record.

- Certified Financial Planner Board of Standards, 888-CFP-MARK (888-237-6275)
- North American Securities Administrators Association, 888-84-NA-SAA (888-846-2722)
- National Association of Insurance Commissioners, 816-842-3600
- National Association of Securities Dealers, 800-289-9999
- National Fraud Exchange (fee involved), 800-822-0416
- Securities and Exchange Commission, 800-732-0330

Checking Credentials

As you look for an advisor, one of the things you want to check is how qualified the person is to do the job. That's not as easy as it seems because there is no single credential that a financial advisor must have, like those of an MD or a CPA.

The most stringent requirements are for brokerage firm employees who sell securities. To be registered representatives (RR), they must pass an exam administered by the National Association of Securities Dealers (NASD). However, that exam tests securities law rather than financial planning expertise. Such a person must also be listed with the Securities and Exchange Commission (SEC) as a registered investment advisor (RIA) or with the securities agencies in the states in which they work.

You can easily access registered advisors' files. Part II of Form ADV (discussed in Chapter 13), contains summaries of the advisor's background and fees. If your advisor is on the list, you can ask to see his or her form by calling the SEC Public Reference Branch. Part I of Form ADV reports certain disciplinary actions against the advisor, but not current complaints, if there are any. The NASD, in association with each state, also tracks credentials of registered advisors.

Warning Signs

You should expect the advisors you interview to be professional and honest, especially if they have the appropriate credentials and you've been referred to them by people you trust. Nevertheless, be wary of any adviser who:

- Guarantees you're going to make a lot of money
- Insists that an uninsured investment has little or no risk
- Advises you to put all of your money in one investment
- Recommends investments you don't recognize, and doesn't try to explain them clearly, or says they're too complicated to understand
- Argues with you or ignores your instructions
- Is vague about the amount of commission or fees he or she will earn
- Asks you to sign any documents you haven't fully read or don't fully understand

Professional Standards

Some financial planning professional organizations have established their own criteria and certify advisors who meet their standards. You may want to look for someone with one of the following designations:

- **Certified Financial Planner (CFP).** This distinction is granted by the Certified Financial Planner Board of Standards and requires passing a comprehensive ten-hour exam and adhering to a code of ethics.
- **Personal Financial Specialist (PFS).** This is a certified public accountant (CPA) who has been accredited as a financial planner by the Institute of Certified Public Accountants.
- **Chartered Financial Analyst (CFA).** This title is granted by the Institute of Chartered Financial Analysts and requires industry experience and passing three six-hour exams over a three-year period.

- **Chartered Financial Consultant (ChFC).** This designation is granted primarily to insurance agents who qualify as financial planners by the American College, Bryn Mawr, Pennsylvania.

Advisors and Separate Accounts: A Marriage Made in Heaven

According to a report from the Boston-based Financial Research Corp., independent advisors who handle separate accounts for their clients develop a much clearer understanding of their clients' life goals than any other financial strategy. The report said that the redemption rates for equities in a separate account are as low as 8 percent and the average hold on assets is ten years versus three years for mutual funds.[4]

SELECTING THE MONEY MANAGER

One of the major benefits of owning a separate account is having access to your own money managers. Most of these money managers have considerable talent and years of experience tending to the investing needs of the superrich and major institutions.

Their job is to make the hard decisions of day-to-day investing. It is your job, with the help of your financial advisor, to find the money managers that complement your diversified portfolio. Diversification in a portfolio means the right allocation between growth and value, domestic and international, fixed income and equity. With the right moves and corrections, the money managers will create the right blend of stability and volatility to maximize returns.

How to Find a Money Manager

In financial circles, the term *due diligence* means simply using an abundance of care to select an investment management firm and its money managers. In spite of the concentration of logic applied, the process is still subjective in nature.

The process begins by you and your advisor screening all money manager candidates based on some general criteria. Factors usually include assets under management (e.g., $200 million), years of experience (e.g., minimum 5 years), job turnover (stability in employment), registration (such as with the SEC), and compliance (no ongoing investigation or litigation that would prove damaging).

After narrowing down the list, you and your advisor should review the management styles of the remaining managers, looking for consistency and performance during different marketing cycles.

Finally, study the past performance of each manager to assess whether you believe this performance can be continued in the future.

The managers that make it through these hoops will receive the recommendation of your advisor. As a client, you need to review these recommendations looking not at short-term performance numbers but at the consistency of results over a period of time.

To support your selection decision, review additional information about each money manager. The SEC utilizes Form ADV to regulate the actions of money managers. This disclosure form provides information on the money manager's credentials, and any disciplinary or legal problems, conflicts of interest, background briefs, etc. Although the SEC does not claim complete disclosure on Form ADV, it created the form to provide basic information about investment managers to potential clients. If you want to know more about a money manager, you can check the employment, education, and court case background of the manager and his firm's principals.

If the manager has more than $100 million assets under management, the SEC requires the quarterly filing of Form 13F. This form covers all the equity positions and shares outstanding. It's a good measurement of a money manager's expected performance position for the coming quarter.

All this due diligence should get you to a point where you and your financial advisor can select the most appropriate manager to service your portfolio.

How Your Money Manager Gets Paid

One of the best things about a fee-based arrangement is that all the players servicing your separate account are paid based on how much they are able to make for you. Their financial interests are in sync with yours. The money manager usually is compensated annually between .20 percent and 1.0 percent. The overall value of your portfolio is the basis for the fee. This is usually paid on a quarterly basis and in advance. Because your money manager is paid on the value of your portfolio, you can see it's in her best interest to increase your net worth.

Transparency Access

You won't find listings of money manager's performance in the stock section of the newspaper. You will, however, have immediate access to your account online where you can track trades and transactions easily.

It's good that you have regular access to your portfolio, but never let daily reporting cloud your vision of where your portfolio is going. The best tool to assess if your portfolio is on track is your quarterly performance report. This is where you can determine if the performance of your securities meets your financial objectives within your defined risk level and time horizon.

The performance report gives you the necessary data to evaluate your progress. It includes year-to-date performance, percentage of returns since inception, asset allocation, and benchmark comparisons. Remember, performance is not only based on return but the risk level you have assigned to attain that rate of return.

Evaluating Your Money Manager

One of the tasks you and your financial advisor must do is judge the performance of your money manager over time. Your quarterly reports will provide a barometer to help you determine if your financial objectives are being met.

Comparisons can be made with other portfolios with similar performance objectives and appropriate market benchmarks.

However, performance should not be the only indicator by which to judge your money manager. Other aspects of your money manager's modus operandi should be factored in as well. For instance, you must look at a money manager's underlying risk factor.

After examining your risk tolerance established in the IPS, you can eliminate managers deemed too risky. The same analysis should be done regarding tax reduction. You want to evaluate if your money manager is sensitive to your needs to eliminate or reduce capital gains taxes and adjust your portfolio accordingly.

Finding Safe Harbor

Putting together a team of advisor, money manager, and broker-dealer is more of an art than a science. In spite of years of experience and know-how, no one is infallible. Mistakes will be made and your investment strategy, whether a separate account or a mutual fund, can hit a speed bump now and then. The separate account process does place you, the investor, in a better position for enhanced performance and increased security of your principal. Therefore, if the strategy is right, then your concentration should be on finding the optimum independent financial advisor and money manager to handle your wealth. Remember, you're the captain of your own financial boat.

15

SHOW THEM THE MONEY

Money is better than poverty, if only for financial reasons.
Woody Allen

Thene is a misconception about separate accounts. There is the mistaken impression among investors that this financial strategy carries a ticket for entrance and maintenance that is too expensive. When you look at the actual numbers, separate accounts are more cost-efficient than mutual funds. Yes, that's what I said.

In the early days of separate accounts for 20 years or more, the original fee or wrap fee as it became known was 3 percent of assets. The cost associated with mutual funds was around 1.5 percent.

The defining factor for separate accounts, however, was that all costs were bundled together—the 3 percent fee included the services of the independent advisor, the money manager, the sponsor firm (brokerage or third-party broker-dealer), and all custody and daily trades of the portfolio. Investment advice was a bonus at no extra charge!

Unfortunately, the financial press played up the 3 percent without examining all the facts. The perception was that because separate accounts were primarily for the rich, they cost more. The fee, however, was most realistic, however, because some execution costs often exceed 3 percent for other financial products, especially commission-based programs.

Today, during this growth phase of separate accounts, rapidly changing technology and increased competition have been adding value and cutting costs at the same time. Executing transactions, recordkeeping, and other administrative tasks all have been streamlined. According to research by McKinsey, a New York consulting firm, the annual client cost of an average separately managed account fell to **1.69 percent in 2004** from 2.12 percent in 1999.[1]

Moreover, as highlighted in many chapters in this book, the tax efficiency of separate accounts is an overshadowing advantage over mutual fund investing. In addition, the pricing structure of mutual funds is in a mess accented by an industry that constantly tries to inflate and hide fees from investors. Most investors, whether due to ignorance or misguided information, have no idea they are paying add-on expenses for their mutual funds.

> *Many mutual fund investors could set up a separate account with a professional money manager and pay a good independent advisor his annual fee for what they lose to Uncle Sam every year!*
>
> **Joe Smith, director of Private Advisor Services, and board member, Money Management Institute**

In separate accounts, there are no loads, redemption fees, 12b-1 marketing fees, trading commissions, or soft-dollar costs that accelerate the cost of mutual funds and propel expenses far higher than is disclosed.

If we must compare, remember that the separate account is fee-based—a straightforward system, fully disclosed, with nothing hidden or disguised to confuse the client. Furthermore, the client receives feedback on her separate account portfolio's progress on a daily and monthly basis.

What you'll find in a separate account, which is understandably debatable, is an asset management strategy that is less expensive to maintain than the mutual fund alternative. When you tally up the expense ratios of mutual funds, you might be startled to know just how little you are taking to the bank.

> *The trouble with mutual funds is that they are rewarded for the amount of money they attract, not the amount of money they earn.*
>
> **George Soros, financier and author**

In addition, with a separate account you are receiving customized and personalized attention from a professional money manager. For the fees mutual funds charge, ordinary investors with as little as $50,000 (or even $25,000 for some accounts) now can sail in the same cruise ship in which the price of entry once was $1 million or more.

WHAT'S IT GOING TO COST YOU REALLY?

In the separate account world, let's first determine who is charging what.

Fee-Based Pricing

First know there's a strong trend in the financial industry to replacing transaction commission fees with fee-based or wrap accounts. This means that sooner or later clients like you will be getting billed based on the amount of assets they have under portfolio management. You'd pay one flat fee annually at a percentage you can live with. You know why there's this trend in the industry? Clients prefer to pay as they go. That says it all.

Fees All Over the Map

Typically, the wire houses like Salomon Smith Barney and Merrill Lynch charge their clients on the average 2 percent, but fees can be as high as 3 percent. Fees can fluctuate at Smith Barney because the minimum investment capital required depends on the portfolio manager(s) chosen. The annual fee depends on whether the client chooses equity or fixed-income accounts and how many services the investor requires. The same goes for Merrill Lynch and most of the other big broker houses. Nevertheless, wire houses' separate account fees have been dropping from 2.42 percent in 1999 to 2.15 percent in 2000, according to Cerulli research.[2]

The new entry of banks into the separate account mix gives them an edge because they charge the lowest fees, around 1.97 percent. Insurance companies (2.0 percent) and regional brokerages (2.26 percent) come in slightly higher. The highest rates are in the third-party sectors at between 2.2 and 3.0 percent.

SAM Fees Are Dropping and Are Negotiable

There you have it. If you're shopping for a firm to set up your separate account, then you now have a feel for the fees. Fees are going down as of this printing and it behooves you to utilize the above information as only a guide.

Furthermore, as I have said before, fees are negotiable. The advertised price, like used cars, is not necessarily what you end up paying. The reduction can be as much as 25 to 30 percent. Ever try negotiating mutual fund fees? It can't be done.

On average, investors receive reduced fees of 25 percent in separate account programs, according to Cerulli Associates.[3] Clients can pay less in fees as assets increase. Fees can also be split according to amounts invested. For instance, say a client begins a separate account program with $500,000. He might pay a 2.5 percent fee on the first $400,000 of assets, and then be charged 2 percent on the final $100,000.

Know the Fee Structure

To gain a better understanding of what you are paying for with a SAM, you need to dissect the individual components of the fee. Here's where your money goes to fund a separate account:

- The independent advisor
- The money manager(s)
- The sponsor
- Custody, clearing, and execution[4]

Explanation is warranted on these elements. The money manager or managers can provide all services or just a few service options. For instance, in a particular portfolio program, one manager may only provide portfolio management. He would bill only a portion of his usual 1 percent for full service in basic points (bps). One hundred basic points equal 1 percent.

The broker or third-party platform (sponsor) also provides services to the advisor/investor and the money manager. Here are some services the sponsor handles:

- Researching money managers
- Asset allocation (initial and ongoing, called rebalancing)
- Separate account generation
- Client reporting (statement/performance)
- Account administration
- Billing (usually quarterly)
- Consultant interface
- Account setup
- End-of-year tax reporting
- Manager monitoring (hiring and firing)

Sponsors can do more. Sometimes the firm offers fiduciary responsibility, consultant training, regulatory compliance, etc.

Custody, clearing, and execution are accomplished by the separate account sponsor. The sponsor keeps separate account securities and keeps the records of the account. The sponsor executes the buy-and-sell orders from the money manager. The clearing function occurs when the money manager executes a block stock trade and delivers it to the custodian for placement in the account.

All of the service fees above are priced on bps (100 basis points + 1 percent of asset value on annual basis); the more assets under management, the lower the pricing. (See Figure 15.1.)

The Full Picture

As covered in earlier chapters, when you consider the tax-saving opportunities, customized service, unblemished transparency, and other important benefits, separate account fees seem to be reasonable. So reasonable, in fact, that a good case can be made that SAMs cost less than mutual funds. Certainly, this is true when you factor in the funds' capital gains tax problems and their performance degradation due to frequent trading. As for performance, a recent FundQuest study revealed that

Figure 15.1 *Fee Structure for a $100,000 Account Total, Annual Fee to Client of 2.50%*

Separate account management fee	0.50%
Sponsor advisory fee	0.50%
Clearing/executive fee	0.25%
Advisor fee	1.00%
Training costs	0.15%
Administrative	0.10%

Are expenses a big deal?
If you invest $10,000 in a mutual fund producing a 10 percent annual return for 20 years, you should have roughly $49,725, assuming annual operating expenses of 1.5 percent. If the fund expenses were only 0.50 percent, then you would end up with $60,858–an 18 percent difference!

Make sure you know what you are paying for!

Source: Erick H. Davidson and Kevin D. Freeman.

mutual funds and separate accounts are neck and neck in return on investment.

Clear up-front fees and no hidden costs make separate accounts even more appealing.

Separate accounts are gaining enough draw to someday become the investment vehicle of choice for millions of Americans currently invested in mutual funds. Over $8 trillion reside in mutual funds presently. That's a long stretch for separate accounts that possess approximately $750 billion presently.

Still, since the middle 1990s, SAMs have been mushrooming twice as fast as mutual fund assets. Investors are getting the message that SAMs provide a better permanent environment for their assets than do mutual funds.

THE COST OF MEMBERSHIP

Granted, to create a separate account you have to be prepared to make an initial investment that is considerably more than the $1,000 to $1,500 average for a mutual fund.

The average separate account investment is in the neighborhood of $250,000, according to Cerulli Associates.[5] Separate accounts with many managers servicing numerous SAMs diversified in different asset classes for one client can be in the millions of dollars. More traditionally, the minimum investment was over $1 million. This is still true for some firms. T. Rowe Price asks for a minimum investment of $2 million to get into a separate account.

However, the steep minimums necessary to buy into a separate account are based more on the economies of scale rather than on elitism. According to some financial schools of thought, the added monetary resources are necessary to spread asset management dollars into different asset classes—value and growth, international and domestic, fixed and equity securities. Doing so provides adequate diversification to reduce risk. Money managers have problems spreading amounts of cash less than $100,000 into proper classifications without having odd lots of stock on the outside of the portfolio. Therefore, the minimum to get into a separate account is set pretty high.

This does not mean it's not possible to secure the safety of principal in today's market environment with a smaller infusion of dollars. An investor in a separate account can expect, with crafted financial objectives and suitable risk tolerance, a quality separate account portfolio for a $100,000, $50,000, or even $25,000 initial investment.

Thus, this is the reason this book was written. The affluent investor can stand alongside the highest-net-worth client and institutions to enjoy the privileges and advantages offered by a separate account with less up-front capital today than was possible even five years ago.

Smith Barney, Merrill Lynch, Bank of America, and others are offering separate account programs with minimums as low as $100,000.

"The recent trend of investors lining up to set up separate accounts occurred before the mutual fund scandal," said Christopher Davis, executive director of Money Management Institute, the prime organization representing the separate account industry. "All things begin with the high-net-worth client and work their way down."[6]

The same can be said for TVs and other electronics that at one time carried high price tags and were only accessible to the well-to-do; eventually their prices fell so everyone could own them.

Most financial experts say that in spite of the growth of smaller minimums to get into separate accounts, an investor who qualifies for a SAM should have enough capital to spread her wealth across at least three different asset classes or managers. This would require around $250,000, depending on the program sponsors you are talking to.

This is not a paltry sum, but it's not Donald Trump money either. Any investor who qualifies should take a look at separate accounts and prompt his advisor to investigate all the possibilities.

Nevertheless, even with a lower minimum investment, the investor can still receive proper diversification, according to some experts. If the client has $100,000 or less, he just might be restricted to only one account. "Keep in mind that the typical separate account usually has 40 to 50 securities," said Kevin Davison, author of *Investing in Separate Accounts*. "This is more than enough, under modern portfolio theory, to achieve necessary diversification."[7]

The Bottom Line

To create a separate account, your initial investment can be anywhere from new industry lows of $25,000 to unlimited capital. Keep in mind, though, that the average separate account minimum most often cited by brokers and advisors is around $250,000. This amount allows your portfolio to have enough asset classes to reduce risk and develop sufficient diversification. Other experts say that $100,000 is adequate to get diversification as long as you are spread across enough asset classes.

From the beginning, you will have unprecedented control over fees, because separate accounts give you an "in your face" fee structure. You know *what* you're paying for. You know *how* you're paying. You know *why* you're paying. With your fees tiered to the asset level of your investment, it's advantageous for your money manager and advisor to make you money!

Separate accounts are based on a sliding scale of basis points; the larger the account, the lower the fees. Contrast this with that of mutual funds, referred to by *Forbes* magazine as "the dirty little secret" of the fund industry. Though it requires no more servicing expense to handle the $1 million account than it does the $10,000 account, investors are charged the same, regardless of their investment level.

Further, your fees cover all transaction costs dealing with your separate account portfolio. These fees also cover the services of your money manager, reporting, custody, administrative control of your portfolio, as well as the services of your financial advisor. There are no additional charges.

When you think about it, a separate account looks better all the time with multiple advantages for the investor including a respectable fee structure. Do not let fees be the only factor in determining if a separate account is for you and your circumstances. Regardless of whether the fees are low or high, look at other factors such as performance, risk, value (alpha) over benchmarks, plus services from your financial advisor and money manager(s).

16

PUTTING POWER IN YOUR PORTFOLIO

Obstacles can't stop you. Problems can't stop you.
Most of all, other people can't stop you. Only you can stop you.

Jeffrey Gitomer

By now you know that significant benefits of a SAM far outweigh any mutual fund or an independent portfolio of stocks. You know you prefer more control (no commingling with other investors), the right to customize your portfolio with stocks in sync with your values system, direct ownership of security positions, and tax savings issues being addressed at your level. All these benefits confirm a separate account is a much better alternative for the investor in the 21st century.

Also, you like the idea of telling your associates and relatives about your business savvy by relating your investment in a separate account rather than "retail" mutual funds. You don't mind saying your wealth is now at a higher portfolio management level serviced by a full-time professional money manager.

A separate account can even help transform you from an irrational investor to a rational one through the prudent influence of your financial advisor and money manager restraining you from fast-trading holdings in your account.

Most experts predict you won't be the only client that moves his wealth into a separate account with all the accolades above. A huge growth expansion of separate accounts is projected and it will be to your advantage.

More large financial services traditionally offering mutual funds are moving into the separate account space. Large banks and insurance companies with fee-based mutual funds are adding SAMs as an investment choice. More independent advisors are becoming more comfortable with the separate account concept either supplementing or downplaying their mutual fund business. As these institutions and firms take up the separate account banner, even major mutual fund families are joining in lockstep. This will guarantee enhanced separate account product selection and lower fees for you.

The competition for separate account investors is intensifying in the marketplace. Separate account platforms are making new technological advances. New separate account options are arising. All this activity means that separate accounts will only become even better for you and your investment circumstances.

What you should keep in mind throughout this chapter is that the traditional separate account involves professional money managers directing the daily performance of your owned securities in your portfolio administrated by a sponsoring entity.

SEPARATE ACCOUNT HYBRIDS: MDA AND UMA

Multiple-disciplined accounts (MDAs), which are fairly new, allow you to keep assets managed by different money managers in the same account. An MDA allows you the option of diversification not only among different asset classes but also among different money managers.

These MDAs have all the benefits of the traditional SAM, including direct ownership of your securities, superior tax efficiency, ability to customize your account, etc. In addition, MDAs come with new capitalization and style categories. For example, an MDA could be made up of three different subportfolios—large-cap growth, large-cap value, and small-cap value—each run by a different manager. If you have a traditional separate account, you might be limited to just one asset class.

Further, MDAs are being offered with lower account minimums. For instance, you could own three or more MDAs for as little as $50,000 each.

Not only do MDAs offer all the advantages of SAMs, but they also allow you to create subportfolios supervised by different managers with different investment styles in different asset classes within a single account.

The unified managed account (UMA) takes the concept of the MDA to the next level. It also has multiple managers servicing the same account, but the difference is a UMA can include other investment options, such as separate stocks, mutual funds, or exchange traded funds (ETFs) in one account.

Why would an investor wish to go outside his or her separate account with its basket of 30 to 80 holdings in a sharply defined investment strategy portfolio?

Increasing diversification may be the main reason. For instance, an advisor may encourage the investor with $100,000 to set up a separate account to supplement part of her portfolio with mutual funds or ETFs in order to spread her securities into more asset classes.

Another reason might be to diversify further in international stocks in which the separate account structure might prove more cumbersome.

An ETF would permit the purchase of a single sector correlated to an index such as precious metals, microcap, commodities, etc. This might make sense for some investors who desire a particular small-cap stock outside of the parameters of a large-cap separate account portfolio.

One approach could be to allocate the major portion of your portfolio to a managed account investing solely in a single asset class. Then you could invest the rest of your money in individual securities or mutual funds.

For example, if your primary investment goal is providing current income, your advisor might suggest a fixed-income managed account for 55 percent of your assets. You might allocate 25 percent to cash in a combination of certificates of deposit (CDs), U.S. Treasury bills, and a money market mutual fund. With the remaining 20 percent, you might buy a diversified portfolio of individual stocks or two or three mutual funds with different investment styles or capitalization characteristics.

If your goals are growth and income, and if the value of your total portfolio is large enough to meet the minimums, you might invest in one separate account focused on income and another account focused on growth.

As I covered earlier, the multimanagement approach of the separate account structure offers the investor the potential for consistent returns and minimized risks utilizing different money managers. Thus, the trend is toward diversification among money managers. This is similar to the principle that created investor interest ten years ago with the introduction of diversification of asset classes.

Both MDAs and UMAs are moving toward having an overlay manager function assigned. An overlay manager's job is to get individual portfolios within the sponsoring firm to perform in unison. He might oversee all the portfolios of the same asset class to be sure all buy-and-sell decisions are embedded in a single pretrade compliance package. These actions reduce trading costs by exchanging stocks between managers and eliminating small trades that do not affect overall performance.

Thus, the overlay manager makes the decisions designed to optimize the portfolio performance of each investor under his responsibility. For example, the overlay manager might police managers responsible for one diversified portfolio to make certain one manager running one asset class does not sell a stock while another manager servicing another asset class buys back the same stock a week later. This is called a wash and it is the overlay manager's responsibility to see that these things don't happen.

Thus, the role of the overlay manager is to function as a traffic cop for separate accounts. It includes even taking the lists of all portfolio holdings from money managers to handle the buying and selling of the securities. In addition, the overlay manager would be sensitive to the tax situations of individual investors by identifying taxable problems brewing to minimize unprofitable gains.

All in all, adding overlay management can enhance the potential of the separate account process and provide significant assistance to improving after-tax performance for clients. They have a bird's-eye view of each account in a firm, making their role ideal to monitor accounts for tax and risk-control situations.

"This will be the managed money structure of the future," says Matt Schott, a senior analyst at TowerGroup, an investment research firm. "Overlay portfolio management allows you to look across the different assets that the client has and manage those in a holistic way, still respecting all different customers requests either in the investment policy statements or in the sponsor's own directives," says Schott.[1]

Exchange-traded fund: A security that tracks an index and represents a basket of stocks like an index fund, but trades like a stock on an exchange, thus experiencing price changes throughout the day as it is bought and sold.

Because it trades like a stock whose price fluctuates daily, an ETF does not have its net asset value (NAV) calculated every day like a mutual fund.

By owning an ETF, you get the diversification of an index fund as well as the ability to sell short, buy on margin, and purchase as little as one share.

Another advantage is that the expense ratios for most ETFs are lower than those of the average mutual fund. When buying and selling ETFs, you have to pay the same commission to your broker that you'd pay on any regular order.

Source: Investopedia.com.

Exchange-traded funds. Exchange-traded funds are similar to index mutual funds but are traded more like stocks. Like the name suggests, an ETF is a basket of securities that are traded on an exchange. Think of an ETF as an index fund that thinks it's a stock.

The advantages of ETFs are that they can be bought throughout the trading day, can be bought on margin, are as inexpensive as the cheapest mutual funds, and have tax efficiency. They are superior to mutual funds in tax advantages. Why? ETFs trade on an exchange so every sale is matched with a purchase. Therefore, the assets do not change.

On the downside, ETFs are like individual stocks triggering commissions at each trade. If you have a large sum in a lump payout and are facing tax problems, ETFs hold an advantage over index funds.

A separate account would be a better investment alternative in most cases because it offers investing in a no-commission environment and has built-in tax efficiency, which would be a wash in an ETF.

Folios. A folio, which is a new investment vehicle in the financial business, is a cross between a discount brokerage and a mutual fund. But unlike in mutual funds, in a folio the individual owns the assets. Just like a separate account, the investor can rail against a particular manager's buy-or-sell decision adjusting her account for specific companies or certain tax strategies.

Seven years ago, Steven M. H. Wallman, a former commissioner of the SEC, founded FOLIO*fn*, an online service. While at the SEC, he became interested in why stock picking is such a mystifying process, keeping many people out of the market. "Online brokers were spending hundreds of millions of dollars publicizing systems that make stock trading faster and cheaper, but they were not really making investing better and easier."[2]

Wallman came up with FOLIO*fn* to make investing easier for a separate account want-to-be online. Individuals can run their own account with most of the advantages a separate account offers by filling a "basket" with up to 50 stocks and other securities.

In this process, investors do not pay commissions, only a monthly or annual membership fee. Members can make up to 200 no-commissions trades per month per basket executed at certain times of the day to keep down trading costs.

In essence, investors can develop their own portfolio or utilize customized portfolios that the FOLIO*fn* site provides with just a point and click of their mouse. I will discuss the phenomenon of online brokering further in Chapter 17.

Hedge funds. Separate accounts mainly offer a conservative approach to investment choices, such as large-cap value and small-cap value asset classes. However, the future of separate accounts will include greater variety, such as registered hedge funds.

A hedge fund is a complex product available to wealthy individuals (with net worth of at least $1 million) and institutions. These funds pursue returns through a number of alternative investment strategies, including hedging against market downturns by holding both long and short positions, investing in derivatives, using arbitrage, and speculating on mergers and acquisitions.

Moving these hedge funds as an available option for separate accounts won't be easy. These complex hedge funds have technical, legal, and other challenges not simple to incorporate into the separate account platform. Hedge funds, by their very nature, have limited transparency, are less liquid, and don't report their performance regularly.

"It's an uneasy fit, but I think separate accounts firms will find a way to include it," said Rick Cortez, president of the private client group at Torrey Funds, a New York hedge firm investor.[3]

Fees are extra and are not included in the basic separate account package. "I don't think it can be wrapped with the separate account," said Cortez.

Your 401(k). Your retirement plan from your employer can be established as a separate account too. Even as we speak, a number of sponsors supporting 401(k)s are enlisting brokerages, mutual fund companies, insurance companies, and banks to create SAM-type programs. For plan years beginning after 2002, the government says an individual can maintain a separate account or annuity under his or her 401(k) to receive voluntary employee contributions. If the separate account or annuity otherwise meets the requirements of a traditional IRA or Roth IRA, it is deemed a traditional IRA or Roth IRA.

Remember your 401(k) consists of pooled assets so you don't have the flexibility of customization and asset allocation that a traditional separate account has.

YOU WANT A SEPARATE ACCOUNT. WHAT'S THE NEXT STEP?

You have decided to put your wealth in the most sensible approach to investing available today in the financial industry. Not an easy decision but information and education are the greatest tools you can have when investing your wealth.

This book is designed to get you to take action toward establishing a productive working relationship with an independent financial advisor who can establish your own separate account. From this chapter, you see that separate accounts methodology is a growing, maturing process that is developing and evolving with new investment options. If you lost money in mutual funds, regard it as a learning experience that taught you the limits of certain investment structures. There are very few limits with a separate account.

Part Four

KEEPING WEALTH IN SEPARATE ACCOUNTS

17

STAY TUNED AND KEEP REGULAR HOURS

Informed decision making comes from a long tradition of guessing and then blaming others for inadequate results.

Scott Adams

One of the major ways you keep your wealth performing with a separate account is to stay wired to the entire asset management process.

I have urged you to stay the course with your investment, committing to the proven buy-and-hold strategy of portfolio management. Buy and hold doesn't mean ignoring your portfolio and financial advisor until tax time. Yes, leave your securities in place but be comfortable with and aware of the state of your separate account portfolio. Work with your advisor watching your wealth.

The long, powerful bull market of the 1980s and 1990s triggered the term *wealth effect.*

The premise is that when the value of stock portfolios rises due to escalating stock prices, investors feel more comfortable and secure about their wealth, causing them to spend more.[1]

The bull market from 1984 through 2000 produced an average return of **16.3 percent** under the S&P 500 Index. Unfortunately, as highlighted a number of times in the pages of this book, the average equity mutual fund investor realized a yearly gain of only **5.3 percent.** It's troubling. Mutual fund investors pocketed a return at the time less than that of Treasury bills during the greatest market in U.S. history.[2]

Still, investors during the big bull market made more money in the stock market than they ever did before. This generation of investors is still a little bruised from the bear market that followed from 2000 to 2003.

The system now has created a new breed of investor more savvy and streetwise than their investor predecessors. These newly affluent investors are, on average, more sophisticated and determined about how and where they put their wealth. They have high expectations and demand results. They know there's money to be made in the market and they have hopes of making it. They are demanding personalized service from their advisors and portfolio managers. They want to know at all times what's going on in their portfolio.

This new class of investor understands the value of having customized institutional professional money management and wants maximum returns and safety from these experts. They're comfortable with elements of investing like diversification, total return, and expense ratios. They're beginning to grasp the effect taxes can have on their portfolio's growth. This understanding is driving their high interest in the customization of their asset management strategy addressing their long-term goals and tax situation.

Does this sound like I'm talking about you?

If so, this chapter will let you know about the myriad means to keep yourself informed on the status of your portfolio.

COMMUNICATION CONNECTS

When you set up your separate account, you'll find a number of ways to keep yourself up-to-date on the status of your portfolio. Lest we forget, mutual fund companies have been weaving a web for years to discourage you from being informed. Their theory has been the uninformed or ignorant investor is a "good" investor. Presently, the fund companies are required by the SEC to show the stocks in client portfolios twice yearly. It is recommended by the SEC they do it quarterly. Even these disclosures are outdated by the time they reach the investor. By that time, the stocks in the portfolios have been reshuffled. Thus, most mutual fund investors have no inkling of the stocks in which they are invested.

The Separate Account Process

Your separate account by design provides openness and transparency. Remember, you're no longer in a pool of fragmented investors. You now own your portfolio of 30 to 80 stocks, which you selected with your money manager(s). Based on the development of your IPS with your advisor, your securities are all tailored to your financial goals and strategy.

Asset Manager Quarterly Reports

Your advisor receives regular, usually quarterly, reports from each money manager handling an account in your overall portfolio. These reports assess the current and near-term economic and financial outlook for the securities markets in general and for those asset classes of the market where your managed accounts are invested. You may prefer that your advisor summarize and interpret the reports for you, or you may want to review them yourself and discuss them with your advisor.

Monthly Account Statements

Your managers' reports, in conjunction with your monthly account statements, can provide guidance for your investment decisions. Note that over time your managers are most effective in assessing the investment climate and adding value; they're the ones who should have the greatest influence on your decisions.

Also note which managers are least effective; that should be a red flag for you and your advisor to consider alternatives, as long as you have allowed adequate time to pass for a good evaluation of their performance.

The quarterly account statement reviews the performance of your securities and analyzes your total portfolio. Look at the bottom line; you'll have a clear picture of how your account performed over the past three months.

You'll be able to evaluate whether you're making progress toward your financial goals. If you notice anything unusual or unexpected, it's always a good idea to consult with your financial advisor. It's also smart to keep a file of your statements so you can use them as the basis for a comprehensive annual review with your advisor, which is what every good advisor should conduct.

The numbers tell an important part of the story about your account. But you'll typically also find an explanation of current market trends, an analysis of the economic factors that influenced investment results, and an overview of historical performance. Your advisor can help you put this information in perspective, and together you can decide if it's time to make any changes in your asset allocation.

You may never see or talk to the broker or firm who sponsors your account. In fact, if you invest through an online account, you may never speak to a person at all. But if you're looking for advice you can trust as you make financial decisions, there's no substitute for a long-term, collaborative relationship with an independent financial advisor. That's my advice after 30 years in the business. Too much is left to chance when you're a do-it-yourself investor. Research time and again shows that investors without advisors consistently bring in poorer returns with their portfolios than investors with a financial advisor in their corner.

Besides bringing access to professional investment managers, financial advisors bring other resources to their client relationships. For example, advisors have access to the research reports and analytical tools of the firms where they work. These resources enable them to take an objective look at the buy-and-sell decisions your asset class managers are making for your accounts, and to assess those decisions in the context of the overall risk-return profile of your portfolio.

USING THE WORD *REVOLUTION* LIGHTLY

With today's technology and the Internet, you're an investor set free. Never before has the genie's bottle been opened to give you instantaneous direct access to Wall Street.

Daily you can easily check company annual reports, track stocks, open accounts, and observe trades in your account. All accomplished while you're still in your bathrobe—online and close to real time.

The Lure of Online Investing

The growth phenomenon of the Internet over the past ten years parallels the growth of the financial services industry in general and separate account management specifically. Historically, individual investors have relied on broker-dealers to buy and sell securities for them. The Internet is breaking the mold.

The most visible form of Internet investing is trading through an online broker. An online broker functions much like a traditional broker except that investors communicate with their online broker online. All in all, trading costs and management fees online are much lower than those of brick-and-mortar brokers.

The online brokers execute trades through the traditional exchanges (e.g., NYSE, AMEX, Nasdaq, CBOE) with the broadest range of investment options for their customers. Not withstanding, they offer lots of advice and market information.

Increasing competition and increasing volume in the online brokerage market has driven online brokerage commissions down to levels unheard of in face-to-face brokerage transactions. Many investors find that this benefit of online trading gives them flexibility because they can execute more trades with the same dollars. Busy investors appreciate the convenience of online brokerage services. Some of the brokers currently online are: Accutrade, Ameritrade, Charles Schwab, Datek, Discover Direct, E*Trade, SureTrade, and TD Waterhouse.

This short assessment of online brokerages serves to demonstrate what is happening on the Internet and how this relatively new way to invest affects separate accounts. Separate accounts are traveling down tracks parallel to online brokerages. Most of the major wire houses offer separate account portfolios online. In fact, even some of the discount online brokers (such as Charles Schwab) are offering separate accounts with minimums as low as $25,000.

Cerulli Associates says of online separate accounts, "Once the exclusive province of only the big wire houses, separate accounts are now available on the Internet. Recognizing the growing popularity and mainstream demand for separate accounts, several online providers have emerged that provide the access to institutional money managers, tax efficiencies, and customization that are characteristic of separate accounts."[3]

With the Internet acting as liaison between the investor and money managers, the wire houses and/or financial firms offer advice and guidance to help investors structure their separate account portfolios. These sites provide basic information on participating managers for Internet investors. The investor has the option of matching his financial objectives with the appropriate managers.

Setting Up a SAM in Cyberspace

Here's how it works. Separate accounts and cyberspace work especially well together. Investors can go online and set up a separate account complete with a diversified group of stocks for a flat fee—no commissions. They can then review a list of professional money managers, evaluate them, and then pick the one they are compatible with. From there, investors complete an online application. In a short time, an asset-managed portfolio will be established once investment minimums are met.

WrapManager (http://wrapmanager.com) is one such site. Investors can go to this site and establish their own separate account, review the credentials of over 150 money managers already prescreened by the Web site from 5,000 listed money management portfolios, and be charged less in fees than those offered by traditional brokers. WrapManager goes even further. The site offers the building of an investment policy statement live through a computer-to-computer interface and phone connection between the potential investor and the investment advisor, according to Gabriel Burczyk, CEO of WrapManager. "We walk the investors through the whole process of determining their asset allocation that is secure, inexpensive, and detailed," he said, "In the end, each investor has a complete customized portfolio built with handpicked professional money managers in tune with their lifestyle goals and tolerance for risk."[4]

The big wire houses are not to be left out of the Internet explosion even if they have over 70 percent of the business. Separate account managers at Salomon Smith Barney and Merrill Lynch have separate accounts available on their Web pages, as do most of the regional brokers and larger financial firms.

Once an investor is committed to a separate account, they have access to their quarterly performance report and, in some cases, can check their portfolio performance 24 hours a day, seven days a week, 365 days a year. Clients can e-mail their money manager an order to sell certain stocks they might not want in their portfolio because of personal or economic reasons, or buy others that interest them.

Online financial management sites give the client plenty of informative materials and investment guidance on separate accounts even defining asset classes to determine the best allocation mix for the client. On some sites, the customer can even run sample portfolio allocations.

Call-in centers are the norm in Internet investing. Service reps for separate accounts can help the client with routine problems, tracking portfolio returns, or rebalancing a portfolio to reapportion securities. The latest communication marvel allows the client and a member of the account team to conduct a live chat online on any relevant issue. In this way, the client can be looking at his account on the computer and communicating with the account representative at the same time.

Snail Mail Is Not Dead Yet

While the Internet is the most promising source of up-to-date financial information, not all investors are sold on it yet. DALBAR Research studied investors and their use of the Internet for financial information. Eighty-three percent of Internet users check the performance of their investments on the Web. Yet, only 18 percent of Web-using customers routinely access statements online in lieu of reviewing mailed copies, and only 17 percent use the Web to get answers to their questions.[5] The telephone and mail service are still the most popular forms of customer contact.

Other Online Sources for Separate Account Investors

Stars for separate accounts. Morningstar, the leading online Web site grading mutual funds, stocks, exchange-traded funds, and variable annuities has announced a new rating system for separate accounts. Does this mean that separate accounts have truly arrived? Some say the service could ramp up interest from on-the-fence investors. Morningstar's rating system for separate accounts is similar to the ratings given to mutual funds. A rating of one to five stars will judge 1,200 separate accounts. The database would reflect 90 percent of the retail separate accounts market and 60 percent of the institutional market by asset and number of composites.

Regulatory agencies. Who is protecting your backside and your pocketbook from Wall Street? A very complicated structure is in place making the financial industry the most regulated business in the nation. Does the system work? It does most of the time. However, headlines are always made when a stockbroker trades an elderly person's retirement money away or a hedge firm is caught trading after the market closes at the expense of multitudes of investors. It makes us wonder.

In any event, it will benefit you to know the players:

- **U.S. Congress.** It passes the major laws affecting the financial industry's modus operandi.
- **SEC.** The Securities and Exchange Commission oversees the industry, registers securities, and handles all filings required of public companies. The agency also supervises all the stock exchanges and all other agencies that sell securities.
- **NASD.** The National Association of Securities Dealers polices the financial industry. It also sets the standards for stockbrokers and other financial professionals.
- **State regulators.** Individual states have regulatory agencies that monitor activities with the industry usually acting on complaints from investors.
- **Self-regulation.** Each agency is required to keep records and perform audits on itself and its employees.

While these protective levels do not guarantee that the investor won't get burned, they do provide reasonable assurance that the industry is working with the government to monitor business practices.[6]

THE NEW INDEPENDENT INVESTOR

Today's typical investor has tasted power that comes from knowledge and control over one's own investments. The industry will never be the same again.

The triad of the emerging affluent savvy investor, the accessibility of contemporaneous financial information available on the Internet, and a separate account chosen after careful due diligence all contribute to a paradigm of the powerful new investor.

With these new resources, the investor can be in total control. The investor has control over his ownership of specific securities. Investors have control over hiring and firing their managers and advisors. They have control over the direction their portfolio takes—up or down. The client is connected, in control, and in management mode.

There is immeasurable satisfaction—and safety—in having control over your wealth.

18

THE ASSET MANAGEMENT RECOVERY PLAN

Procrastination is the bad habit of putting off until the day after
tomorrow what should have been done the day before yesterday.

Napoleon Hill

You are now equipped with knowledge of a newly viable, innovative investment strategy, and profound reasons why a separate account is a superior asset management vehicle to a mutual fund. You also know the recent troubles and scandals that have befallen the mutual fund industry.

That being said, mutual funds have their place. There are a few funds out there that do outperform the market (at last count, around 20 percent). And there are funds available that offer some tax-saving options.

Mutual funds make sense for people who don't have any clue what to do with their money. Even below-market returns can be better than the less-than-1-percent return you'd receive from a savings account at your local bank. Mutual funds also make sense for investors who don't possess the necessary resource minimum to qualify for an alternative means of investing. If you don't have at least $25,000 as the initial capital outlay to set up a separate account, most advisors would advise you to stay with mutual funds. In fact, many advisors would go further and say you shouldn't open a separate account without funds ranging from $100,000 to $250,000. The average separate account was $237,000 in 2004, according to the Money Management Institute.[1]

For the remainder of U.S. mutual fund investors, accepting the poor performance of returns, inflated hidden fees, and unnecessarily high tax bills doesn't make sense. Sadly, most of those investors have not learned much from the dot-com implosion of 1999 and 2000. Nor did they depart in large numbers from mutual funds when word of a major scandal was brewing in late September 2003 and the continuing investigative probes still making headlines today.

As a result, American investors are still chasing the performance fantasy of mutual funds, As evidence, the mutual fund companies had record sales in 2004.

MUTUAL FUNDS: STORIES OF THEIR DEATH ARE GREATLY EXAGGERATED

If this dissection of the faults intrinsic in mutual funds has you thinking the industry will soon shut its doors, think again. The $8 trillion industry can take more than a few hits and still remain strong. In fact, being the great marketers they are, the fund companies have joined in lockstep with the separate account business in setting up their own SAM accounts. The fund companies, recognizing the strength of SAMs, intend to protect assets from leaving their mutual fund portfolios. If the competition is jumping in with both feet, that should show you the strength of separate account asset management.

The End of Mutual Fund Domination?

Both separate accounts and mutual funds have a place in the financial marketplace, and both serve an important function—fueling the lifestyles and retirements of millions of Americans.

It should be said: Mutual funds are an American icon. Since the first mutual fund was formed, this building block of our country's investment strategy is home for some 93 million Americans today.

From an investment pattern whose concept developed slowly, Americans put about 20 percent of their discretionary wealth into mutual funds during the 1970s and 1980s. By the 1990s, investors were investing at a rate of 25 percent. By 1996, the rate rose to 60 percent. At the end of the century in 2000, the rate of investment into mutual funds by Americans climbed to 82 percent.

During the time between 1999 and 2001, American investors had saved $385 billion yearly . . . and put $320 billion of it in mutual funds! They took a lot of money out during the dot-com implosion, but they have put it back into mutual funds as memories dimmed and, frankly, there was no other investment vehicle for the average investor that made as much sense in theory—but not in practical terms.

This $8 trillion business embraced by the American investor is not going to go anywhere. In spite of the poor performance, high and hidden fees, lack of transparency, and lately the uncovering of deceit and deception toward the mutual fund investor, there are always going to be funds. Millions of American investors will continue to put their hard-earned wealth into the mutual fund vehicle. They don't get the message. (See Figure 18.1.)

But now you do, and now you have greater options to accumulate future wealth, leading to a comfortable retirement. The more you accumulate by the time you retire, the more freedom and comfort you'll have to stay on that vacation a week longer, or see the grandkids in Vermont three times a year instead of just one.

MAKING SAMS THE BETTER INVESTING OPTION

The Big Population Bulge

If you're a baby boomer born between 1945 and 1965 you have a lot of clout in the financial industry.

Baby boomers with $17 trillion of investable assets today will have $30 trillion by 2010. As the first boomers are coming into retirement, they are and will be there to liquefy their retirement plans, sell their small businesses, exercise stock options, sell their large homes, and move into smaller less-expensive digs.

What this means for you—boomer or not—is that separate accounts are becoming a big business. By the end of 2004, total assets in SAMs reached $576.1 billion, nearly 16 percent higher than 2003 figures, according to a

Figure 18.1 *Comparison of Separate Accounts and Mutual Funds*

	Mutual Funds	Separate Accounts
General Features		
Access to professional money managers	Yes	Yes
Diversified portfolio	Yes	Yes
Ability to customize portfolio	No	Yes, investors can restrict specific securities from their portfolios
Manager independence from the "herd instinct"	No, if clients want to redeem shares, fund managers must sell to raise the cash to do so	Yes, money managers can buy when the herd is selling and vice versa, customizing the decision to the client's asset class objectives
Unlimited withdrawals/ redemptions	No, most funds have restrictions	Yes
Typical account minimum	$1,000	$25,000–$250,000 plus
Liquidity	Typically, next day	Three-day settlement of trades
Access to asset classes	Numerous	Somewhat more limited than funds
Performance-Reporting Features		
Ownership of securities reporting	Typically semi-annual, some more frequent	Customized performance reporting available daily, monthly depending on program
Customized performance reporting	No, investors must calculate their own performance, which is problematic, particularly for investors who use dollar cost averaging	Yes, automatically sent to investors every quarter, includes performance of individual portfolios and of aggregate of multiple portfolios

Figure 18.1 *Comparison of Separate Accounts and Mutual Funds*

	Mutual Funds	Separate Accounts
Tax-related Features		
Separately held securities	No, investor owns one security, the fund, which in turn owns a diversified portfolio	Yes, investor owns securities in an account managed by his money managers
Unrealized gains	Yes, average U.S. mutual fund has a 20% imbedded, unrealized capital gain	No, cost basis of each security in the portfolio is established at time of purchase
Customized to control taxes	No, most funds are managed for pre-tax returns, and investors pay a proportionate share of taxes on capital gains	Yes, investors can instruct money managers to take gains or losses as available, to manage their tax liability
Tax-efficient handling of low-cost basis stocks	No, stocks cannot be held in an investor's mutual fund account, so there is no opportunity to manage low-cost basis stocks	Yes, the handling of low-cost basis stocks can be customized to the client's situation, liquidating in concert with offsetting losses, etc.
Gain/loss distribution	Virtually all gains must be distributed; losses cannot be distributed	Realized gains and losses are reported in the year recorded
Cost-related Features		
Expenses (excluding brokerage costs)	1.42%[1,3]	1.00%
Expenses (including brokerage costs)	1.56% average[2, 3]	1.25%[3]

Figure 18.1 *Comparison of Separate Accounts and Mutual Funds*

	Mutual Funds	**Separate Accounts**
Volume fee discounts	No, all investors pay the same expense ratio	Yes, larger investors enjoy fee discounts
Other costs	12b-1, sales loads, redemption fees, etc.	None

¹ Morningstar Principia Plus for Windows, February 2002
² Brokerage costs estimated at 0.13% for the 10 largest funds
³ Costs do not include advisor fee, which will vary

Source: Money Management Institute.

report released by the Money Management Institute.[2] The institute predicts the separate account business will reach $1.3 trillion by 2008.

With this upward trend in the business, separate account management will become more innovative, more tailored to your investment needs by offering an improved array of financial products, and more competitive in terms of pricing and minimums. All these factors will make separate accounts an even better way to manage your stock market assets than is the way you are doing it today.

> *After three decades of wealth accumulation by baby boomers,*
> *we're gearing up to deal with those turning 60 who are starting to retire.*
> *They're winding down; they've sold their businesses. They're seeking*
> *cash-flow generation rather than wealth accumulation.*
> **Len Reinhart, president of Lockwood Financial**

The Evolution of Managed Accounts: A Recap

In the early days, the "wrap" account was created to bundle multiple services under a charge of one total fee. It was tailored to the high-net-worth and institutional investor market.

Most things of value can't be hidden forever, so when the wrap account began dropping the initial minimums required and computer tracking software advanced, it evolved into the more mainstream product we're seeing emerging today.

The description of a wrap account has matured to the more inclusive **separately managed account.**

Managed account: A managed account is a portfolio of stocks or bonds owned by an individual investor and overseen by a professional investment manager(s) who makes buy-and-sell decisions. Each managed account has an investment objective, and each manager oversees specific asset classes invested to meet the client's overall objectives.

While managed accounts resemble mutual funds in some ways, there are differences. With a managed account you own individual securities rather than shares of a common fund. You may also ask the manager to make certain investments or avoid others, which you can't do with a mutual fund. You can ask the manager to sell certain holdings in your account to realize capital gains or losses. And you are not vulnerable to phantom gains, which can occur if a fund realizes a profit on an investment it sells and credits you with a capital gain even if you haven't actually realized a gain in account value.

Source: Investopedia.com.

But managed money went a step further. The concept also altered the role of the traditional stockbroker—the investment specialist who matched buyers and sellers with securities for a commission. Because of the nature of the fee-based wrap account, the role of the broker handling such accounts changed. No longer reaping commissions for their services, brokers became advisors. They began to offer *portfolio management* for the client.

Today, in a managed account, you receive the benefit of ongoing consultation with a professional financial advisor in exchange for a predictable, disclosed ongoing fee. The advisor's services include managing your financial plan and scrutinizing your managers. The advisor serves you, the client, by understanding your overall financial situation and then by determining your risk tolerance, helping you set goals, and adjusting asset allocation in accordance with those goals. From there, your advisor helps you chose managers by asset class, and monitors your portfolio and progress toward your goals.

You can call it a wrap account. You can call it a managed account. They are one in the same. In exchange for one set fee that covers all services, you receive with a separate account what all financial products

Wrap account: A wrap account is a professionally managed investment plan in which all expenses, including brokerage commissions, management fees, and administrative costs, are "wrapped" into a single annual charge, usually amounting to 2 percent to 3 percent of the value of the assets in the account.

Wrap accounts usually combine the services of an independent advisor who helps the client; a professional money manager who manages a personalized portfolio of stocks, bonds, mutual funds, and other investments; and a brokerage firm or a third-party platform firm, which takes care of the trading and recordkeeping on the account.

Source: Investopedia.com.

should deliver: the peace of mind of having many people checking on your assets for a lower annual cost than mutual funds can deliver.

Price for Admission Is Dropping, Technology Is Climbing

As with most products in the marketplace, catching on with the mainstream audience stimulates competition and opportunities for program improvement. Separate accounts are no exception. From its origins of an initial outlay of millions of dollars to get into a separate account by well-heeled superrich clients and institutions, today a separate account requires a minimum as low as $50,000 for admission. Even packages with $25,000 minimums are out there on a limited basis.

As discussed, the fees for all services offered by a separate account are also being reduced. Unlike with mutual funds, the client, depending on his individual investment situation and size of his account, can negotiate a separate account package fee discounted as much as 30 percent.

Minimums and fees are also dropping due to the increased competition of major wire houses, insurance companies, banks, independent financial advisors, and mutual fund companies all getting on the separate account bandwagon. It's certain that separate account investors will gain new product options as well as lower fees.

New technology continues to level the playing field. An individual advisor can service a client's account with tools available that are capable of handling thousands of individual portfolios. The only thing holding back a significant number of advisors is their becoming familiar with the separate accounts process over the tried-and-true practice of selling mutual funds.

The Advisor Sits on the Same Side of the Desk with the Client

The executive desk has always been a handicap to good communication between businessperson and client. The separate account process removes any barriers between advisor and client. Unlike the matter-of-fact dealing of buying and selling mutual funds and individual securities, a separate account builds a bridge between the advisor and the client so they work mutually toward the success of the client's portfolio. The advisor really becomes an "advisor" to retain the faith and trust of the client.

For example, the advisor is paid on a percentage of assets under management. This means she has a stake in the success of your portfolio. If you have $100,000 in your portfolio and your advisor's fee is 1 percent, then you would pay your advisor $1,000 a year. If your portfolio grows to a value of $200,000, under the same fee structure, you would pay $2,000 a year. Understandably, the advisor's incentive is to seek the best financial program or platform of managers for your separate account. Commissions come and go, but this is building an asset management strategy to satisfy your entire life's goals and objectives.

Growth of the Internet Fuels Interest in Separate Accounts

Harnessing the power of the Internet has fueled further the effectiveness of a separate account for the individual client. Clients can receive their statements, confirmations, performance reviews of their money managers, and individual reviews of securities owned and even financial advice. All this information (and more) is available in real time, 365 days a year. The Internet is shifting the power to the investor away from the providers who no longer hold all the cards in the deck. The Internet has equipped the investor with more information than has ever previously been available. The financial products that meet the expectations of these new knowledge-empowered investors demand more personalized service, tax management, and accountability.

Fee-based Business Is Replacing Commissions

Fee-based pricing is intrinsic to separate accounts. The growth of wrap accounts in which one fee is "wrapped" around the investment portfolio offering a multitude of services is the wave of the future. Investors do not like commissions—the traditional way brokers charge for buy-and-sell trading—and seem to welcome this fee-based option.

> *Professional management and regular reporting for one asset-based fee appeals to people. These are some of the key reasons we hear from both our investment advisors, as well as customers, for the growing popularity of managed accounts.*
> **Stephen Bodurtha, head of investment products, Merrill Lynch**

Today's client puts emphasis on consistent performance and accountability. The fee-based system allows the transparency and up-front understanding of fees that investors want and demand. Mutual funds with their myriad fees are out of sync with these investors. Separate accounts offer what investors of today want. (See Figure 18.2.)

WRAP IT UP

The number one reason for setting up a separate account is tax efficiency. Most taxable investors lose the benefit of their mutual fund performance due to taxes. It is the responsibility of you and your advisor to hire the money manager who is tax-sensitive to accounts similar to yours. With the newer MDAs discussed in Chapter 17, increased focus can be put on tax efficiencies, especially if your sponsor has overlay managers servicing the accounts. Remember, the money manager must manage your account with the goals of tax efficiency and achieving performance returns.

Take full advantage of the customization benefit offered by your separate account. You can restrict the stocks you have in your portfolio. If you wish to eliminate "sin" stocks (e.g., tobacco or alcohol) or support socially responsible companies, instruct your advisor to relay your instructions to your money manager who is responsible for your account.

In a professional separate account portfolio, will all investors and institutions receive the same rate of return? It's possible but very unlikely. This is because tax preferences sometimes will differ with each investor,

Figure 18.2 *The Growth in Popularity of Managed Accounts*

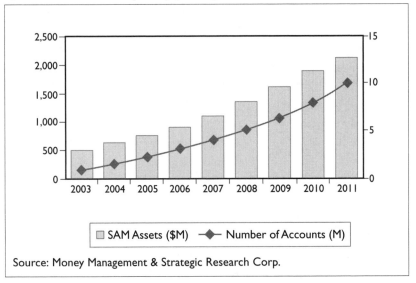

SAM Assets ($M) — Number of Accounts (M)

Source: Money Management & Strategic Research Corp.

due to customization restrictions and the like. The timing between portfolio transactions could differ even if the same money manager is responsible for the accounts. Remember, you are receiving customized investment strategies based on your financial goals and objectives.

When it comes to your bottom line, separate account fees are compatible with mutual fund fees, and are even lower in many cases because of the hidden and incidental fees inherent in mutual funds. With separate accounts, clients can negotiate fees. With mutual funds, they cannot.

Is a Separate Account Right for You?

Hopefully, you will come away from this book knowing if a separate account is right for you. My purpose was to introduce you to an alternative asset management strategy superior to the mutual fund platform for managing your wealth in the stock market. But a separate account is not for every investor.

Separate accounts are for the long-term investor. If you're not willing to take at least a three-year or five-year time horizon to stabilize your account holdings, a separate account may not be for you.

In addition, you have to be willing to delegate the day-to-day hands-on trading to your professional money manager(s). Conversely, if you've been accustomed to having a concentrated portfolio with more aggressive group stocks, a separate account would require you to slow down and possess a more highly diversified portfolio of individual securities.

Thus, restricting the longer time line and desiring a more concentrated grouping of stocks may not make you a good candidate for a separate account. Generally, the way to find out what type of SAM portfolio is for you is by completing a risk questionnaire (like the one in Chapter 13) to learn if you are a conservative, moderate, growth, or aggressive investor.

SET UP YOUR SEPARATE ACCOUNT

When you turn over your assets to a financial advisor and selected money manager(s), you should experience improved returns and less risk, obtain newly found control, and possibly most important, free up time for you to enjoy other aspects of your life.

Managed money offers a renewed relationship with your financial advisor. You and your advisor move to the same side of the desk, both of you working in unison to make your portfolio an investment success. The advisor becomes a true watchdog of your assets.

If you fit the investor profile I have outlined throughout this book, then a separate account could be an excellent, viable investment vehicle for you.

Welcome to a new investment opportunity, one that will give you control over your money, increase your wealth, and decrease taxes and unnecessary fees. Welcome to the best asset management option for your future.

SAMPLE INVESTMENT POLICY STATEMENT

Proposal and Investment Policy Statement

Prepared for: **Sample Client**

> 123 Penny Lane Suite 1
> Anywhere, MI 49123
> *Phone:* 333-444-5555
> *E-mail:* sample.client@abc.co
> *Date:* 08/24/2004

Proposal Name: Sample Proposal
Proposal ID: P0000000

Your Financial Professional is:

Sample Financial Professional
financial.professional@ABC.com

333-444-5566

ABC capital

INTRODUCTION

ABC Capital guides you and your Financial Professional through a comprehensive, four-step process toward helping you identify and achieve your financial objectives. With a separate account, you invest in a portfolio of securities you own directly, run by professional money managers. You have the flexibility to accommodate your investment strategy to your changing financial needs and objectives as they arise throughout life.

The ABC Capital process is designed to assist you and your Financial Professional in monitoring your progress and achieving your objectives. Here's how the process works.

STEP ONE   IDENTIFYING YOUR FINANCIAL GOALS

Objectives - Your first step in creating an effective investment program is working with your Financial Professional to determine your overall financial goals and the time over which you aim to achieve them. Your objectives are based upon your individual life situation, including age, marital and family status, discretionary income, tax situation, and income requirements. As your life changes, so will your objectives.

Risk Tolerance - This is your comfort level when it comes to accepting the uncertainties, complexities, and volatility typically inherent in the stock market. Your risk tolerance is based on your life situation, investment time horizon, and your comfort with variations in the value of your account.

Investment Time Horizon - The time frame over which you plan to work toward attaining your financial goals. Typically, the longer your investment time horizon, the higher the risk you're willing to accommodate, while a shorter time horizon results in a less aggressive investment plan.

STEP TWO   STRATEGY DEVELOPMENT

Asset Allocation - You and your Financial Professional choose an asset allocation model based on your goals, time horizon, and risk tolerance, designed to earn an acceptable rate of return through diversification over a range of asset types. ABC Capital periodically updates your asset allocation to adjust to changing economic conditions.

ABC Capital LLC A Registered Investment Advisor

Manager Selection - ABC Capital selects money managers based on their expertise in specific investment styles best suited to your asset allocation strategy. The managers buy and sell securities in your separate account. ABC Capital regularly reviews manager performance and replaces those who do not meet our criteria with consistency.

Securities Exclusion - Since you directly own the holdings in your portfolio, you may place reasonable restrictions on which securities or sectors you do not want in your account.

STEP THREE   IMPLEMENTATION

Investment Philosophy - Once you and your Financial Professional have identified your financial goals, your time line for working toward them, and an asset allocation strategy, your Financial Professional prepares an investment proposal for your evaluation, which outlines the overall purpose and goals of your separate account. The proposal, once approved, serves as the Investment Policy Statement (IPS) for your account. The IPS specifies the guidelines for managing your account. Typically, the IPS also contains guidelines for you, in terms of adhering to a long-term investment strategy and keeping your Financial Professional informed of any material changes in your financial situation, investment objectives, or securities exclusions.

STEP FOUR   MONITORING

Regular Reports - You can track your separate account performance with in-depth monthly statements and quarterly reports.

Typically, you also have access to your statements and performance reports. Performance is measured in relation to the economy, capital markets, and relevant benchmarks.

Account Rebalancing - Your investment managers periodically rebalance the securities in their portfolios based on market and other economic conditions. ABC Capital periodically rebalances the allocation among money managers in your account to maintain optimal target weightings.

Section 1:   PURPOSE of INVESTMENT POLICY STATEMENT

This Investment Policy Statement is designed to help you and your Financial Professional work toward achieving your financial goals over a specified time frame. Your objectives are based upon your individual life situation, including age, marital and family status, discretionary income, and tax situation and income requirements. As your life changes, so will your objectives. This Investment Policy Statement is set forth in order that:

1. You have a clear understanding of the nature, purpose, and goals of this account.
2. You and your Financial Professional have agreed upon a basis for evaluation of the performance of the Account's assets and respective investment managers.
3. Your Financial Professional is provided with guidance regarding the execution of duties to achieve the Investment objectives as stated in the policy.
4. You understand the roles and responsibilities of ABC Capital, the money managers, and your Financial Professional.

Background Information

Account Type:	Rollover IRA
Federal Tax Bracket:	28% to 35%
State Tax Bracket:	Greater than 9%
Annual Income:	$100,000
Approximate Net Worth:	$2,000,001 to $5,000,000
Total Investable Amount:	$100,000

Section 2:   GUIDELINES and INVESTMENT POLICY

Time Horizon

The time frame over which you plan to work toward attaining your financial goals is an important factor in determining an appropriate investment policy.

Other factors that may impact your time horizon include liquidity needs, emergency fund availability, and substantial contributions or withdrawals to or from the account.

Based upon your responses to the time horizon questions, you have indicated a long-term investment time horizon.

Risk Tolerance

In addition to your time horizon, your willingness to accept the uncertainties, complexities, and volatility typically inherent with investments is important in determining a suitable investment policy. Factors influencing your risk tolerance include, though are not limited to: 1. Comfort with variations in the value of your account. 2. Your current financial situation. 3. Your investment goals. 4. Your life situation.

After taking into account these factors, you have indicated by your responses to a risk-profiling questionnaire, a risk tolerance score of 71 out of 100.

Your risk tolerance assessment is exhibited in the Suitability Questionnaire and Response Summary.

Investment Policy

The primary objectives of the recommended investment policy have been determined by an in-depth review of your financial situation, resources, investment goals, risk tolerance, and time horizon.

Moderate Aggressive
- Moderate to High Risk
- Medium to Long Term
- Moderate to Large Price Fluctuations
- Moderate to High Growth Potential

Asset Class Preferences

You have identified a preference to include the following asset categories in your portfolio:

International Equities

High-Yield Bonds

Investment Methodology

Based on your identified investment objective and asset class preferences, you have selected Moderate Aggressive as your investment methodology.

Section 3:   ASSET ALLOCATION

The ABC Capital investment process is built upon strategic asset allocation. Asset allocation is the process of spreading your investments across a broad range of asset classes. This is commonly known as diversification. While a diversified portfolio may not reap the maximum return of a rising market, it possesses an element of safety during periods of market volatility and corrections.

While ABC Capital does not actively attempt to time short-term investment fluctuations, ABC Capital implements changes in strategic asset allocation periodically to adjust the portfolio to changing market and client conditions.

The following asset allocation has been identified, based upon client financial resources, goals, time horizon, tax status, asset class constraints, and risk tolerance, and is meant to be a long-term strategy for working toward attaining your investment goals.

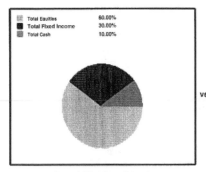

Total Equities	60.00%
Total Fixed Income	30.00%
Total Cash	10.00%

vs.

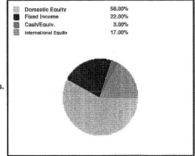

Domestic Equity	58.00%
Fixed Income	22.00%
Cash/Equiv.	3.00%
International Equity	17.00%

Current Allocation of Assets   Recommended Allocation of Assets

Section 4:   HYPOTHETICAL RANGE OF RETURNS

We designed your selected portfolio allocation based on the historical performance of asset classes as measured by commonly accepted indices. Specifically, we structured the portfolio by taking your investment objectives and instructions on how you want to balance risk and return and matching them to asset classes that historically have displayed similar risk-return characteristics.

The chart below shows the hypothetical range of returns of a portfolio with an asset allocation that resembles the asset allocation of your selected portfolio over different time periods. The chart is merely an indication of how the asset allocation might have performed in the past if a similar asset allocation portfolio had been constructed.

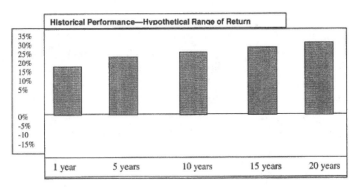

Historical Performance—Hypothetical Range of Return

The actual performance of your portfolio will vary from the hypothetical range of return set forth in the graph above. This chart does not reflect the performance of actual accounts, but rather, it reflects only the performance of asset classes as measured by commonly accepted indices. The information set forth in the chart above is limited in a number of respects, including: (i) the investment disciplines used to develop your portfolio did not exist during most of the period in which the historical data used in the above presentation was derived; (ii) your portfolio returns will be affected by the deduction of your wrap fee and other expenses (as described in our brochure) that, when compounded over the years, will further decrease your portfolio's actual

Proposal and Investment Policy Statement	
	Prepared for: Sample Client Proposa ID: C000000 Page 8 of 15 8/24/05

performance; (iii) the presentation assumes reinvestment of dividends and other income into the asset classes generating the income; and (iv) the presentation assumes that the assets in the portfolio are allocated consistently over the given period. Portfolios inevitably experience drift from the original model allocation upon which they were based. Accordingly, as our Model Portfolios drift from the performance of the asset classes they represent, we will substitute or change the securities comprising the portfolio. More important, investors revise their allocations to reflect current events and changing market and economic conditions. We will likely change our portfolio allocations and Model Portfolios as we believe necessary. Performance will not necessarily be constant, and there could be significant multiyear losses. **PAST RESULTS ARE NOT INDICATIVE OF FUTURE RETURNS.**

Section 5:   MANAGER SELECTION

Investment managers are selected based upon their expertise in managing assets to a specific style. The following managers have been selected based upon the recommended asset allocation strategy and your authorization. These managers have undergone rigorous screening to ascertain their qualifications to participate in the ABC Capital investment program, and undergo regular, periodic review to ensure their adherence to the investment philosophy and fulfillment of client performance expectations.

ABC capital

Section 8: FEES

Prepared for: Sample Client
Proposal ID: 00000000
Page 9 of 15   8/24/05

Domestic Equity	58.00 %
Large-Cap Growth	**18.47 %**
ABC Large-Cap Growth PSP	12.31 %
Sands Capital Management	6.16 %
Small-/Mid-Cap Growth	**4.36 %**
ABC Small-Cap Growth PSP	2.18 %
Fred Alger Small-Cap Growth	8.22 %
Large-Cap Core	**12.33 %**
ABC Capital Large-Cap Core	4.11 %
Sosnoff Capital Large Cap	8.22 %
Large-Cap Value	**18.48 %**
ABC Large-Cap Value PSP	12.33 %
ABC Capital Large-Cap Value	6.16 %
Small-/Mid-Cap Value	4.36 %
CM Asset Mgmt Small-Cap Value	2.18 %
ABC Smal-Cap Value PSP	2.18 %
Fixed Income	**22.00 %**
High-Yield Bond	3.00 %
High-Yield Fixed Income	3.00 %
Intermediate-Term Fixed Income	19.00 %
Fixed Income Model	19.00%
Cash/Equivalent	**3.00 %**
Cash/Equivalent	3..00%

ABC Capital

Proposal and Investment Policy Statement

International Equity	17.00%
International Equity	17.00%
Deutsche International Large-Cap Gr	4.25%
ABC Large-Cap ADR PSP	0.65%
ABC International Value ADR ABC	4.25%
International Mid-Cap ADR PS	0.85%

Section 6:   MONITORING and REVIEW

Investment monitoring is conducted periodically, evaluating, account performance in relation to stated investment objectives. Relative performance measurement is also utilized to evaluate portfolio management in relation to the economy, capital markets, and relevant benchmarks.

An Investment Policy Statement is a dynamic document that changes over time to reflect your changing life circumstances. Such changes naturally affect your goals, needs, time horizons, and levels of risk tolerance.

You should meet with your Financial Professional to review your IPS at least once each year, or more often if necessary.
Review meetings typically cover:

1. Any adjustments which may be necessary to your account.
2. Existing and recommended asset allocation.
3. Review of present and prospective economic factors affecting the portfolio.
4. Review of level of risk represented in the portfolio and asset allocation strategy.
5. Review of portfolio performance with respect to investment objectives.

Since the nature of the investment program is long term, periodic adjustments will be small.

Section 7:   PORTFOLIO CUSTOMIZATION

Among the primary attributes of a managed account program are the abilities to:

1. **Control of account rebalancing** whenever asset allocation is modified. ABC Capital will periodically adjust or rebalance portfolios based on market and economic conditions. You may opt to rebalance concurrently with ABC Capital adjustments and on a periodic calendar schedule (annually or semiannually) based upon specific goals and objectives.

You have selected an Annual rebalancing schedule.

2. Securities exclusions are based on a social rationale, for example, the securities of tobacco, gambling, firearms, military contractors, and nuclear power companies. Additionally, you may exclude the securities of specific companies altogether from the investment program. You have identified the following categories you wish excluded from your portfolio: **Tobacco**

Section 8:   FEES

Fees are based on a percentage of overall assets under management in the account.

Your fees are based on the investment amount and selected model.

- Based on your investment selection, your total wrap fee is: 2.90%

Money manager rates, which are included in your total wrap fee, are a blended average of the individual managers selected for your account. The actual fee for money managers may vary over time, depending on factors including:

1. Fee schedule for each money manager.

2. Each manager's percentage of the overall assets in your account.

3. Quantitative and active managers employed in your account.

CONCLUSION

This Investment Policy Statement is not a contractual obligation, but a guideline and tool to assist you, your Financial Professional, and selected investment managers in thoroughly understanding and working toward the objectives of your account. As such, it is important to remember that keeping your Financial Professional informed of any material changes in your financial situation, investment objectives, and securities exclusions is critical to the success of your investment strategy. A prudent plan calls for communicating with your Financial Professional on a quarterly basis.

Remember, investing is a multistep process. ABC Capital helps you and your Financial Professional assess your financial characteristics and objectives, enabling you to properly evaluate what you want to accomplish with your investment strategy. It also helps you and your Financial Professional create objective guidelines to help you at critical times when perhaps emotions may tempt you to react against your best interests during market volatility. Once you've put the investment process into motion, you're actively working toward attaining your financial goals.

ACCEPTANCE AND ADOPTION

| Proposal and Investment Policy Statement | ABC Capital |

Prepared for: Sample Client
Proposal ID. 00000000
Page 13 of 15   8/24/05

I (we) have reviewed, approved, and adopted this Investment Policy Statement for the investment program prepared with the assistance of Sample Financial Professional.

INVESTOR'S SIGNATURE   DATE

Sample Client

SUITABILITY QUESTIONAIRE AND RESPONSE SUMMARY

Given your investment objective, how many years from now do you wish to begin making withdrawals from this investment?

C) 10+ years

Once you begin to take withdrawals from this account, over how many years do you expect withdrawals to continue?

D) 10+ years

Which statement best summarizes your response towards fluctuations in the value of your investment account?

D) My primary objective is to increase the potential for higher returns on my portfolio. I realize that in order to achieve this goal, there may be significant fluctuations in the value of my portfolio.

Please specify your preferences regarding the impact of inflation on your investment portfolio.

B) I am willing to accept moderate fluctuations in my investment portfolio for the potential that my investment portfolio may moderately outpace inflation.

The graph above is a hypothetical illustration that does not show the probability that investing in specific securities will produce a desired result. It is only designed to gauge a client's risk tolerance. For each portfolio, the potential gain and loss at the end of a one-year period for a $100,000.00 investment is shown. The number above each bar shows the potential gain, while the number below the bar shows the potential loss. Considering that this is the only information that you have on these hypothetical portfolios, which one would you choose to invest in?

D) Portfolio 4

The table below displays the worst, most likely, and best expected returns for five hypothetical investment portfolios over a three-year holding period. Which of the following portfolios would you be most comfortable holding?

D) Portfolio 4

One of the most important risks investors face is the risk of losing money on their investment portfolio. However, history has shown that investments with higher risk of losing money in the short term generally have provided higher returns over the long run. As a result, investors must balance the trade-off between return potential and risk when building their investment portfolio. Based upon your stated investment amount of $100,000.00, the possible gain estimate and probability of losing money after one year are shown for five hypothetical portfolios. Based upon the trade-off below, which of these five hypothetical portfolios contain the potential gain/chance of loss characteristics that you find most suitable?

D) Portfolio 4

Securities from companies domiciled outside the United States (international securities) have additional risk factors not normally associated with domestic securities, like currency risk, political risk, and information risk. However, when combined with a well-rounded domestic portfolio, international securities can potentially benefit your portfolio by expanding the investment set and by providing diversification benefits. What statement best illustrates your opinion on incorporating international securities in your portfolio?

A)   I wish to include international securities in my portfolio. These international securities included in my portfolio may be in the form of American Depository Receipts (Dears), exchange-traded funds (ETFs), or mutual funds. I am aware of the diversification benefits these securities can provide.

Industry Associations

The Financial Planning Association
Membership organization created in 2000 by combining Certified
Financial Planners (CFP) and the International Association for
Financial Planning (IAFP). This organization furthers the cause of
financial planning as a profession. It can locate suitable planners
for investors.
http://www.fpanet.org
800-322-4237

National Association of Insurance and Financial Advisors (NAIFA)
Founded in 1890, NAIFA is the nation's largest financial services membership association. Its mission is to advocate for a positive legislative and regulatory environment, enhance business and professional
skills, and promote the ethical conduct of its members. The investors section of the Web site gives financial guidance and sources for
advisors.
http://www.naifa.org
703-770-8100

The National Association of Personal Financial Advisors (NAPFA)
The National Association of Personal Financial Advisors is the nation's
leading organization of fee-only comprehensive financial planning
professionals. Since 1983, NAPFA's ranks have enjoyed steady
growth, operating under a strict *code of ethics* and *fiduciary oath*.
NAPFA members are trusted, objective financial advisors for consumers and institutions alike. The investors section on the Web site
gives financial advice and includes a fee-only advisor search.
http://www.napfa.org
800-366-2732

Money Management Institute (MMI)
This national organization represents the separately managed account and wealth-management industry. Organized in 1997, it serves as a forum for the separately managed account industry's leaders to address common concerns, discuss industry issues, and work together to better serve investors. The institute is the leading advocate for the industry on regulatory and legislative issues.
http://www.moneyinstitute.com
202-822-4949

Investment Company Institute (ICI)
This national association represents mutual fund investment companies. Founded in 1940, its mutual fund members represent 87.7 million individual shareholders and manage $7.959 trillion in investor assets. The Web site includes numerous education sections for investors.
http://www.ici.org
202-326-5890

Regulating Agencies

National Association of Security Dealers (NASD)
For more than 60 years, NASD has served as the primary private-sector regulator of America's securities industry. The agency oversees the activities of more than 5,100 brokerage firms, approximately 100,400 branch offices, and more than 660,000 registered securities representatives. In addition, it provides outsourced regulatory services to a number of stock markets and exchanges.
http://www.nasd.com
301-590-6500

Securities and Exchange Commission (SEC)
The SEC is the agency responsible for administering federal securities laws in the United States.
http://www.sec.gov
800-SEC-0330 (800-732-0330)

Financial Research Firms

Cerulli Associates
Cerulli Associates is a Boston-based research and consulting firm specializing exclusively in the financial services industry. It is recognized throughout the industry as a leading source of guidance, information, and data for different markets it covers, especially in the area of separately managed accounts.
http://www.cerulli.com
617-437-0084

Financial Research Corporation (FRC)
Based in Boston, FRC is a full-service product and distribution research firm that works to support its 200 client-based business goals. It concentrates in eight expert subject areas including mutual funds, managed accounts, retirement accounts, college savings, and variable annuities.
http://www.frcnet.com
617-824-1325

DALBAR Research
For over 25 years, DALBAR, Inc., has concentrated its research services in the financial services industry. Headquartered in Boston, with an additional office in Toronto, DALBAR develops standards and provides research for the mutual fund, broker-dealer, discount brokerage, life insurance, and banking industries.
http://www.dalbarinc.com
617-723-6400

Lipper
Lipper, a Reuters company, is a global leader in supplying mutual fund information, analytical tools, and commentary. Lipper's benchmarking assists asset managers, fund companies, financial intermediaries, traditional media, Web sites, and individual investors.
http://www.lipperweb.com
877-955-4773

Morningstar

Morningstar is a source for insightful information on stocks, mutual funds, variable annuities, closed-end funds, exchange-traded funds, separate accounts, hedge funds, and 529 college savings plans. It operates in 16 countries, and currently tracks more than 125,000 investment offerings worldwide. It is a good resource for investors.

http://www.morningstar.com

312-384-4000

Tiburon Strategic Advisors

Tiburon was formed in 1998 to offer market research, strategy consulting, and other related services primarily to financial services firms. It is based in Tiburon, California.

http://www.tiburonadvisors.com

415-789-2540

Resources for Investors

Personal Fund, Inc., gives investors up-to-date information on how to invest successfully. It provides a number of tools to help investors determine the right portfolio mix. One of its strongest tools is allowing the investor to determine all fees incurred with any mutual fund.

http://www.personalfund.com

Investopedia.com has a substantial glossary of financial terms but more than that, it educates all levels of investors on the latest trends in financial management.

http://www.investopedia.com

CCH's Web site contains a Financial Planning Toolkit providing numerous financial tools and calculators to assist investors in retirement planning, investing principals, etc.

http://www.finance.cch.com

All consumers will have the right to examine free copies of their credit reports by end of the year. The Fed is phasing in this process so all consumers will have right to examine credit reports at no charge.
http://www.annualcreditreport.com

Beginners and expert investors alike can get answers to financial questions at this Web site. A free investing newsletter is available.
http://www.invest-faq.com

The Internet Legal Resource Guide is a resource index for any investor in need of legal advice and appropriate legal forms.
http://www.ilrg.com

The American Saving Education Council provides numerous retirement planning tools to give retirees a clearer picture of their financial futures.
http://www.asec.org

The *Fund Police* takes a hard-nosed look at why you should be getting out of mutual funds. It offers a critical report titled, "Mutual Funds Unmasked."
http://www.fundpolice.com

Gain Keeper arms you with accurate tax cost data, capital gains analysis, and trade decision tools to maximize after-tax returns.
http://www.gainskeeper.com

The *Bond Market Association's* Web site provides information about bonds for investors who are looking for safer investments.
http://investinginbonds.com

Chapter 1

1. Paul Ferrell, "It's the Expenses, Stupid," retrieved from http://cbs.marketwatch.com/news/print_story.asp?print+1&guid=[9F36107-90B4-46DB- AD63-FD657E288583]&siteid-mtw.

Chapter 2

1. Arthur Levitt, *Take On the Street* (Pantheon Books, 2002), 43.

2. John C. Bogle, *Common Sense on Mutual Funds* (John Wiley & Sons, 2003), 34.

3. John Bogle, "Saint Jack on the Attack," retrieved from http://www.fortune.com/fortune/print/0.15935.406061.00.html. © 2003 Time, Inc. All rights reserved.

4. Richard Karlgarrd, "Sorry I Stank," *Forbes,* January 13, 2000.

5. John Bogle, "Saint Jack on the Attack."

6. Arthur Levitt, statement during appearance at congressional hearing on mutual fund fraud, November 4, 2003, retrieved from http://www.pbs.org/newshour/bb/business/july-dec03/mutual_11-4.html.

Chapter 3

1. "Industry Scandal Hits American Funds," statement from vice chairman of NASD, Mary L. Schapiro, retrieved from http://www.marketwatch.com/news/print_story.asp?print=1&guid={DD%DBA06-F28A-4CDC-8D20-A33CD9C

2. Jason Greene, retrieved September 11, 2003, from http://www.moneycentral.msn.com.

3. Russel Kinnel, "Unfinished Business from the Fund Scandal," Morningstar, retrieved from http://news.morningstar.com/doc/document/print/1.3651.125808,00.html.

4. "More Mutual Funds Disclosure Is Coming," *Investment News,* April 23, 2005.

5. AMG annual flow summary, AMG Data Services, retrieved April 22, 2005, from http://www.amgdata.com.

6. Hersh M. Shefrin, Santa Clara University professor, retrieved April 23, 2005, from http://www.nytimes.com/2004/01/11/business/mutfund/11fund.html.

7. Don Cassidy, senior research analyst, Lipper, Inc., retrieved April 23, 2005, from http://www.nytimes.com/2004/01/11/business/mutfund/11fund.html.

Chapter 4

1. Paul B. Ferrell, "Ten Habits of Highly Irrational Investors," *MarketWatch,* December 14, 2004, retrieved from http://www.cbsmarket watch.com/news/print.asp?print-1&guid-(75C6ECIF-C19D-4BOF-A36E-2C62CV257739F)&SITEID-mkrw.

2. Whitney Tilson, "The Perils of Investor Overconfidence," quote from Warren Buffett, retrieved March 21, 2005, from http://www.fool.com/Boringport/1999?BoringPort990920.htm.

3. Brad Barber, "Do Individual Day Traders Make Money: Evidence from Taiwan," February 1, 2005, retrieved March 28, 2005, from http://www.fool.com/Boringport/1999?BoringPort990920.htm.

4. Ibid.

5. "Quantitative Analysis of Investor Behavior," DALBAR Research, retrieved April 2, 2005, from http://www.dalbarinc.com/content/show page.asp?pages+2001062100.htm.

Chapter 5

1. Erick H. Davison and Kevin D. Freeman. *Investing in Separate Accounts* (McGraw-Hill, 2002), 25.

2. Cerulli Associates, compiled from published research.

Chapter 6

1. Investment Company Institute, retrieved March 15, 2005, from http://www.ici.com.

2. SEC ruling.

3. Fatima Sulaiman, "SEC Adopts Final Rule Requiring Disclosure of Mutual Fund After-Tax Returns," retrieved December 28, 2004, from http://www.cybersecuritieslaw.com/KL/sulaiman1.htm.

4. "Many Investors Not Aware of SEC Rule on Fund After-Tax Disclosure," 3rd annual Easton Vance survey, retrieved December 24, 2004, from http://www.womenfinance.com/mutualfunds/secrule.shtml.

5. Brooke A. Masters, "Regulators Reach Deal with Strong, Fund Firm," May 20, 2004, retrieved April 20, 2005, from http://www.washingtonpost.com.

6. John Waggoner, "Seek Good Return, Low Turnover," *USA TODAY*, June 6, 2000, from Lipper study, retrieved from http://www.usatoday.com/money/perfi/columist/waggon/0017.htm.

7. Stefan Sharkansky, "Mutual Fund Costs: Risk Without Reward," *Personal Fund Inc.*, July 2002. Also interview with author, March 2005.

8. Richard Rutner, *The Trouble with Mutual Funds*, 2d ed. (Elton Wolfe Publishing, 2002), 60–61.

9. Louis Corrigan, "Fool on the Hill—Buy and Hold Beats Rapid Trading," retrieved from http://www.fool.com/eveningnews/foth/1998/foth980610.htm.

Chapter 7

1. Lipper Analytical Services, retrieved from http//lipperweb.com.

2. Richard Rutner, *The Trouble with Mutual Funds*, 2d ed. (Elton Wolfe Publishing, 2002), 25.

3. David M. Stein "Separate Is More Than Equal," *Financial Planning*, October 1, 2002, retrieved from http://www.financial-planning.com. Also interview with author, March 21, 2005.

4. Paul Royce, "Navigating the Mutual Fund Industry through Challenging Times," retrieved from http://www.see.gov/news/speech491 .htm.

5. Margaret Myers, "Information Disclosure Regulation and the Return to Active Management in the Mutual Fund Industry," retrieved from http://www.mit.edu/faculty/poterba/files/copycatoct2001.pdf.

6. Lorie Richards, SEC inspections official, retrieved from available research.

7. *Barron's*, retrieved from http://www.financial–planning.com/ cgi bin/print.

Chapter 8

1. "Few Actually Use SMA Customization," *Financial Planning*, retrieved from http://www.financial-planning.com/cgi-bin/print.pl.

Chapter 9

1. Richard Rutner, *The Trouble with Mutual Funds*, 2d ed. (Elton Wolfe Publishing, 2002), 31.

Chapter 10

1. Peter Tedstrom, Brown & Tedstrom, interview with author, April 6, 2005.

2. David Thompson, Phoenix Marketing International, retrieved from available research.

3. Troy Daum, Wealth Analytics, retrieved from available research.

Chapter 11

1. Max Rottersman, http://www.fundforensics.com, interview with author, March 16, 2005.

2. Richard Rutner, *The Trouble with Mutual Funds,* 2d ed. (Elton Wolfe Publishing, 2002), 58.

3. David Gardner and Tom Gardner, *The Feeling Isn't Mutual: The Motley Fool Investment Guide* (Simon & Schuster).

4. "Portfolio Transactions Cost at U.S. Equity Mutual Funds," Zero Alpha Group study, November 17, 2004, retrieved from http://www.ze roalphagroup.com/headlines/hiddenstudy111704.html.

5. Bob Enright, partner in Burton/Enright Group, interview with author, April 5, 2005.

6. Kieran Beer, "Held to Account," *Bloomberg Wealth Manager*, December 2004, 60.

7. "Interest in IMAs Continues to Grow," *Ticker*, June 2002, 20.

Chapter 12

1. Robert B. Jorgensen, *Individually Managed Accounts: An Investor's Guide* (John Wiley & Sons, Inc., 2003), 47.

2. Scott MacKillop, Trivium Consulting, retrieved from available data.

3. Richard Rutner, *The Trouble with Mutual Funds*, 2d ed. (Elton Wolfe Publishing, 2002), 32.

Chapter 13

1. Cerulli Associates, interview with author March 23, 2005.

2. Comment from Cerulli Associates, retrieved from http://www .thestreet.com/pf/funds/belowradar/10009217.html.

3. Chris Consentino, Money Management Institute, interview with author March 23, 2005.

4. Money Management Institute, retrieved January 3, 2005, from http://www.moneymarketinstitute.com.

5. Robert B. Jorgensen, *Individually Managed Accounts* (John Wiley & Sons, 2003), 118.

6. Larry Chambers, *Separate Account Management* (John Wiley & Sons, 2003), 87.

7. J. E. Grable and R. H. Lytton, "Financial Risk Tolerance Revisited: The Development of a Risk Assessment Instrument," *Financial Services Review* 8 (1999):163–81.

Chapter 14

1. Paul Fullerton, Cerulli Associates, interview with author, March 20, 2005.

2. Larry Chambers, *Separate Account Management* (John Wiley & Sons, 2003), 29.

3. Ibid., 38.

4. Laurie Kulikowski, *Financial Planning,* December 2001, 26.

Chapter 15

1. Kieran Beer, "Held to Account," *Bloomberg Wealth Magazine,* January 2005, 60.

2. Cerulli Associates, compiled from published research.

3. Ibid.

4. Larry Chambers, *Separate Account Management* (John Wiley & Sons 2003), 161.

5. Cerulli Associates, compiled from published research.

6. Christopher Davis, Money Management Institute, retrieved from published research.

7. Erik H. Davison and Kevin D. Freeman, *Investing in Separate Accounts* (McGraw-Hill, 2002), 34.

Chapter 16

1. Matt Schott, TowerGroup, interview with author, March 2005.

2. "Investment Folio for the Average Joe," retrieved March 25, 2005, from http://www.wired.com/news/print/0,1294,65869,00.html.

3. Rick Cortez, "Hedge Funds Likely in Managed Accounts," November 7, 2003, retrieved from http://yahoo.com/ap/041107/managing_money_hedge_funds_1.htm.

Chapter 17

1. "The Wealth Effect," retrieved from http://www.investopedia
.com/terms/w/wealtheffect.asp.

2. Len Lockhart and Chris Farrell, "Remembering the Pre-Millennium Bull Run," March 6, 2002, retrieved from http://www.rightonthe money.org/docs/commentary0307.html.

3. "Market Update: The Managed Account and Wrap Industry," research paper by Cerulli Associates.

4. Gabriel Burezyk, WrapManager, Inc., interview with author, April 5, 2005.

5. "Consumer Use of the Internet for Financial Services," DALBAR Research (2001), retrieved March 21, 2005, from http://www.dalbar inc.com/content/showpage.asp?page=200111011101.html.

6. Ken Little, "Who's Watching Your Back," *Your Guide to Stocks*, re trieved from http://www.stocks.about.com/od/tradingbasics/a/Regulat()11705_p.htm.

Chapter 18

1. Money Management Institute, retrieved from http://www.money managementinstitute.com.

2. "SMA Assets Continue to Climb in 2004," Money Management Institute, retrieved from http://www.moneymanagmentinstitute.com.

accredited investor A term used by the SEC under Regulation D to define investors who are financially sophisticated and have no need for the protection provided by certain government filings; also knows as a *qualified purchaser.*

acquisition cost Cost of acquiring a property, in addition to the purchase price, such as title insurance and lender's fees (e.g., with FHA, acquisition is a set amount based on the appraised value of the property).

active investing An investment strategy involving the ongoing buying and selling actions of the investor. Active investors will purchase investments and continuously monitor their activity in order to exploit profitable conditions.

advisor An individual or firm that usually charges fees for services versus commissions.

asset allocation Deciding how much of an investor's funds will be put into stocks, bonds, or any other investment based on goals, time frame, and degree of risk.

asset class A specific category of assets or investments, such as stocks, bonds, and real estate.

back office Administration and support personnel in a financial services company. They carry out functions like settlements, clearances, record maintenance, regulatory compliance, and accounting. When order processing is slow due to high volume, it is commonly referred to as *back office crunch.*

balanced return A portfolio allocation and management method aimed at balancing risk and return.

basis point A unit for measuring a bond's yield that is equal to $\frac{1}{100}$ of 1 percent of yield; also known as *bps.*

basis risk The risk that offsetting investments in a hedging strategy will not experience price changes in entirely opposite directions from each other. This imperfect correlation between the two investments creates the potential for excess gains or losses in a hedging strategy, thus adding risk to the position.

bear market A market condition in which the prices of securities are falling or are expected to fall. Although figures can vary, a downturn of 15 percent to 20 percent or more in multiple indexes (Dow or S&P 500) is considered an entry into a bear market.

behavior finance A field of finance that proposes psychology-based theories to explain stock market anomalies. Within behavioral finance it is assumed that the information structure and the characteristics of market participants systematically influence individuals' investment decisions as well as market outcomes.

Black Tuesday On this day, October 29, 1929, the Dow Jones Industrial Average fell 12 percent—one of the largest one-day drops in stock market history. More than 16 million shares were traded in a panic sell-off.

board of directors A group of individuals who are elected by stockholders to establish corporate management policies and make decisions on major company issues, such as dividend policies.

bottom-up investing An investment approach that de-emphasizes the significance of economic and market cycles. This approach focuses on the analysis of individual stocks.

broker An individual or firm that charges a fee or commission for executing buy-and-sell orders submitted by an investor.

broker-dealer A person or firm in the business of buying and selling securities operating as both a broker and dealer depending on the transaction.

bull market A financial market of a certain group of securities in which prices are rising or are expected to rise. The term *bull market* is most often used in respect to the stock market, but really can be applied to anything that is traded, such as bonds, currencies, commodities, etc.

business cycle The recurring and fluctuating levels of economic activity that an economy experiences over a long period of time. The five stages of the business cycle are growth (expansion), peak, recession (contraction), trough, and recovery. At one time, business cycles were thought to be extremely regular, with predictable durations. But today business cycles are widely known to be irregular, varying in frequency, magnitude, and duration.

buy and hold A passive investment strategy with which an investor buys stocks and holds them for a long period regardless of fluctuations in the market.

Certified Financial Planner (CFP) An individual who successfully completes the Certified Financial Planner Board's initial and ongoing CFP certification requirements.

Chartered Financial Analyst A professional designation given by the Chartered Financial Analyst Institute (formerly AIMR), a group that measures the competence and integrity of financial analysts. Candidates are required to pass three levels of exams covering areas such as accounting, economics, ethics, money management, and security analysis.

churning An unethical practice employed by some brokers to increase their commissions by excessively trading in a client's account. This practice violates the NASD fair practice rules. It is also referred to as *twisting*.

closet indexing A portfolio strategy used by some portfolio managers to achieve returns similar to those of their benchmark index, without exactly replicating the index.

The CNN Effect The temporary shifting of consumer spending that occurs as a result of gripping news.

commingled fund A type of mutual fund consisting of assets from several accounts that are blended together; sometimes called a *pooled fund*.

cook the books A fraudulent activity done by some corporations to falsify their financial statements.

derivative A security, such as an option or futures contract, whose value depends on the performance of an underlying security or asset.

direct rollover A distribution of eligible rollover assets from a qualified plan, 403(b) plan, or a governmental 457 plan to a traditional IRA, qualified plan, 403(b) plan, or a governmental 457 plan; or a distribution from an IRA to a qualified plan, 403(b) plan, or a governmental 457 plan.

diversification A risk management technique that mixes a wide variety of investments within a portfolio. It is designed to minimize the impact of any one security on overall portfolio performance.

dollar cost averaging The technique of buying a fixed dollar amount of a particular investment on a regular schedule, regardless of the share price. More shares are purchased when prices are low, and fewer shares are bought when prices are high.

dot-com A company that embraces the Internet as the key component in its business.

Dow Jones Industrial Average The Dow Jones Industrial Average (DJIA) is a price-weighted average of 30 significant stocks traded on the New York Stock Exchange and the Nasdaq. Charles Dow created the DJIA back in 1896.

due diligence An investigation or audit of a potential investment. Due diligence serves to confirm all material facts in regards to a sale. Generally, due diligence refers to the care a reasonable person should take before entering into an agreement or transaction with another party.

eat well, sleep well An adage that, referring to the risk/return trade-off, says that the type of security an investor chooses depends on whether he or she wants to eat well or sleep well.

fiduciary A person legally appointed and authorized to hold assets in trust for another person. The fiduciary manages the assets for the benefit of the other person rather than for his or her own profit.

financial planner A qualified investment professional who assists individuals and corporations to meet their long-term financial objectives by analyzing the client's status and setting a program to achieve these goals. They are specialized in tax planning, asset allocation, risk management, retirement planning, and/or estate planning.

financial risk The risk that a company will not have adequate cash flow to meet financial obligations.

financial supermarket A company offering a wide range of financial services (e.g., stocks, insurance, and real-estate brokerage).

Form ADV A form that is kept on file with the SEC that contains critical financial information about a registered investment advisor.

fund manager The person responsible for investing a mutual fund's assets, implementing its investment strategy, and managing the day-to-day portfolio trading.

gross national product An economic statistic that includes gross domestic product (GDP), plus any income earned by residents from overseas investments, minus income earned within the domestic economy by overseas residents.

growth stock A diversified portfolio of stocks that has capital appreciation as its primary goal, and thereby invests in companies that reinvest their earnings into expansion, acquisitions, and/or research and development.

hedge fund An aggressively managed fund portfolio taking positions in both safe and speculative opportunities.

herd instinct A mentality characterized by a lack of individuality, causing people to think and act like the general population.

income stock A stock with a history of regular dividend payments that constitute the largest portion of the stock's overall return.

index fund A portfolio of investments that are weighted the same as a stock-exchange index in order to mirror its performance. This process is also referred to as *indexing*.

inside trading The buying or selling of a security by someone who has access to material, nonpublic information about the security.

institutional fund A mutual fund targeting high-value investors with low fees, but high minimum requirements.

Investment Act of 1940 The federal law enforced and interpreted by the Securities and Exchange Commission (SEC) that governs investment advisors.

load fund A mutual fund with shares sold at a price including a large sales charge. This sales fee may range from 3 percent to as high as 8 percent of the full purchase.

managed account An investment account that is owned by an individual investor and looked after by a hired professional money manager and a financial advisor. In contrast to mutual funds (which are professionally managed on behalf of many mutual fund holders), managed accounts are personalized investment portfolios tailored to the specific needs of the account holder.

managed money An investor's portfolio assets that are turned over to the direction of a professional money manager, who in turn makes the investment decisions for the assets. Generally available through major brokerage firms, managed money gives the individual investor the opportunity to invest with reputable money managers. This quality of private portfolio management is available typically for a single all-inclusive annual fee. Instead of being transaction oriented, the management fee is calculated as a percentage of the assets under administration. The annual fees generally range from 1 percent to 3 percent and pay for the services of the investment advisor, who has full discretion over the active management of the account in accordance with the investor's stated objectives.

market timing The act of attempting to predict the future direction of the market, typically through the use of technical indicators or economic data. Also, the practice of switching among mutual fund asset classes in an attempt to profit from the changes in their market outlook.

mid-cap Short for "middle capitalization," mid-cap refers to stocks with a market capitalization of between $2 billion to $10 billion.

modern portfolio theory A theory on how risk-averse investors can construct portfolios in order to optimize market risk for expected returns, emphasizing that risk is an inherent part of higher reward; also called *portfolio theory* or *portfolio management theory*.

money management The process of managing money. It is typically performed by professional money managers (also known as *portfolio managers*) who oversee and have full discretion over large investment portfolios of pension funds, endowments, and institutional and individual investors; also known as *investment management*.

money manager A business or bank responsible for managing the securities portfolio of an individual or institutional investor. Typically, a money manager employs people with various expertise ranging from research and selection of investment options to monitoring the assets and deciding when to sell them. In return for a fee, the money manager has the fiduciary duty to choose and manage investments prudently for his or her clients, including developing an appropriate investment strategy, and buying and selling securities to meet those goals. Also known as *portfolio manager* or *investment manager*.

mutual fund A security that gives small investors access to a well-diversified portfolio of equities, bonds, and other securities. Each shareholder participates in the gain or loss of the fund. Shares are issued and can be redeemed as needed. The fund's net asset value (NAV) is determined each day. Each mutual fund portfolio is invested to match the objective stated in the prospectus.

mutual fund timing A legal but frowned-upon practice whereby traders attempt to profit from the short-term differences between the daily closing prices of a mutual fund. Timing occurs when investors attempt to gain short-term profits from buying and selling mutual funds. This has a negative effect on the fund's long-term holders, as they will be subjugated to higher fees due to the short-term trading. In order to prevent this, many mutual funds will impose a short-term trading penalty upon the sale of funds that are not held for a minimum period of time. This transfers the short-term costs of buying and selling new shares within the fund's portfolio to those investors not planning to stay with the fund for the long term. Don't confuse mutual fund timing with *market timing*. Market timing is a practice of trying to predict the best time to buy and sell stocks for the purpose of a short-term gain. Mutual fund timing is a practice publicly frowned upon by many mutual fund companies in their prospectuses.

online trading Making trades via the Internet.

portfolio management The art and science of making decisions about investment mix and policy, matching investments to objectives, asset allocation for individuals and institutions, and balancing risk versus performance.

prospectus A formal legal document describing the details of a corporation. The prospectus is generally created for a proposed offering (usually an IPO), but it can still be obtained from existing businesses as well. The prospectus includes company facts that are vitally important to potential investors.

return on assets A useful indicator of how profitable a company is relative to its total assets. Calculated by dividing a company's annual earnings by its total assets, return on assets (ROA) is displayed as a percentage. Sometimes this is referred to as *return on investment*.

Securities and Exchange Commission The Securities and Exchange Commission (SEC) is a government commission created by Congress to regulate the securities markets and protect investors. In addition to regulation and protection, it also monitors corporate takeovers in the United States. The SEC is composed of five commissioners appointed by the president of the United States and approved by the Senate. The statutes administered by the SEC are designed to promote full public disclosure and protect the investing public against fraudulent and manipulative practices in the securities markets. Generally, most issues of securities offered in interstate commerce, through the mail, or on the Internet must be registered with the SEC.

S&P 500 An index consisting of 500 stocks chosen for market size, liquidity, and industry group representation, among other factors. The S&P 500 is designed to be a leading indicator of U.S. equities, and it is meant to reflect the risk/return characteristics of the large-cap universe.

Companies included in the index are selected by the S&P Index Committee, which is a team of analysts and economists at Standard and Poor's. The S&P 500 is a market value weighted index, which means each stock's weight in the index is proportionate to its market value.

tax-loss harvesting A process of selling securities at a loss to offset a capital gains tax liability. It is typically used to limit the recognition of short-term capital gains, which are normally taxed at higher federal income-tax rates than long-term capital gains. Also known as *tax-loss selling*.

volatility A statistical measure of the tendency of a market or security to rise or fall sharply within a period of time.

Warren Buffett Known as "the Oracle of Omaha," Buffett is chairman of Berkshire Hathaway and arguably the greatest investor of all time. His wealth fluctuates with the performance of the market, but for the last few years he has been reported to be worth over $30 billion, making him the second richest man in the world.

wealth management A professional service that is the combination of financial/asset management advice, accounting/tax services, and legal/estate planning for one fee.

Sources and Quotations

AMG annual flow summary. AMG Data Services. Retrieved April 22, 2005, from http://www.amgdata.com.

Aronson, Ted. Retrieved August 2003, from http://www.cbsmarket watch.com.

Baer, George, and Gary Bungler. *The Great Mutual Fund Trap.* Broadway Books, 2002.

Barber, Brad. "Do Individual Day Traders Make Money: Evidence from Taiwan," February 1, 2005. Retrieved March 28, 2005, from http://www.fool.com/Boringport/1999?BoringPort990920.htm.

Barron's. Retrieved from http://www.financialplanning.com/cgi-bin/print.

Beer, Kieran. "Held to Account." *Bloomberg Wealth Manager,* December 2004, 60.

Bevis, Charles. "The Future of the Mutual Fund Industry." October 2002. Study by Financial Research Corp.

Bodurtha, Stephen. Retrieved from research data.

Bogle, John C. *Common Sense on Mutual Funds.* John Wiley & Sons, 1999.

Bogle, John. "Saint Jack on the Attack." Retrieved from http://www.for tune.com.

Bullard, Mercer. Retrieved September 11, 2003, from http://www.mon eycentral.msn.com.

Burczyk, Gabriel. WrapManager, Inc. Interview with author, April 5, 2005.

Carlson, Gregory. Carlson Capital Management. Retrieved from available research.

Cassidy, Don. Senior research analyst at Lipper, Inc. Retrieved April 23, 2005, from http://www.nytimes.com/2004/01/11/business/mut fund/11fund.html.

Cerulli Associates. "Total Separate Accounts Industry Assets and Growth, Proprietary and Third-Party." Bar chart.

Cerulli Associates. Quote from research.

Chambers, Larry. *Separate Account Management*. John Wiley & Sons, 2003, 87.

Consentino, Chris. Money Management Institute. Interview with author, March 23, 2005.

Corrigan, Louis. "Fool on the Hill—Buy and Hold Beats Rapid Trading." Retrieved from http://www.fool.com/eveningnews/foth/1998/foth980610.htm.

DALBAR Research. "Consumer Use of the Internet for Financial Services," 2001. Retrieved March 21, 2005, from http://www.dalbarinc .com/con tent/showpage. asp?page=200111011101.html.

——. "Quantitative Analysis of Investor Behavior 2001." Retrieved from http://www.dalbar.com.

——. "Quantitative Analysis of Investor Behavior." Retrieved April 2, 2005, from http://www.dalbarinc.com/content/showpage.asp? pages+2001062100.htm.

——. "Quantitative Analysis of Investor Behavior 2005." 2005 annual DALBAR study. E-mailed to author by Lou Harvey, president of DALBAR.

Damato, Karen. "Mutual Funds' Relatively Untainted Image May Be Lost." *Wall Street Journal*, September 9, 2003.

Daum, Troy. *Wealth Analytics*. Retrieved from available research.

Davidson, Erick H., and Kevin D. Freeman. *Investing in Separate Accounts*. McGraw-Hill, 2002.

Davis, Christopher. Money Management Institute. Retrieved from published research.

Dell'orfano, Scott. Retrieved from http://www.financialplanning.com.

Dew, Jim. *Dew Wealth Management*. Interview with author, April 27, 2005.

Dixon, Joel, and John Shoven. "Ranking Mutual Funds on an After-Tax Basis." Working Paper Number 4393, National Bureau of Economic Research, 1993.

"Documents to Detail Dot-com Accusations." *USA TODAY,* April 28, 2003.

"Don't Expect Special Attention with 'Separate Accounts.'" Comment from Cerulli Associates. Retrieved from http://www.thestreet.com/ pf/funds/belowradar/10009217.html.

Enright, Bob. Partner in Burton/Enright Group. Phone interview with author, April 5, 2005.

Evans, Mike. Finance Research Corporation. Interview with author, March 17, 2005.

———. "Asset Trends Show Direction of the Industry." In *Individually Managed Accounts,* Robert B. Jorgensen (John Wiley & Sons, 2003).

"Exhibit G: SMA Assets by Distribution Channel." Money Management Institute member report 4Q 2004.

Ferrell, Paul. "It's the Expenses, Stupid." Retrieved from http://cbs.mar-ketwatch.com/news/print_story.asp?print+1&guid=[9F36107-90B4-46 ,DB-AD63-FD657E288583]&siteid-mtw.

———. "Ten Habits of Highly Irrational Investors." *MarketWatch,* December 14, 2004. Retrieved from http://www.cbsmarketwatch.com/ news/print.asp?print-1&guid-(75C6ECIF-C19D-4BOF-A36E-2C62 CV257739F)&SITEID-mkrw.

"Few Actually Use SMA Customization." Financial Planning. Retrieved from http://www.financial-planning.com/cgi-bin/print.pl.

Fisher, Kenneth L. *Forbes,* August 2001.

Fullerton, Paul. Cerulli Associates. Interview with author, March 20, 2005.

"Funds Trading Abuses Go Unpunished." Retrieved from http://www .lipper.com.

Gardner, David, and Tom Gardner. *The Feeling Isn't Mutual: The Motley Fool Investment Guide* (Simon & Schuster).

Grable, J. E., and R. H. Lytton. "Financial Risk Tolerance Revisited: The Development of a Risk Assessment Instrument." *Financial Services Review* 8 (1999):163-81.

Greene, Jason. Retrieved September 11, 2003, from http://www.money central.msn.com.

Gresham. Stephen. *The Managed Account Handbook: How to Build Your Financial Advisory Practice Using Separately Managed Accounts* (Phoenix Investment Partners, 2002).

Haaga, Paul G. Jr. "With Mutual Funds, Is the Investor Number 1?" *Wall Street Journal,* September 5, 2003.

IAFP/DALBAR, Inc. "The Value of Advice." 1997. Retrieved from http://www.fpanet.org.

"Industry Scandal Hits American Funds." Statement from vice chairman of NASD, Mary L. Schapiro. Retrieved from http://www.mar ketwatch.com/news/print_story.asp?print=1&guid={DD%DBA06-F28A-4CDC-8D20-A33CD9CCC13C}&siteit-mtw.

"Interest in IMAs Continues to Grow." *Ticker,* June 2002, 20.

"In the World of Managed Accounts, Few One-of-a-Kinds." *Wall Street Journal,* July 7, 2003.

Investment Company Institute. Retrieved March 15, 2005, from http://www.ici.com.

Israel, Sam. NASD chief counsel for enforcement. Retrieved from research data.

Jorgensen, Robert B. *Individually Managed Accounts* (John Wiley & Sons, 2003), 47, 118.

Karlgaard, Richard. "Sorry, I Stank." *Forbes,* January 13, 2000.

Keil, Jeffery. Vice president, Global Fiduciary Review, Lipper Inc. Interview with author, April 18, 2005.

Kinnel, Russel. "Unfinished Business from the Fund Scandal." Morningstar. Retrieved from http://news.morningstar.com/doc/document /print/1.3651.125808,00.html.

———. Morningstar. Retrieved from research data.

Kulikowski, Laurie. *Financial Planning,* December 2001, 26.

Levitt, Arthur. *Take On the Street.* Pantheon Books, 2002.

———. Statement during appearance at congressional hearings on mutual fund fraud, November 4, 2003. Retrieved from http://www.pbs.org.

Lipper Analytical Services. Retrieved from http//lipperweb.com.

Little, Ken. "Who's Watching Your Back." *Your Guide to Stocks.* Retrieved from http://www.stocks.about.com/od/tradingbasics/a/Regulat() 11705_p.htm.

Lockhart, Len, and Chris Farrell. "Remembering the Pre-Millennium Bull Run." March 6, 2002. Retrieved from http://www.rightonthe money.org/docs/commentary0307.html.

MacKillop, Scott. Trivium Consulting. "Separate Accounts: A Different Tune." *Investment Advisor,* November 2000.

"Many Investors Not Aware of SEC Rule on Fund After-Tax Disclosure." 3rd annual Easton Vance survey. Retrieved December 24, 2004, from http://www.womenfinance.com/mutualfunds/secrule.shtml.

Marino, Vivian. "These Accounts Aren't Just for Millionaires Anymore." *New York Times.* Retrieved from http://www.nytimes.com/2005/ 02/13/business/yourmoney/13smas/htm.

"Market Update: The Managed Account and Wrap Industry." Research paper by Cerulli Associates.

Masters, Brooke A. "Regulators Reach Deal with Strong, Fund Firm." May 20, 2004. Retrieved April 20, 2005, from http://www.washing tonpost.com.

Money Management Institute. "SMA Assets Continue to Climb in 2004." Retrieved from http://www.moneyinstitute.com.

———. Retrieved January 3, 2005, from http://www.moneymarketinstitute .com.

"More Mutual Funds Disclosure Is Coming." *Investment News,* April 23, 2005.

Mulville, Michael. "A Question of Trust." *Morningstar Mutual Funds,* August 30, 1996.

"Mutual Funds: What's Wrong." *BusinessWeek,* January 24, 2000.

Myers, Margaret. "Information Disclosure Regulation and the Returns to Active Management in the Mutual Fund Industry." Retrieved from http://www.mit.edu/faculty/poterba/files/copycatoct2001.pdf.

Newsline, newsletter from American Funds, June 30, 2003.

"Portfolio Transactions Cost at U.S. Equity Mutual Funds." Zero Alpha Group Study, November 17, 2004. Retrieved from http://www.zero alphagroup.com/headlines/hiddenstudy111704.html.

Reinhart, Len. Retrieved from available research.

Revell, Janice. "Road Kill: Mutual Funds Have Flattened Investors . . ." *Fortune,* November 11, 2002.

Richards, Lorie. SEC inspections official. Retrieved from available research.

Robinson, David. Robinson, Tigue, Sponcil & Associates. Interview with author, April 5, 2005.

Roland, Mary. *The New Commonsense Guide to Mutual Funds* (Bloomberg Press, 1998).

Rottersman, Max. Retrieved from http://www.fundforensics.com. Also interview with author, March 16, 2005.

Royce, Paul. "Navigating the Mutual Fund Industry though Challenging Times." Retrieved from http://www.see.gov/news/speech491.htm.

Rutner, Richard. *The Trouble with Mutual Funds.* 2d ed. (Elton Wolfe Publishing, 2002).

"Scandal Tarnishes Mutual Funds." Comments from Eliot Spitzer, attorney general of New York. Retrieved from http://www.yourlawyer.com/practice/printnews.htm.

"Scandals Run Deep in Fund World." *Investment News,* November 22, 2001, 1.

Schuster, Lars. Financial Research Corp. Interview with author, April 4, 2005.

SEC. Retrieved March 15, 2005, from http://www.sec.gov.

Selz, Marica, PhD. Interview with author, April 2005.

Sharkansky, Stefan. "Mutual Fund Costs: Risk Without Reward." *Personal Fund Inc.,* July 2002. Interview with author, March 2005.

Shefrin, Hersh. M. Santa Clara University professor. Retrieved April 23, 2005, from http://www.nytimes.com/2004/01/11/business/mut fund/11fund.html.

Sores, George. "The Case for an Open Society." Speech, John F. Kennedy School of Government, Harvard University.

Spitzer, Eliot. *USA TODAY,* September 9, 2003.

Stein, David M. "Separate Is More Than Equal." *Financial Planning,* October 1, 2002. Retrieved from http://www.financial-planning .com. Also interview with author, March 20, 2005.

Sulaiman, Fatima. "SEC Adopts Final Rule Requiring Disclosure of Mutual Fund After-Tax Returns." Retrieved December 28, 2004, from http://www.cybersecuritieslaw.com/KL/sulaiman1.htm.

Tedstrom, Peter F. Brown & Tedstrom. Interview with author, April 6, 2005.

Thompson, David. Phoenix Marketing International. Retrieved from available research.

Tigue, Keith. Robinson, Tigue, Sponcil and Assoc. Interview with author, April 27, 2005.

Tilson, Whitney. "The Perils of Investor Overconfidence," February 1, 2005. Retrieved March 21, 2005, from http://www.fool.com/Bor ingport/1999?BoringPort990920.htm.

Wade, Jerry. "Mutual Funds Unmasked—What the Fund Industry Does Not Want Investors to Know." Report retrieved from http://www .wadefolios.com.

Waggoner, John. "Seek Good Return, Low Turnover." *USA TODAY,* June 6, 2000. Lipper study. Retrieved from http://usatoday.com/ money/perfi/columist/waggon/0017.htm.

——. "Funds' Image Battered by Trading Scandal," September 30, 2003. Retrieved from http://www.usatoday.com.

"The Wealth Effect." Retrieved from http://www.investopedia.com/ terms/w/wealtheffect.asp.

Wirner, Daniel. Retrieved from https://www.iplacereports.com.

Yeske, David. "Investment Expectations." *Military Officer Magazine,* March 2003.